Franklin c

Franklin on Faith

The Definitive Guide to the Religion of the First American

Bill Fortenberry

"I am conscious I believe in Christ, and exert my best Endeavours to understand his Will aright, and strictly to follow it."

- Benjamin Franklin

Table of Contents

Introduction – The Conversion of Benjamin Franklin

Benjamin Franklin was raised in a Christian home, but according to his autobiography, he decided to become a deist at the age of fifteen after reading several books on the subject. He soon began to doubt this decision, however, and he wrote that "I began to suspect that this doctrine, though it might be true, was not very useful." Franklin moved to London at the age of seventeen while still a deist, and during that stay, he published a pamphlet with the motto, "Whatever is, is right." It was during this time, that Franklin really began to doubt the truth of deism, and he recorded in his autobiography that he "doubted whether some error had not insinuated itself unperceived into my argument." He then said that he "grew convinced that truth, sincerity, and integrity in dealings between man and man were of the utmost importance to the felicity of life." It was about his conclusions of this time that Franklin wrote, "Revelation had indeed no weight with me, as such;" and he concluded that it was "the kind hand of Providence" which preserved him during this "dangerous time of youth."

Franklin returned from London in 1726, and two years later he wrote out his "Articles of Belief." The wording of this document is consistent with the time period after his rejection of deism but before his acceptance of the Bible as revelation from God. This transitional phase appears to have continued through 1731 when Franklin wrote his outline of "Doctrine to be Preached." In the mere ten lines of this outline that have been recovered, there is no reference to Scripture. There is, however, a marked difference between this outline and the "Articles of Belief" which Franklin had written three years prior. In this outline, Franklin completely abandoned his earlier concept of God as merely the God of our solar system with other God's above Him and instead fully embraced a single God whom he identified as the "Father of the Universe." Franklin's "Doctrine to be Preached" described God as "infinitely good, Powerful and wise" as well as "omnipresent." At this time, Franklin also recognized the existence of an afterlife and wrote that men "are made more happy or miserable after this Life according to their Actions."

This brings us to the consideration of Franklin's 1732 article "On the Providence of God in the Government of the World" in which he argued for the intervention of God in the affairs of men. This argument agrees with Franklin's "Doctrine to be Preached" of the previous year in that it was predicated on "the Existence of a Deity and that he is the Creator of the Universe." It also agreed in the claim that God is infinitely wise, powerful and good. The 1732 article, however, introduced several additional concepts which are not seen in the remnants of the earlier outline, though they might have been in the portions which have been lost. In particular, Fanklin's 1732 article included the conclusion "that the Deity sometimes interferes by his particular Providence, and sets aside the Events which would otherwise have been produc'd in the Course of Nature, or by the Free Agency of Men." This conclusion marks the first indication that Franklin recognized God's direct interference in the actions of men, and it is also the first evidence of Franklin's acknowledgement of the free will of man. This article also marks the first record we have of Franklin saying that men should pray to God for "his Favour and Protection." His previous prayer in the "Articles of Belief" was primarily focused on praising God, and the request in that prayer was only for aid in maintaining good virtue. The 1732 article, by contrast, stated that men should pray for God's direct intervention in their lives.

About two years after Franklin's article on the providence of God, a new preacher by the name of Hemphill arrived in Philadelphia, and Franklin wrote in his autobiography that "I became one of his constant hearers." It was shortly after Mr. Hemphill's arrival that Franklin published an article entitled "Self-Denial is not the Essence of Virtue." In that article, we find Franklin denying a doctrine that had been fundamental to his beliefs up to this time. He denied his previous claim that men would be rewarded by God according to their virtues. In this February 18, 1735, article, he wrote that "We do not pretend to merit any thing of God, for he is above our Services; and the Benefits he confers on us, are the Effects of his Goodness and Bounty."

Less than two months later, the Gazette published an article that many attribute to Franklin entitled "Dialogue between Two Presbyterians." If, as is frequently assumed, the character in this dialogue represented by the initial S. conveys Franklin's own opinions, then this dialogue shows that at this point in 1735, Franklin was still struggling with the proper relationship between virtue and belief in regards to salvation. In the dialogue, S. claims that "Morality or Virtue is the End, Faith only a Means to obtain that End." S. also said, "The whole, says he, need not a Physician, but they that are sick; and, I come not to call the Righteous, but Sinners, to Repentance: Does not this imply, that there were good Men, who, without Faith in him, were in a State of Salvation?" We will see in a moment that Franklin quickly resolved this error, but it is important to note that if Franklin actually did use S. to convey his own opinions, then this dialogue marks the first time that Franklin chose to support his theological writings with quotes from Scripture. Nor is this statement the only reference to the Bible in the dialogue. Throughout the course of the discussion, S. directly quoted nine passages of Scripture in support of his position. This is a significant change from Franklin's earlier statement that "Revelation had indeed no weight with me."

There is another even more significant change which should be noted at this point. In the dialogue, S. made the statement, "I suppose you think no Doctrine fit to be preached in a Christian Congregation, but such as Christ and his Apostles used to preach," and a few paragraphs later, he said, "Our Saviour was a Teacher of Morality or Virtue, and they that were deficient and desired to be taught, ought first to believe in him as an able and faithful Teacher." If these are the opinions of Franklin himself, then this dialogue marks the first recorded instance that I know of in which he referred to Jesus as the Savior and as the Christ.

In addition to publishing the "Dialogue between Two Presbyterians," Franklin also published three pamphlets in defense of Hemphill. In those pamphlets, we find Franklin shedding the last vestiges of his previously held deism and fully adopting biblical Christianity. The third of these pamphlets was entitled "A Defense of Mr. Hemphill's Observations," and in it, Franklin declared in no uncertain terms that "Christ by his Death and Sufferings has purchas'd for us those easy Terms and Conditions of our Acceptance with God, propos'd in the Gospel, to wit, Faith and Repentance." Here at last, he had arrived at pure Christian doctrine. He finally understood that there is a God, that sin separates men from Him, that no man is virtuous enough to regain fellowship with God, that the penalty for this failure is death, that Christ paid that penalty for all men through His own death on the cross and that it is only by placing faith in His sacrifice and repenting of our own failures that we can be brought back into favor with God. Here, Franklin speaks not as a mere deist or theist but as a true follower of Jesus Christ.

Franklin's defenses of Hemphill mark a radical change in the way that he wrote about Christianity. Prior to this point, Franklin had no use whatsoever for the Scriptures. He gave little if any consideration to the work of Christ. He believed in a God of his own creation, and he lived by the morals of his own choosing. From this point forward, however, Franklin's writings are dramatically different. He accepted the Bible as the inspired and authoritative Word of God. He praised Christ for His sacrificial death and referred to Him as the Savior. He proclaimed the God of the Bible as the one true God, and he grounded his view of morality on the commands of Scripture. In short, Franklin's writings reveal that a significant spiritual change took place in his life sometime during the year 1735, and I believe that this year can rightly be identified as the year that Franklin became a Christian.

In this book, I have attempted to collect everything that Franklin wrote which could be used to determine his religious beliefs. His letters and essays are presented in chronological order intermixed with excerpts from his autobiography, and my commentary has been relegated to the footnotes. It is my hope that this format will allow you to follow the progression of Franklin's own accounts of his beliefs and to arrive at a more complete understanding of his faith.

Autobiography

This obscure Family of ours was early in the Reformation, and continu'd Protestants thro' the Reign of Queen Mary, when they were sometimes in Danger of Trouble on Account of their Zeal against Popery. They had got an English Bible, and to conceal and secure it, it was fastned open with Tapes under and within the Frame of a Joint Stool. When my Great Great Grandfather read in it to his Family, he turn'd up the Joint Stool upon his Knees, turning over the Leaves then under the Tapes. One of the Children stood at the Door to give Notice if he saw the Apparitor coming, who was an Officer of the Spiritual Court. In that Case the Stool was turn'd down again upon its feet, when the Bible remain'd conceal'd under it as before. This Anecdote I had from my Uncle Benjamin. The Family continu'd all of the Church of England till about the End of Charles the 2ds Reign, when some of the Ministers that had been outed for Nonconformity, holding Conventicles in Northamptonshire, Benjamin and Josiah adher'd to them, and so continu'd all their Lives. The rest of the Family remain'd with the Episcopal Church.

Josiah, my Father, married young, and carried his Wife with three Children unto New England, about 1682. The Conventicles having been forbidden by Law, and frequently disturbed, induced some considerable Men of his Acquaintance to remove to that Country, and he was prevail'd with to accompany them thither, where they expected to enjoy their Mode of Religion with Freedom.[1] By the same Wife he had 4 Children more born there, and by a second Wife ten more, in all 17, of which I remember 13 sitting at one time at his Table, who all grew up to be Men and Women, and married. I was the youngest Son and the youngest Child but two, and was born in Boston, N. England.

---

[1] As we will see later, Franklin was a strong advocate for religious freedom. Historians often claim that this was a result of his enlightenment education, but it is much more likely to have been the product of a childhood spent listening to his godly parents tell of the persecutions that their families faced in both the old world and the new as a result of their beliefs.

My Mother the 2d Wife was Abiah Folger, a Daughter of Peter Folger,[2] one of the first Settlers of New England, of whom honourable mention is made by Cotton Mather, in his Church History of that Country, (entitled Magnalia Christi Americana) as a *godly learned Englishman,* if I remember the words rightly. I have heard that he wrote sundry small occasional Pieces, but only one of them was printed which I saw now many Years since. It was written in 1675, in the homespun Verse of that Time and People, and address'd to those then concern'd in the Government there. It was in favour of Liberty of Conscience, and in behalf of the Baptists, Quakers, and other Secretaries, that had been under Persecution; ascribing the Indian Wars and other Distresses, that had befallen the Country to that Persecution, as so many Judgments of God, to punish so heinous an Offence; and exhorting a Repeal of those uncharitable Laws. The whole appear'd to me as written with a good deal of Decent Plainness and manly Freedom. The six last concluding Lines I remember, tho' I have forgotten the two first of the Stanza, but the Purport of them was that his Censures proceeded from *Goodwill,* and therefore he would be known as the Author,

because to be a Libeller, (says he)
I hate it with my Heart.
From Sherburne Town where now I dwell,
My Name I do put here,
Without Offence, your real Friend,
It is Peter Folgier.

My elder Brothers were all put Apprentices to different Trades. I was put to the Grammar School at Eight Years of Age, my Father intending to devote me as the Tithe of his Sons to the Service of the Church. My early Readiness in learning to read (which must have been very early, as I do not remember when I could not read) and the Opinion of all his Friends that I should certainly make a good

---

[2] Peter Foulger was a Baptist missionary in Nantucket, Massachusetts. He died 16 years before Franklin was born, but his daughter (Franklin's mother) likely conveyed several of his doctrines to her son. This Baptist influence in Franklin's life could be the source of some of his later statements in defense of Samuel Hemphill.

Scholar, encourag'd him in this Purpose of his. My Uncle Benjamin too approv'd of it, and propos'd to give me all his Shorthand Volumes of Sermons I suppose as a Stock to set up with, if I would learn his Character. I continu'd however at the Grammar School not quite one Year, tho' in that time I had risen gradually from the Middle of the Class of that Year to be the Head of it, and farther was remov'd into the next Class above it, in order to go with that into the third at the End of the Year. But my Father in the mean time, from a View of the Expence of a College Education which, having so large a Family, he could not well afford, and the mean Living many so educated were afterwards able to obtain, Reasons that he gave to his Friends in my Hearing, altered his first Intention, took me from the Grammar School, and sent me to a School for Writing and Arithmetic kept by a then famous Man, Mr. Geo. Brownell, very successful in his Profession generally, and that by mild encouraging Methods. Under him I acquired fair Writing pretty soon, but I fail'd in the Arithmetic, and made no Progress in it.

Autobiography

Before I enter upon my public Appearance in Business it may be well to let you know the then State of my Mind, with regard to my Principles and Morals, that you may see how far those influenc'd the future Events of my Life. My Parents had early given me religious Impressions, and brought me through my Childhood piously in the Dissenting Way. But I was scarce 15 when, after doubting by turns of several Points as I found them disputed in the different Books I read, I began to doubt of Revelation it self. Some Books against Deism fell into my Hands; they were said to be the Substance of Sermons preached at Boyle's Lectures. It happened that they wrought an Effect on me quite contrary to what was intended by them: For the Arguments of the Deists which were quoted to be refuted, appeared to me much stronger than the Refutations. In short I soon became a thorough Deist.[3] My Arguments perverted some

---

[3] It is interesting to note that, like many other impetuous teenagers, Franklin accepted the principles of Deism because of the weakness of the arguments which he read against it and not because of the strength of any arguments in its favor. The errors which he soon discovered in this philosophy not only led him to

others, particularly Collins and Ralph: but each of them having afterwards wrong'd me greatly without the least Compunction and recollecting Keith's Conduct towards me, (who was another Freethinker) and my own towards Vernon and Miss Read which at Times gave me great Trouble, I began to suspect that this Doctrine tho' it might be true, was not very useful. My London Pamphlet, which had for its Motto those Lines of Dryden

———Whatever is, is right.———
Tho' purblind Man
Sees but a Part of the Chain, the nearest Link,
His Eyes not carrying to the equal Beam,
That poizes all, above.

And from the Attributes of God, his infinite Wisdom, Goodness and Power concluded that nothing could possibly be wrong in the World, and that Vice and Virtue were empty Distinctions, no such Things existing: appear'd now not so clever a Performance as I once thought it; and I doubted whether some Error had not insinuated itself unperceiv'd into my Argument, so as to infect all that follow'd, as is common in metaphysical Reasonings.[4] I grew convinc'd that *Truth, Sincerity and Integrity* in Dealings between Man and Man, were of the utmost Importance to the Felicity of Life, and I form'd written Resolutions, (which still remain in my Journal Book) to practice them ever while I lived. Revelation had indeed no

---

abandon Deism, but also to adopt the more mature approach of reserving judgment in religious matters until he had studied both sides of the issue. This habit stayed with him his entire life, and it explains why, at the end of his life, he informed Dr. Styles that he was not dogmatic on the subject of the divinity of Christ.

[4] One historian writes of Franklin that "he never gave reason to think that he ever departed from the convictions acquired as a youthful bibliophile" (Stewart, 471). This claim is directly contradicted by Franklin's autobiography, and in fact, Franklin later wrote that he was so embarrassed by these early defenses of Deism that he burned every copy of this pamphlet that he had except one which he kept because the margin contained some notes from one of his friends (To Benjamin Vaughan – Nov. 9, 1779).

weight with me as such;[5] but I entertain'd an Opinion, that tho' certain Actions might not be bad *because* they were forbidden by it, or good *because* it commanded them; yet probably those Actions might be forbidden *because* they were bad for us, or commanded *because* they were beneficial to us, in their own Natures, all the Circumstances of things considered. And this Persuasion, with the kind hand of Providence, or some guardian Angel, or accidental favourable Circumstances and Situations, or all together, preserved me (thro' this dangerous Time of Youth and the hazardous Situations I was sometimes in among Strangers, remote from the Eye and Advice of my Father) without any *wilful* gross Immorality or Injustice that might have been expected from my Want of Religion. I say *wilful,* because the Instances I have mentioned, had something of *Necessity* in them, from my Youth, Inexperience, and the Knavery of others. I had therefore a tolerable Character to begin the World with, I valued it properly, and determin'd to preserve it.

Silence Dogood No. 9 – July 23, 1722

It has been for some Time a Question with me, Whether a Commonwealth suffers more by hypocritical Pretenders to Religion, or by the openly Profane? But some late Thoughts of this Nature, have inclined me to think, that the Hypocrite is the most dangerous Person of the Two, especially if he sustains a Post in the Government, and we consider his Conduct as it regards the Publick. The first Artifice of a *State Hypocrite* is, by a few savoury Expressions which cost him Nothing, to betray the best Men in his Country into an Opinion of his Goodness; and if the Country wherein he lives is noted for the Purity of Religion, he the more easily gains his End, and consequently may more justly be expos'd and detested. A notoriously profane Person in a private Capacity, ruins himself, and perhaps forwards the Destruction of a few of his

---

[5] Franklin would later abandon his youthful disregard for Revelation. Beginning in 1735 (Dialogue between Two Presbyterians), and continuing throughout the rest of his life, Franklin frequently cited the Bible as authoritative and once referred to it as "the most faithful of all histories" (To the Editor of the Federal Gazette – April 8, 1788).

Equals; but a publick Hypocrite every day deceives his betters, and makes them the Ignorant Trumpeters of his supposed Godliness: They take him for a Saint, and pass him for one, without considering that they are (as it were) the Instruments of publick Mischief out of Conscience, and ruin their Country for God's sake.

This Political Description of a Hypocrite, may (for ought I know) be taken for a new Doctrine by some of your Readers; but let them consider, that *a little Religion, and a little Honesty, goes a great way in Courts.* 'Tis not inconsistent with Charity to distrust a Religious Man in Power, tho' he may be a good Man; he has many Temptations "to propagate *publick Destruction* for *Personal Advantages* and Security": And if his Natural Temper be covetous, and his Actions often contradict his pious Discourse, we may with great Reason conclude, that he has some other Design in his Religion besides barely getting to Heaven. But the most dangerous Hypocrite in a Common-Wealth, is one who *leaves the Gospel for the sake of the Law*: A Man compounded of Law and Gospel, is able to cheat a whole Country with his Religion, and then destroy them under *Colour of Law*: And here the Clergy are in great Danger of being deceiv'd, and the People of being deceiv'd by the Clergy, until the Monster arrives to such Power and Wealth, that he is out of the reach of both, and can oppress the People without their own blind Assistance. And it is a sad Observation, that when the People too late see their Error, yet the Clergy still persist in their Encomiums on the Hypocrite; and when he happens to die *for the Good of his Country,* without leaving behind him the Memory of *one good Action,* he shall be sure to have his Funeral Sermon stuff'd with *Pious Expressions* which he dropt at such a Time, and at such a Place, and on such an Occasion; than which nothing can be more prejudicial to the Interest of Religion, nor indeed to the Memory of the Person deceas'd. The Reason of this Blindness in the Clergy is, because they are honourably supported (as they ought to be) by their People, and see nor feel nothing of the Oppression which is obvious and burdensome to every one else.

But this Subject raises in me an Indignation not to be born; and if we have had, or are like to have any Instances of this Nature in New

England, we cannot better manifest our Love to Religion and the Country, than by setting the Deceivers in a true Light, and undeceiving the Deceived, however such Discoveries may be represented by the ignorant or designing Enemies of our Peace and Safety.

I shall conclude with a Paragraph or two from an ingenious Political Writer in the *London Journal,* the better to convince your Readers, that Publick Destruction may be easily carry'd on by *hypocritical Pretenders to Religion.*

"A raging Passion for immoderate Gain had made Men universally and intensely hard-hearted: They were every where devouring one another. And yet the Directors and their Accomplices, who were the acting Instruments of all this outrageous Madness and Mischief, set up for wonderful pious Persons, while they were defying Almighty God, and plundering Men; and they set apart a Fund of Subscriptions for charitable Uses; that is, they mercilessly made a whole People Beggars, and charitably supported a few *necessitous* and *worthless* Favourites. I doubt not, but if the Villany had gone on with Success, they would have had their Names handed down to Posterity with Encomiums; as the Names of other *publick Robbers* have been! We have *Historians* and Ode Makers now living, very proper for such a Task. It is certain, that most People did, at one Time, believe the *Directors* to be *great and worthy Persons*. And an honest Country Clergyman told me last Summer, upon the Road, that Sir John was an excellent publick-spirited Person, for that he had beautified his Chancel.

"Upon the whole we must not judge of one another by their best Actions; since the worst Men do some Good, and all Men make fine Professions: But we must judge of Men by the whole of their Conduct, and the Effects of it. Thorough Honesty requires great and long Proof, since many a Man, long thought honest, has at length proved a Knave. And it is from judging without Proof, or false Proof, that Mankind continue Unhappy." I am, Sir, Your humble Servant,

On Titles of Honor – Feb. 1723

There is nothing in which Mankind reproach themselves more than in their Diversity of Opinions. Every Man sets himself above another in his own Opinion, and there are not two Men in the World whose Sentiments are alike in every thing. Hence it comes to pass, that the same Passages in the Holy Scriptures or the Works of the Learned, are wrested to the meaning of two opposite Parties, of contrary Opinions, as if the Passages they recite were like our Master Janus, looking *two ways at once,* or like Lawyers, who with equal Force of Argument, can plead either for the *Plaintiff* or *Defendant.*

A Dissertation on Liberty and Necessity – 1725

Sir,

I have here, according to your Request, given you my *present* Thoughts of the *general State of Things* in the Universe.[6] Such as

---

[6] Franklin stated both in his autobiography and in a letter to Benjamin Vaughan (Nov. 9, 1779) that this pamphlet was the product of his youthful folly. Soon after writing it, he burned every copy of it but one which he kept solely because of some notes jotted down on it by one of his friends. In spite of this, many historians still refer to this pamphlet as an example of Franklin's view of religion. One historian wrote of Franklin that:

"His own opinions about religion, significantly liberal for his day are best presented in two works, *A Dissertation on Liberty and Necessity, Pleasure and Pain* (1725), [an] early satirical work in which he lampooned contemporary religion, and *Articles of Belief and Acts of Religion* (1728), the most complete statement of his personal spiritual beliefs, with obvious deistic leanings." (Melton, 174)

Even those historians who admit that Franklin eventually abandoned the philosophy presented in his *Dissertation* often insist that he maintained the same attitude toward Christianity. Remsberg, for example, quoted the portion of Franklin's autobiography in which Franklin wrote of his rejection of the arguments in the *Dissertation*, but Remsberg was quick to add: "His unbelief in Christianity, however, remained unchanged" (Remsburg, 160)

they are, you have them, and are welcome to 'em; and if they yield you any Pleasure or Satisfaction, I shall think my Trouble sufficiently compensated. I know my Scheme will be liable to many Objections from a less discerning Reader than your self; but it is not design'd for those who can't understand it. I need not give you any Caution to distinguish the hypothetical Parts of the Argument from the conclusive: You will easily perceive what I design for Demonstration, and what for Probability only. The whole I leave entirely to you, and shall value my self more or less on this account, in proportion to your Esteem and Approbation.

Sect. I. Of Liberty and Necessity.

I. *There is said to be a* First Mover, *who is called* God, *Maker of the Universe.*

II. *He is said to be all-wise, all-good, all powerful.*

These two Propositions being allow'd and asserted by People of almost every Sect and Opinion; I have here suppos'd them granted, and laid them down as the Foundation of my Argument; What follows then, being a Chain of Consequences truly drawn from them, will stand or fall as they are true or false.

III. *If He is all-good, whatsoever He doth must be good.*

IV. *If He is all-wise, whatsoever He doth must be wise.*

The Truth of these Propositions, with relation to the two first, I think may be justly call'd evident; since, either that infinite Goodness will act what is ill, or infinite Wisdom what is not wise, is too glaring a Contradiction not to be perceiv'd by any Man of common Sense, and deny'd as soon as understood.

In reality, the *Dissertation on Liberty and Necessity* should be viewed as nothing more than the vainglorious ranting of a rebellious youth. That is how Franklin himself viewed it in his own reflections, and he was certainly more knowledgeable of the author's state of mind than we can ever hope to be.

V. If He is all-powerful, there can be nothing either existing or acting in the Universe against *or* without *his Consent; and what He consents to must be good, because He is good; therefore* Evil *doth not exist.*

Unde Malum? has been long a Question, and many of the Learned have perplex'd themselves and Readers to little Purpose in Answer to it. That there are both Things and Actions to which we give the Name of *Evil,* is not here deny'd, as *Pain, Sickness, Want, Theft, Murder,* &c. but that these and the like are not in reality *Evils, Ills,* or *Defects* in the Order of the Universe, is demonstrated in the next Section, as well as by this and the following Proposition. Indeed, to suppose any Thing to exist or be done, *contrary* to the Will of the Almighty, is to suppose him not almighty; or that Something (the Cause of *Evil*) is more mighty than the Almighty; an Inconsistence that I think no One will defend: And to deny any Thing or Action, which he consents to the existence of, to be good, is entirely to destroy his two Attributes of *Wisdom* and *Goodness.*

There is nothing done in the Universe, say the Philosophers, *but what God either does, or* permits *to be done.* This, as He is Almighty, is certainly true: But what need of this Distinction between *doing* and *permitting?* Why, first they take it for granted that many Things in the Universe exist in such a Manner as is not for the best, and that many Actions are done which ought not to be done, or would be better undone; these Things or Actions they cannot ascribe to God as His, because they have already attributed to Him infinite Wisdom and Goodness; Here then is the Use of the Word *Permit;* He *permits* them to be done, *say they.* But we will reason thus: If God permits an Action to be done, it is because he wants either *Power* or *Inclination* to hinder it; in saying he wants *Power,* we deny Him to be *almighty;* and if we say He wants *Inclination* or *Will,* it must be, either because He is not Good, or the Action is not *evil,* (for all Evil is contrary to the Essence of *infinite Goodness.*) The former is inconsistent with his before-given Attribute of Goodness, therefore the latter must be true.

It will be said, perhaps, that *God permits evil Actions to be done, for* wise *Ends and Purposes*. But this Objection destroys itself; for whatever an infinitely good God hath wise Ends in suffering to *be*, must be good, is thereby made good, and cannot be otherwise.

VI. *If a Creature is made by God, it must depend upon God, and receive all its Power from Him; with which Power the Creature can do nothing contrary to the Will of God, because God is Almighty; what is not contrary to His Will, must be agreeable to it; what is agreeable to it, must be good, because He is Good; therefore a Creature can do nothing but what is good.*

This Proposition is much to the same Purpose with the former, but more particular; and its Conclusion is as just and evident. Tho' a Creature may do many Actions which by his Fellow Creatures will be nam'd *Evil,* and which will naturally and necessarily cause or bring upon the Doer, certain *Pains* (which will likewise be call'd *Punishments*;) yet this Proposition proves, that he cannot act what will be in itself really Ill, or displeasing to God. And that the painful Consequences of his evil Actions (*so call'd*) are not, as indeed they ought not to be, *Punishments* or Unhappinesses, will be shewn hereafter.

Nevertheless, the late learned Author of *The Religion of Nature,* (which I send you herewith) has given us a Rule or Scheme, whereby to discover which of our Actions ought to be esteem'd and denominated *good,* and which *evil*: It is in short this, "Every Action which is done according to *Truth,* is good; and every Action contrary to Truth, is evil: To act according to Truth is to use and esteem every Thing as what it is, &c. Thus if *A* steals a Horse from *B,* and rides away upon him, he uses him not as what he is in Truth, viz. the Property of another, but as his own, which is contrary to Truth, and therefore *evil*." But, as this Gentleman himself says, (Sect. I. Prop. VI.) "In order to judge rightly what any Thing is, it must be consider'd, not only what it is in one Respect, but also what it may be in any other Respect; and the whole Description of the Thing ought to be taken in:" So in this Case it ought to be consider'd, that *A* is naturally a *covetous* Being, feeling an

Uneasiness in the want of *B*'s Horse, which produces an Inclination for stealing him, stronger than his Fear of Punishment for so doing. This is *Truth* likewise, and *A* acts according to it when he steals the Horse. Besides, if it is prov'd to be a *Truth,* that *A* has not Power over his own Actions, it will be indisputable that he acts according to Truth, and impossible he should do otherwise.

I would not be understood by this to encourage or defend Theft; 'tis only for the sake of the Argument, and will certainly have no *ill Effect.* The Order and Course of Things will not be affected by Reasoning of this Kind; and 'tis as just and necessary, and as much according to Truth, for *B* to dislike and punish the Theft of his Horse, as it is for *A* to steal him.

VII. *If the Creature is thus limited in his Actions, being able to do only such Things as God would have him to do, and not being able to refuse doing what God would have done; then he can have no such Thing as Liberty, Free-will or Power to do or refrain an Action.*

By *Liberty* is sometimes understood the Absence of Opposition; and in this Sense, indeed, all our Actions may be said to be the Effects of our Liberty: But it is a Liberty of the same Nature with the Fall of a heavy Body to the Ground; it has Liberty to fall, that is, it meets with nothing to hinder its Fall, but at the same Time it is necessitated to fall, and has no Power or Liberty to remain suspended.

But let us take the Argument in another View, and suppose ourselves to be, in the common sense of the Word, *Free Agents.* As Man is a Part of this great Machine, the Universe, his regular Acting is requisite to the regular moving of the whole. Among the many Things which lie before him to be done, he may, as he is at Liberty and his Choice influenc'd by nothing, (for so it must be, or he is not at Liberty) chuse any one, and refuse the rest. Now there is every Moment something *best* to be done, which is alone then *good,* and with respect to which, every Thing else is at that Time *evil*. In order to know which is best to be done, and which not, it is requisite that we should have at one View all the intricate Consequences of every Action with respect to the general Order and Scheme of the Universe, both present and future; but they are innumerable and incomprehensible by any Thing but Omnis-cience. As we cannot know these, we have but as one Chance to ten thousand, to hit on the right Action; we should then be perpetually blundering about in the Dark, and putting the Scheme in Disorder; for every wrong Action of a Part, is a Defect or Blemish in the Order of the Whole. Is it not necessary then, that our Actions should be over-rul'd and govern'd by an all-wise Providence? How exact and regular is every Thing in the *natural* World! How wisely in every Part contriv'd! We cannot here find the least Defect! Those who have study'd the mere animal and vegetable Creation, demonstrate that nothing can be more harmonious and beautiful! All the heavenly Bodies, the Stars and Planets, are regulated with the utmost Wisdom! And can we suppose less Care to be taken in the Order of the *moral* than in the *natural* System? It is as if an ingenious Artificer, having fram'd a curious Machine or Clock, and put its many intricate Wheels and Powers in such a Dependance on one another, that the whole might move in the most exact Order and Regularity, had nevertheless plac'd in it several other Wheels endu'd with an independent *Self-Motion,* but ignorant of the general Interest of the Clock; and these would every now and then be moving wrong, disordering the true Movement, and making continual Work for the Mender; which might better be prevented, by depriving them of that Power of Self-Motion, and placing them in a Dependance on the regular Part of the Clock.

VIII. *If there is no such Thing as Free-Will in Creatures, there can be neither Merit nor Demerit in Creatures.*

IX. *And therefore every Creature must be equally esteem'd by the Creator.*

These Propositions appear to be the necessary Consequences of the former. And certainly no Reason can be given, why the Creator should prefer in his Esteem one Part of His Works to another, if with equal Wisdom and Goodness he design'd and created them all, since all Ill or Defect, as contrary to his Nature, is excluded by his Power.

We will sum up the Argument thus, When the Creator first design'd the Universe, either it was His Will and Intention that all Things should exist and be in the Manner they are at this Time; or it was his Will they should *be* otherwise i.e. in a different Manner: To say it was His Will Things should be otherwise than they are, is to say Somewhat hath contradicted His Will, and broken His Measures, which is impossible because inconsistent with his Power; therefore we must allow that all Things exist now in a Manner agreeable to His Will, and in consequence of that are all equally Good, and therefore equally esteemed by Him.

I proceed now to shew, that as all the Works of the Creator are equally esteem'd by Him, so they are, as in Justice they ought to be, equally us'd.

Sect. II. Of Pleasure and Pain.

I. *When a Creature is form'd and endu'd with Life, 'tis suppos'd to receive a Capacity of the Sensation of* Uneasiness *or* Pain.

It is this distinguishes Life and Consciousness from unactive unconscious Matter. To know or be sensible of Suffering or being acted upon is *to live*; and whatsoever is not so, among created Things, is properly and truly *dead*.

All *Pain* and *Uneasiness* proceeds at first from and is caus'd by Somewhat without and distinct from the Mind itself. The Soul must first be acted upon before it can re-act. In the Beginning of Infancy it is as if it were not; it is not conscious of its own Existence, till it has receiv'd the first Sensation of *Pain*; then, and not before, it begins to feel itself, is rous'd, and put into Action; then it discovers its Powers and Faculties, and exerts them to expel the Uneasiness. Thus is the Machine set on work; this is Life. We are first mov'd by *Pain* and the whole succeeding Course of our Lives is but one continu'd Series of Action with a View to be freed from it. As fast as we have excluded one Uneasiness another appears, otherwise the Motion would cease. If a continual Weight is not apply'd, the Clock will stop. And as soon as the Avenues of Uneasiness to the Soul are choak'd up or cut off, we are dead, we think and act no more.

II. *This Uneasiness, whenever felt, produces* Desire *to be freed from it, great in exact proportion to the Uneasiness.*

Thus is *Uneasiness* the first Spring and Cause of all Action; for till we are uneasy in Rest, we can have no Desire to move, and without Desire of moving there can be no voluntary Motion. The Experience of every Man who has observ'd his own Actions will evince the Truth of this; and I think nothing need be said to prove that the *Desire* will be equal to the *Uneasiness,* for the very Thing implies as much: It is not *Uneasiness* unless we desire to be freed from it, nor a great *Uneasiness* unless the consequent Desire is great.

I might here observe, how necessary a Thing in the Order and Design of the Universe this *Pain* or *Uneasiness* is, and how beautiful in its Place! Let us but suppose it just now banish'd the World entirely, and consider the Consequence of it: All the Animal Creation would immediately stand stock still, exactly in the Posture they were in the Moment Uneasiness departed; not a Limb, not a Finger would henceforth move; we should all be reduc'd to the Condition of Statues, dull and unactive: Here I should continue to sit motionless with the Pen in my Hand thus——and neither leave my Seat nor write one Letter more. This may appear odd at first View, but a little Consideration will make it evident; for 'tis impossible to assign any other Cause for the voluntary Motion of an Animal than its *uneasiness* in Rest. What a different Appearance then would the Face of Nature make, without it! How necessary is it! And how unlikely that the Inhabitants of the World ever were, or that the Creator ever design'd they should be, exempt from it!

I would likewise observe here, that the VIIIth Proposition in the preceding Section, viz. *That there is neither Merit nor Demerit,* &c. is here again demonstrated, as infallibly, tho' in another manner: For since *Freedom from Uneasiness* is the End of all our Actions, how is it possible for us to do any Thing disinterested? How can any Action be meritorious of Praise or Dispraise, Reward or Punishment, when the natural Principle of *Self-Love* is the only and the irresistible Motive to it?

III. *This* Desire *is always fulfill'd or satisfy'd.*

In the *Design* or *End* of it, tho' not in the *Manner:* The first is requisite, the latter not. To exemplify this, let us make a Supposition; A Person is confin'd in a House which appears to be in imminent Danger of Falling, this, as soon as perceiv'd, creates a violent *Uneasiness,* and that instantly produces an equal strong *Desire,* the *End* of which is *freedom from the Uneasiness,* and the *Manner* or Way propos'd to gain this *End,* is *to get out of the House.* Now if he is convinc'd by any Means, that he is mistaken, and the House is not likely to fall, he is immediately freed from his *Uneasiness,* and the *End* of his Desire is attain'd as well as if it had been in the *Manner* desir'd, viz. *leaving the House.*

All our different Desires and Passions proceed from and are reducible to this one Point, *Uneasiness,* tho' the Means we propose to ourselves for expelling of it are infinite. One proposes *Fame,* another *Wealth,* a third *Power,* &c. as the Means to gain this *End;* but tho' these are never attain'd, if the Uneasiness be remov'd by some other Means, the *Desire* is satisfy'd. Now during the Course of Life we are ourselves continually removing successive Uneasiness as they arise, and the *last* we suffer is remov'd by the *sweet Sleep* of Death.

IV. *The fulfilling or Satisfaction of this* Desire, *produces the Sensation of* Pleasure, *great or small in exact proportion to the* Desire.

Pleasure is that Satisfaction which arises in the Mind upon, and is caus'd by, the accomplishment of our *Desires,* and by no other Means at all; and those Desires being above shewn to be caus'd by our *Pains* or *Uneasinesses,* it follows that *Pleasure* is wholly caus'd by *Pain,* and by no other Thing at all.

V. *Therefore the Sensation of* Pleasure *is equal, or in exact proportion to the Sensation of* Pain.

As the *Desire* of being freed from Uneasiness is equal to the *Uneasiness,* and the *Pleasure* of satisfying that Desire equal to the *Desire,* the *Pleasure* thereby produc'd must necessarily be equal to the *Uneasiness* or *Pain* which produces it: Of three Lines, *A, B,* and *C,* if *A* is equal to *B,* and *B* to *C,* must be equal to *A.* And as our *Uneasinesses* are always remov'd by some Means or other, it follows that *Pleasure* and *Pain* are in their Nature inseparable: So many Degrees as one Scale of the Ballance descends, so many exactly the other ascends; and one cannot rise or fall without the Fall or Rise of the other: 'Tis impossible to taste of *Pleasure,* without feeling its preceding proportionate *Pain*; or to be sensible of *Pain,* without having its necessary Consequent *Pleasure:* The *highest Pleasure* is only Consciousness of Freedom from the *deepest Pain,* and Pain is not Pain to us unless we ourselves are sensible of it. They go Hand in Hand; they cannot be divided.

You have a View of the whole Argument in a few familiar Examples: The *Pain* of Abstinence from Food, as it is greater or less, produces a greater or less *Desire* of Eating, the Accomplishment of this *Desire* produces a greater or less *Pleasure* proportionate to it. The *Pain* of Confinement causes the *Desire* of Liberty, which accomplish'd, yields a *Pleasure* equal to that *Pain* of Confinement. The *Pain* of Labour and Fatigue causes the *Pleasure* of Rest, equal to that *Pain.* The *Pain* of Absence from Friends, produces the *Pleasure* of Meeting in exact proportion. &c.

This is the *fixt Nature* of Pleasure and Pain, and will always be found to be so by those who examine it.

One of the most common Arguments for the future Existence of the Soul, is taken from the generally suppos'd Inequality of Pain and Pleasure in the present; and this, notwithstanding the Difficulty by outward Appearances to make a Judgment of another's Happiness, has been look'd upon as almost unanswerable: but since *Pain* naturally and infallibly produces a *Pleasure* in proportion to it, every individual Creature must, in any State of *Life*, have an equal Quantity of each, so that there is not, on that Account, any Occasion for a future Adjustment.

Thus are all the Works of the Creator *equally* us'd by him; And no Condition of Life or Being is in itself better or preferable to another: The Monarch is not more happy than the Slave, nor the Beggar more miserable than Croesus. Suppose *A, B,* and *C,* three distinct Beings; *A* and *B,* animate, capable of *Pleasure* and *Pain, C* an inanimate Piece of Matter, insensible of either. *A* receives ten Degrees of *Pain,* which are necessarily succeeded by ten Degrees of *Pleasure: B* receives fifteen of *Pain,* and the consequent equal Number of *Pleasure: C* all the while lies unconcern'd, and as he has not suffer'd the former, has no right to the latter. What can be more equal and just than this? When the Accounts come to be adjusted, *A* has no Reason to complain that his Portion of *Pleasure* was five Degrees less than that of *B,* for his Portion of *Pain* was five Degrees less likewise: Nor has *B* any Reason to boast that his *Pleasure* was five Degrees greater than that of *A,* for his *Pain* was proportionate: They are then both on the same Foot with *C,* that is, they are neither Gainers nor Losers.

It will possibly be objected here, that even common Experience shews us, there is not in Fact this Equality: "Some we see hearty, brisk and chearful perpetually, while others are constantly burden'd with a heavy Load of Maladies and Misfortunes, remaining for Years perhaps in Poverty, Disgrace, or Pain, and die at last without any Appearance of Recompence." Now tho' 'tis not necessary, when a Proposition is demonstrated to be a general Truth, to shew in what manner it agrees with the particular Circumstances of Persons, and indeed ought not to be requir'd; yet, as this is a common Objection, some Notice may be taken of it: And here let it be observ'd, that we cannot be proper Judges of the good or bad Fortune of Others; we are apt to imagine, that what would give us a great Uneasiness or a great Satisfaction, has the same Effect upon others: we think, for Instance, those unhappy, who must depend upon Charity for a mean Subsistence, who go in Rags, fare hardly, and are despis'd and scorn'd by all; not considering that Custom renders all these Things easy, familiar, and even pleasant. When we see Riches, Grandeur and a chearful Countenance, we easily imagine Happiness accompanies them, when oftentimes 'tis quite otherwise: Nor is a constantly sorrowful Look, attended with continual Complaints, an infallible Indication of Unhappiness. In short, we can judge by nothing but Appearances, and they are very apt to deceive us. Some put on a gay chearful Outside, and appear to the World perfectly at Ease, tho' even then, some inward Sting, some secret Pain imbitters all their Joys, and makes the Ballance even: Others appear continually dejected and full of Sorrow; but even Grief itself is sometimes *pleasant,* and Tears are not always without their Sweetness: Besides, Some take a Satisfaction in being thought unhappy, (as others take a Pride in being thought humble), these will paint their Misfortunes to others in the strongest Colours, and leave no Means unus'd to make you think them thoroughly miserable; so great a *Pleasure* it is to them *to be pitied*; Others retain the Form and outside Shew of Sorrow, long after the Thing itself, with its Cause, is remov'd from the Mind; it is a Habit they have acquir'd and cannot leave. These, with many others that might be given, are Reasons why we cannot make a true Estimate of the *Equality* of the Happiness and Unhappiness of others; and unless we could, Matter of Fact cannot be opposed to this Hypothesis. Indeed, we are sometimes apt to think, that the Uneasinesses we ourselves have had, outweigh our Pleasures; but the Reason is this, the Mind takes no Account of the latter, they slip away unremark'd, when the former leave more lasting Impressions on the Memory. But suppose we pass the greatest part of Life in Pain and Sorrow, suppose we die by Torments and *think no more,* 'tis no Diminution to the Truth of what is here advanc'd; for the *Pain,* tho' exquisite, is not so to the *last* Moments of Life, the Senses are soon benumm'd, and render'd incapable of transmitting it so sharply to the Soul as at first; She perceives it cannot hold long, and 'tis an *exquisite Pleasure* to behold the immediate Approaches of Rest. This makes an Equivalent tho' Annihilation should follow: For the Quantity of *Pleasure* and *Pain* is not to be measur'd by its Duration, any more than the Quantity of Matter by its Extension; and as one cubic Inch may be made to contain, by Condensation, as much Matter as would fill ten thousand cubic Feet, being more expanded, so one single Moment of *Pleasure* may outweigh and compensate an Age of *Pain*.

It was owing to their Ignorance of the Nature of Pleasure and Pain that the Antient Heathens believ'd the idle Fable of their Elizium, that State of uninterrupted Ease and Happiness! The Thing is intirely impossible in Nature! Are not the Pleasures of the Spring made such by the Disagreeableness of the Winter? Is not the Pleasure of fair Weather owing to the Unpleasantness of foul? Certainly. Were it then always Spring, were the Fields always green and flourishing, and the Weather constantly serene and fair, the Pleasure would pall and die upon our Hands; it would cease to be Pleasure to us, when it is not usher'd in by Uneasiness. Could the Philosopher visit, in reality, every Star and Planet with as much Ease and Swiftness as he can now visit their Ideas, and pass from one to another of them in the Imagination; it would be a *Pleasure* I grant; but it would be only in proportion to the *Desire* of accomplishing it, and that would be no greater than the *Uneasiness* suffer'd in the Want of it. The Accomplishment of a long and difficult Journey yields a great *Pleasure*; but if we could take a Trip to the Moon and back again, as frequently and with as much Ease as we can go and come from Market, the Satisfaction would be just the same.

The *Immateriality* of the Soul has been frequently made use of as an Argument for its *Immortality*; but let us consider, that tho' it should be allow'd to be immaterial, and consequently its Parts incapable of Separation or Destruction by any Thing material, yet by Experience we find, that it is not incapable of Cessation of *Thought*, which is its Action. When the Body is but a little indispos'd it has an evident Effect upon the Mind; and a right Disposition of the Organs is requisite to a right Manner of Thinking. In a sound Sleep sometimes, or in a Swoon, we cease to think at all; tho' the Soul is not therefore then annihilated, but *exists* all the while tho' it does not *act*; and may not this probably be the Case after Death? All our Ideas are first admitted by the Senses and imprinted on the Brain, increasing in Number by Observation and Experience; there they become the Subjects of the Soul's Action. The Soul is a mere Power of Faculty of *contemplating* on, and *comparing* those Ideas when it has them;

hence springs Reason: But as it can *think* on nothing but Ideas, it must have them before it can *think* at all. Therefore as it may exist before it has receiv'd any Ideas, it may exist before it *thinks*. To remember a Thing, is to have the Idea of it still plainly imprinted on the Brain, which the Soul can turn to and contemplate on Occasion. To forget a Thing, is to have the Idea of it defac'd and destroy'd by some Accident, or the crouding in and imprinting of great variety of other Ideas upon it, so that the Soul cannot find out its Traces and distinguish it. When we have thus lost the Idea of any one Thing, we can *think* no more, or *cease to think,* on that Thing; and as we can lose the Idea of one Thing, so we may of ten, twenty, a hundred, &c. and even of all Things, because they are not in their Nature permanent; and often during Life we see that some Men, (by an Accident or Distemper affecting the Brain,) lose the greatest Part of their Ideas, and remember very little of their past Actions and Circumstances. Now upon *Death,* and the Destruction of the Body, the Ideas contain'd in the Brain, (which are alone the Subjects of the Soul's Action) being then likewise necessarily destroy'd, the Soul, tho' incapable of Destruction itself, must then necessarily *cease to think* or *act,* having nothing left to think or act upon. It is reduc'd to its first inconscious State before it receiv'd any Ideas. And to cease to *think* is but little different from *ceasing to be.*

Nevertheless, 'tis not impossible that this same *Faculty* of contemplating Ideas may be hereafter united to a new Body, and receive a new Set of Ideas; but that will no way concern us who are now living; for the Identity will be lost, it is no longer that same *Self* but a new Being.

I shall here subjoin a short Recapitulation of the Whole, that it may with all its Parts be comprehended at one View.

1. *It is suppos'd that God the Maker and Governour of the Universe, is infinitely wise, good, and powerful.*

2. *In consequence of His infinite Wisdom and Goodness, it is asserted, that whatever He doth must be infinitely wise and good;*

3. *Unless He be interrupted, and His Measures broken by some other Being, which is impossible because He is Almighty.*

4. *In consequence of His infinite Power, it is asserted, that nothing can exist or be done in the Universe which is not agreeable to His Will, and therefore good.*

5. *Evil is hereby excluded, with all Merit and Demerit; and likewise all preference in the Esteem of God, of one Part of the Creation to another.* This is the Summary of the first Part.

Now our common Notions of Justice will tell us, that if all created Things are equally esteem'd by the Creator, they ought to be equally us'd by Him; and that they are therefore equally us'd, we might embrace for Truth upon the Credit, and as the true Consequence of the foregoing Argument. Nevertheless we proceed to confirm it, by shewing *how* they are equally us'd, and that in the following Manner.

1. *A Creature when endu'd with Life or Consciousness, is made capable of Uneasiness or Pain.*

2. *This Pain produces Desire to be freed from it, in exact proportion to itself.*

3. *The Accomplishment of this Desire produces an equal Pleasure.*

4. *Pleasure is consequently equal to Pain.*

From these Propositions it is observ'd,

1. *That every Creature hath as much Pleasure as Pain.*

2. *That Life is not preferable to Insensibility; for Pleasure and Pain destroy one another: That Being which has ten Degrees of Pain subtracted from ten of Pleasure, has nothing remaining, and is upon an equality with that Being which is insensible of both.*

3. As the first Part proves that all Things must be equally us'd by the Creator because equally esteem'd; so this second Part demonstrates that they are equally esteem'd because equally us'd.

4. Since every Action is the Effect of Self-Uneasiness, the Distinction of Virtue and Vice is excluded; and Prop. VIII. *in* Sect. I. *again demonstrated.*

5. No State of Life can be happier than the present, because Pleasure and Pain are inseparable.

Thus both Parts of this Argument agree with and confirm one another, and the Demonstration is reciprocal.

I am sensible that the Doctrine here advanc'd, if it were to be publish'd, would meet with but an indifferent Reception. Mankind naturally and generally love to be flatter'd: Whatever sooths our Pride, and tends to exalt our Species above the rest of the Creation, we are pleas'd with and easily believe, when ungrateful Truths shall be with the utmost Indignation rejected. "What! bring ourselves down to an Equality with the Beasts of the Field! with the *meanest* part of the Creation! 'Tis insufferable!" But, (to use a Piece of *common* Sense) our *Geese* are but *Geese* tho' we may think 'em *Swans*; and Truth will be Truth tho' it sometimes prove mortifying and distasteful.

Articles of Belief and Acts of Religion – Nov. 20, 1728

Here will I hold—If there is a Pow'r above us (And that there is, all Nature cries aloud, Thro' all her Works), He must delight in Virtue And that which he delights in must be Happy.   Cato.
Part I. Philada. Nov. 20 1728.

First Principles

I Believe there is one Supreme most perfect Being, Author and Father of the Gods themselves.[7]

For I believe that Man is not the most perfect Being but One, rather that as there are many Degrees of Beings his Inferiors, so there are many Degrees of Beings superior to him.

Also, when I stretch my Imagination thro' and beyond our System of Planets, beyond the visible fix'd Stars themselves, into that Space that is every Way infinite, and conceive it fill'd with Suns like ours, each with a Chorus of Worlds for ever moving round him, then this little Ball on which we move, seems, even in my narrow Imagination, to be almost Nothing, and my self less than nothing, and of no sort of Consequence.

When I think thus, I imagine it great Vanity in me to suppose, that the *Supremely Perfect,* does in the least regard such an inconsiderable Nothing as Man. More especially, since it is impossible for me to have any positive clear Idea of that which is infinite and incomprehensible, I cannot conceive otherwise, than that He, *the Infinite Father,* expects or requires no Worship or Praise from us, but that he is even infinitely above it.

---

[7] Scholars are divided over whether Franklin actually embraced polytheism in this essay or just used it as a metaphor for a distant God (Walters, 78-79). I personally think that Franklin did accept polytheism at this point in his life. This essay seems to fit well within the framework of a young man who has come to recognize the futility inherent in deistic determinism, but who is not yet willing to admit his error in renouncing the Christianity of his parents. This view is supported by the fact that Franklin's "Articles" were written a mere three years after his *Dissertation* but also a mere three years prior to his "Doctrine to be Preached" (1731). In his *Dissertation*, Franklin presented a deterministic and indifferent God while in his "Doctrine to be Preached" he described the Almighty as personal, loving and benevolent. The polytheistic system in the "Articles" is exactly between these two with an impersonal God ruling over the universe as a whole and a more considerate god ruling over our solar system.

But since there is in all Men something like a natural Principle which enclines them to Devotion or the Worship of some unseen Power;

And since Men are endued with Reason superior to all other Animals that we are in our World acquainted with;

Therefore I think it seems required of me, and my Duty, as a Man, to pay Divine Regards to Something.

I conceive then, that the Infinite has created many Beings or Gods, vastly superior to Man, who can better conceive his Perfections than we, and return him a more rational and glorious Praise. As among Men, the Praise of the Ignorant or of Children, is not regarded by the ingenious Painter or Architect, who is rather honour'd and pleas'd with the Approbation of Wise men and Artists.

It may be that these created Gods, are immortal, or it may be that after many Ages, they are changed, and Others supply their Places.

Howbeit, I conceive that each of these is exceeding wise, and good, and very powerful; and that Each has made for himself, one glorious Sun, attended with a beautiful and admirable System of Planets.

It is that particular wise and good God, who is the Author and Owner of our System, that I propose for the Object of my Praise and Adoration.

For I conceive that he has in himself some of those Passions he has planted in us, and that, since he has given us Reason whereby we are capable of observing his Wisdom in the Creation, he is not above caring for us, being pleas'd with our Praise, and offended when we slight Him, or neglect his Glory.

I conceive for many Reasons that he is a *good Being,* and as I should be happy to have so wise, good and powerful a Being my Friend, let me consider in what Manner I shall make myself most acceptable to him.

Next to the Praise due, to his Wisdom, I believe he is pleased and delights in the Happiness of those he has created; and since without Virtue Man can have no Happiness in this World, I firmly believe he delights to see me Virtuous, because he is pleas'd when he sees me Happy.

And since he has created many Things which seem purely design'd for the Delight of Man, I believe he is not offended when he sees his Children solace themselves in any manner of pleasant Exercises and innocent Delights, and I think no Pleasure innocent that is to Man hurtful.

I *love* him therefore for his Goodness and I *adore* him for his Wisdom.

My good Father,
And of my Devotion;

(1)

Powerful Goodness, &c.

O Creator, O Father, I believe that thou art Good, and that thou art *pleas'd with the Pleasure* of thy Children. Praised be thy Name for Ever.

(2)

By thy Power hast thou made the glorious Sun, with his attending Worlds; from the Energy of thy mighty Will they first received [their prodigious] Motion, and by thy Wisdom hast thou prescribed the wondrous Laws by which they move. Praised be thy Name for ever.

(3)

By thy Wisdom hast thou formed all Things, Thou hast created Man, bestowing Life and Reason, and plac'd him in Dignity superior to thy other earthly Creatures. Praised be thy Name for ever.

(4)

Thy Wisdom, thy Power, and thy Goodness are every where clearly seen; in the Air and in the Water, in the Heavens and on the Earth; Thou providest for the various winged Fowl, and the innumerable Inhabitants of the Water; Thou givest Cold and Heat, Rain and Sunshine in their Season, and to the Fruits of the Earth Increase.Praised be thy Name for ever.

(5)

I believe thou hast given Life to thy Creatures that they might Live, and art not delighted with violent Death and bloody Sacrifices.centerPraised be thy Name for ever.

(6)

Thou abhorrest in thy Creatures Treachery and Deceit, Malice, Revenge, [*Intemperance*] and every other hurtful Vice; but Thou art a Lover of Justice and Sincerity, of Friendship, Benevolence and every Virtue. Thou art my Friend, my Father, and my Benefactor. Praised be thy Name for ever. Amen.

After this, it will not be improper to read part of some such Book as Ray's Wisdom of God in the Creation or Blacmore on the Creation, or the Archbishop of Cambray's Demonstration of the Being of a God; &c. or else spend some Minutes in a serious Silence, contemplating on those Subjects.

Then Sing Milton's Hymn to the Creator
These are thy Glorious Works, Parent of Good!
Almighty: Thine this Universal Frame,
Thus wondrous fair! Thy self how wondrous then!
Speak ye who best can tell, Ye Sons of Light,

Angels, for ye behold him, and with Songs,
And Choral Symphonies, Day without Night
Circle his Throne rejoicing. You in Heav'n,
On Earth, join all Ye Creatures to extol
Him first, him last, him midst and without End.
  Fairest of Stars, last in the Train of Night,
If rather thou belongst not to the Dawn,
Sure Pledge of Day! That crown'st the smiling Morn
With thy bright Circlet; Praise him in thy Sphere
While Day arises, that sweet Hour of Prime.
  Thou Sun, of this Great World both Eye and Soul
Acknowledge Him thy Greater, Sound his Praise
In thy Eternal Course; both when thou climb'st,
And when high Noon hast gain'd, and when thou fall'st.
Moon! that now meet'st the orient Sun, now fly'st
With the fix'd Stars, fix'd in their Orb that flies,
And ye five other Wandring Fires, that move
In mystic Dance, not without Song, resound
His Praise, that out of Darkness call'd up Light.
Air! and ye Elements! the Eldest Birth
Of Nature's Womb, that in Quaternion run
Perpetual Circle, multiform; and mix
And nourish all Things, let your ceaseless Change
Vary to our great Maker still new Praise.
Ye Mists and Exhalations! that now rise
From Hill or steaming Lake, dusky or grey,
Till the Sun paint your fleecy Skirts with Gold,
In Honour to the World's Great Author rise.
Whether to deck with Clouds th' uncolour'd Sky
Or wet the thirsty Earth with falling Show'rs,
Rising or falling still advance his Praise.
His Praise, ye Winds! that from 4 Quarters blow,
Breathe soft or loud; and wave your Tops ye Pines!
With every Plant, in Sign of Worship wave.
Fountains! and ye that warble as ye flow
Melodious Murmurs, warbling tune his Praise.
Join Voices all ye living Souls, ye Birds!
That singing, up to Heav'n's high Gate ascend,

Bear on your Wings, and in your Notes his Praise.
Ye that in Waters glide! and ye that walk
The Earth! and stately Tread, or lowly Creep;
Witness *if I be silent,* Ev'n or Morn,
To Hill or Valley, Fountain or Fresh Shade,
Made Vocal by my Song, and taught his Praise.

Here follows the Reading of some Book or part of a Book
Discoursing on and exciting to Moral Virtue

Petition.

In as much as by Reason of our Ignorance We cannot be Certain that
many Things Which we often hear mentioned in the Petitions of
Men to the Deity, would prove real Goods if they were in our
Possession, and as I have Reason to hope and believe that the
Goodness of my Heavenly Father will not withold from me a
suitable Share of Temporal Blessings, if by a Virtuous and Holy
Life I merit his Favour and Kindness, There-fore I presume not to
ask such Things, but rather Humbly, and with a sincere Heart
express my earnest Desires that he would graciously assist my
Continual Endeavours and Resolutions of eschewing Vice and
embracing Virtue; Which kind of Supplications will at least be thus
far beneficial, as they remind me in a solemn manner of my
Extensive

Duty. Prel. That I may be preserved from Atheism and Infidelity,
Impiety and Profaneness, and in my Addresses to Thee carefully
avoid Irreverence and Ostentation, Formality and odious Hypocrisy,
Help me, O Father That I may be loyal to my Prince, and faithful to
my Country, careful for its Good, valiant in its Defence, and
obedient to its Laws, abhorring Treason as much as Tyranny, Help
me, O Father That I may to those above me be dutiful, humble, and
submissive, avoiding Pride, Disrespect and Contumacy, Help me, O
Father That I may to those below me, be gracious, Condescending
and Forgiving, using Clemency, protecting *Innocent Distress,*
avoiding Cruelty, Harshness and Oppression, Insolence and
unreasonable Severity, Help me, O Father That I may refrain from

Calumny and Detraction; that I may avoid and abhor Deceit and Envy, Fraud, Flattery and Hatred, Malice, Lying and Ingratitude, Help me, O Father That I may be sincere in Friendship, faithful in Trust, and impartial in Judgment, watchful against Pride, and against Anger (that momentary Madness), Help me, O Father That I may be just in all my Dealings and temperate in my Pleasures, full of Candour and Ingenuity, Humanity and Benevolence, Help me, O Father That I may be grateful to my Benefactors and generous to my Friends, exerting Charity and Liberality to the Poor, and Pity to the Miserable, Help me, O Father That I may avoid Avarice, Ambition, and Intemperance, Luxury and Lasciviousness, Help me, O Father That I may possess Integrity and Evenness of Mind, Resolution in Difficulties, and Fortitude under Affliction; that I may be punctual in performing my Promises, peaceable and prudent in my Behaviour, Help me, O Father That I may have Tenderness for the Weak, and a reverent Respect for the Ancient; That I may be kind to my Neighbours, good-natured to my Companions, and hospitable to Strangers, Help me, O Father That I may be averse to Craft and Overreaching, abhor Extortion, Perjury, and every kind of Wickedness, Help me, O Father That I may be honest and Openhearted, gentle, merciful and Good, chearful in Spirit, rejoicing in the Good of Others, Help me, O Father That I may have a constant Regard to Honour and Probity; That I may possess a perfect Innocence and a good Conscience, and at length become Truly Virtuous and Magnanimous, Help me, Good God, Help me, O Father

And forasmuch as Ingratitude is one of the most odious of Vices, let me not be unmindful gratefully to acknoledge the Favours I receive from Heaven.

Thanks.

For Peace and Liberty, for Food and Raiment, for Corn and Wine, and Milk, and every kind of Healthful Nourishment, *Good God, I Thank thee.*

For the Common Benefits of Air and Light, for useful Fire and delicious Water, *Good God, I Thank thee.*

For Knowledge and Literature and every useful Art; for my Friends and their Prosperity, and for the fewness of my Enemies, *Good God, I Thank thee.*

For all thy innumerable Benefits; For Life and Reason, and the Use of Speech, for Health and Joy and every Pleasant Hour, *my Good God, I thank thee.*

Epitaph – 1728

The Body of B. Franklin, Printer; Like the Cover of an old Book, Its Contents torn out, And stript of its Lettering and Gilding, Lies here, Food for Worms. But the Work shall not be wholly lost: For it will, as he believ'd, appear once more, In a new & more perfect Edition, Corrected and amended By the Author.[8]

---

[8] George Whitefield read a copy of this epitaph in 1755 and wrote the following in a letter to Franklin:

"I have seen your Epitaph. Believe on Jesus, and get a feeling possession of God in your heart, and you cannot possibly be disappointed of your expected second edition finely corrected, and infinitely amended. Verbum sapienti sat est. I could say more, but time is short."

Notice the emphasis on a "feeling possession." Many scholars mention the fact that Whitefield and Franklin shared different religious views, but most attribute that difference to the erroneous conclusion that Franklin remained a Deist throughout his life. Stout, for example, makes the following observation of this friendship:

"Such was their mutual affection that Franklin forever encouraged Whitefield to look after the state of his badly deteriorating health, while Whitefield continually encouraged Franklin to look after the state of his badly deteriorating soul ... On the face of it, there could have been no more unusual a combination for friendship than the creed-despising Franklin and the deist-despising Whitefield. Each was on public record as opposing much of the philosophy the other stood for." (Stout 222)

Doctrine to be Preached – 1731

That there is one God Father of the Universe.[9]

That he [is] infinitely good, Powerful and wise.

That he is omnipresent.

That he ought to be worshipped, by Adoration Prayer and Thanksgiving both in publick and private.

That he loves such of his Creatures as love and do good to others: and will reward them either in this World or hereafter.

That Men's Minds do not die with their Bodies, but are made more happy or miserable after this Life according to their Actions.

That Virtuous Men ought to league together to strengthen the Interest of Virtue, in the World: and so strengthen themselves in Virtue.

That Knowledge and Learning is to be cultivated, and Ignnorance dissipated.

Such claims, however, completely overlook the substance of Franklin and Whitefield's religious disagreement. What really separated these two men was Whitefield's insistence that an emotional experience of spiritual pangs and convulsions was a necessary component of salvation. It was this type of conversion that Whitefield would urge Franklin to have and of which Franklin later tells us that Whitefield "never had the Satisfaction of believing that his Prayers were heard."

[9] Franklin was 25 years old when he wrote this list of doctrines, and though we only have a small portion of it remaining to us, that portion is sufficient to demonstrate that, by this time, his view of God and religion was dramatically different from that which he had expressed during his teen years. Then, he viewed God as distant and indifferent while here he describes God as ever present and loving.

That none but the Virtuous are wise.

That Man's Perfection is in Virtue. [*Remainder lost*]

Standing Queries for the Junto – 1732

Qu. Can a Man arrive at Perfection in this Life as some Believe; or is it impossible as others believe?

A. Perhaps they differ in the meaning of the Word Perfection.

I suppose the Perfection of any Thing to be only the greatest the Nature of that Thing is capable of;

different Things have different Degrees of Perfection; and the same thing at different Times.

Thus an Horse is more perfect than an Oyster yet the Oyster may be a perfect Oyster as well as the Horse a perfect Horse.

And an Egg is not so perfect as a Chicken, nor a Chicken as a Hen; for the Hen has more Strength than the Chicken, and the C[hicken] more Life than the Egg: Yet it may be a perfect Egg, Chicken and Hen.

If they mean, a Man cannot in this Life be so perfect as an Angel, it is [*written above*: may be] true; for an Angel by being incorporeal is allow'd some Perfections we are at present incapable of, and less liable to some Imperfections that we are liable to.

If they mean a Man is not capable of being so perfect here as he is capable of being in Heaven, that may be true likewise. But that a Man is not capable of being so perfect here, as he is capable of being here; is not Sense; it is as if I should say, a Chicken in the State of a Chicken is not capable of being so perfect as a Chicken is capable of being in that State. In the above Sense if there may be a perfect Oyster, a perfect Horse, a perfect Ship, why not a perfect Man? that is as perfect as his present Nature and Circumstances admit?

37

On the Providence of God - 1732

When I consider my own Weakness, and the discerning Judgment of those who are to be my Audience, I cannot help blaming my self considerably, for this rash Undertaking of mine, it being a Thing I am altogether ill practis'd in and very much unqualified for; I am especially discouraged when I reflect that you are all my intimate Pot Companions who have heard me say a 1000 silly Things in Conversations, and therefore have not that laudable Partiality and Veneration for whatever I shall deliver that Good People commonly have for their Spiritual Guides; that You have no Reverence for my Habit, nor for the Sanctity of my Countenance; that you do not believe me inspir'd or divinely assisted, and therefore will think your Selves at Liberty to assent or dissent agree [*written above*: approve] or disagree [*written above*: disapprove] of any Thing I advance, canvassing and sifting it as the private Opinion of one of your Acquaintance. These are great Disadvantages and Discouragements but I am enter'd and must proceed, humbly requesting your Patience and Attention.

I propose at this Time to discourse on the Subject of our last Conversation: the Providence of God in the Government of the World. I shall not attempt to amuse you with Flourishes of Rhetorick, were I master of that deceitful Science because I know ye are Men of substantial Reason and can easily discern between sound Argument and the false Glosses of Oratory; nor shall I endeavour to impose on your Ears, by a musical Accent in delivery, in the Tone of one violently affected with what he says; for well I know that ye are far from being superstitious [or] fond of unmeaning Noise, and that ye believe a Thing to be no more true for being sung than said. I intend to offer you nothing but plain Reasoning, devoid of Art and Ornament; unsupported by the Authority of any Books or Men how sacred soever; because I know that no Authority is more convincing to Men of Reason than the Authority of Reason itself. It might be judg'd an Affront to your Understandings should I go about to prove this first Principle, the Existence of a Deity and that he is the Creator of the Universe, for that would suppose you ignorant of what all Mankind in all Ages have agreed in. I shall therefore proceed to observe: 1. That he must be a Being of great Wisdom; 2. That he must be a Being of great Goodness and 3. That he must be a Being of great Power.

That he must be a Being of infinite Wisdom, appears in his admirable Order and Disposition of Things, whether we consider the heavenly Bodies, the Stars and Planets, and their wonderful regular Motions, or this Earth compounded of such an Excellent mixture of all the Elements; or the admirable Structure of Animal Bodies of such infinite Variety, and yet every one adapted to its Nature, and the Way of Life it is to be placed in, whether on Earth, in the Air or in the Waters, and so exactly that the highest and most exquisite human Reason, cannot find a fault and say this would have been better so or in another Manner, which whoever considers attentively and thoroughly will be astonish'd and swallow'd up in Admiration.

2. That the Deity is a Being of great Goodness, appears in his giving Life to so many Creatures, each of which acknowledge it a Benefit by their unwillingness to leave it; in his providing plentiful Sustenance for them all, and making those Things that are most useful, most common and easy to be had; such as Water necessary for almost every Creature's Drink; Air without which few could subsist, the inexpressible Benefits of Light and Sunshine to almost all Animals in general; and to Men the most useful Vegetables, such as Corn, the most useful of Metals as Iron, and the most useful Animals, as Horses, Oxen and Sheep, he has made easiest to raise, or procure in Quantity or Numbers: each of which particulars if considered seriously and carefully would fill us with the highest Love and Affection.

3. That he is a Being of infinite Power appears, in his being able to form and compound such Vast Masses of Matter as this Earth and the Sun and innumerable Planets and Stars, and give them such prodigious Motion, and yet so to govern them in their greatest Velocity as that they shall not flie off out of their appointed Bounds nor dash one against another, to their mutual Destruction; but 'tis easy to conceive his Power, when we are convinc'd of his infinite Knowledge and Wisdom; for if weak and foolish Creatures as we

are, by knowing the Nature of a few Things can produce such wonderful Effects; such as for instance by knowing the Nature only of Nitre and Sea Salt mix'd we can make a Water which will dissolve the hardest Iron and by adding one Ingredient more, can make another Water which will dissolve Gold and render the most Solid Bodies fluid—and by knowing the Nature of Salt Peter Sulphur and Charcoal those mean Ingredient mix'd we can shake the Air in the most terrible Manner, destroy Ships Houses and Men at a Distance and in an Instant, overthrow Cities, rend Rocks into a Thousand Pieces, and level the highest Mountains. What Power must he possess who not only knows the Nature of every Thing in the Universe, but can make Things of new Natures with the greatest Ease and at his Pleasure!

Agreeing then that the World was at first made by a Being of infinite Wisdom, Goodness and Power, which Being we call God; The State of Things ever since and at this Time must be in one of these four following manners, viz.

1. Either he unchangeably decreed and appointed every Thing that comes to pass; and left nothing to the Course [of] Nature, nor allow'd any Creature free agency. or

2. Without decreeing any thing, he left all to general Nature and the Events of Free Agency in his Creatures, which he never alters or interrupts. or

3. He decreed some Things unchangeably, and left others to general Nature and the Events of Free agency, which also he never alters or interrupts; or

4. He sometimes interferes by his particular Providence and sets aside the Effects which would otherwise have been produced by any of the Above Causes.

I shall endeavour to shew the first 3 Suppositions to be inconsistent with the common Light of Reason; and that the 4th is most agreeable to it, and therefore most probably true.

In the 1. place. If you say he has in the Beginning unchangeably decreed all Things and left Nothing to Nature or free Agency. These Strange Conclusions will necessarily follow; 1. That he is now no more a God. 'Tis true indeed, before he had made such unchangeable Decree, he was a Being of Power, Almighty; but now having determin'd every Thing, he has divested himself of all further Power, he has done and has no more to do, he has ty'd up his Hands, and has now no greater Power than an Idol of Wood or Stone; nor can there be any more Reason for praying to him or worshipping of him, than of such an Idol for the Worshippers can be never the better for such Worship. Then 2. he has decreed some things contrary to the very Notion of a wise and good Being; Such as that some of his Creatures or Children shall do all Manner of Injury to others and bring every kind of Evil upon them without Cause; that some of them shall even blaspheme him their Creator in the most horrible manner; and, which is still more highly absurd that he has decreed the greatest Part of Mankind, shall in all Ages, put up their earnest Prayers to him both in private and publickly in great Assemblies, when all the while he had so determin'd their Fate that he could not possibly grant them any Benefits on that Account, nor could such Prayers be any way available. Why then should he ordain them to make such Prayers? It cannot be imagined they are of any Service to him. Surely it is not more difficult to believe the World was made by a God of Wood or Stone, than that the God who made the World should be such a God as this.[10]

In the 2. Place. If you say he has decreed nothing but left all things to general Nature, and the Events of Free Agency, which he never alters or interrupts. Then these Conclusions will follow; He must either utterly hide him self from the Works of his Hands, and take no Notice at all of their Proceedings natural or moral; or he must be as undoubtedly he is, a Spectator of every thing; for there can be no Reason or Ground to suppose the first—I say there can be no Reason to imagine he would make so glorious a Universe meerly to abandon it. In this Case imagine the Deity looking on and beholding

---

[10] This is not only a rejection of Franklin's own beliefs as a teenager but also a rejection of Calvinism.

the Ways of his Creatures; some Hero's in Virtue he sees are incessantly indeavouring the Good of others, they labour thro vast difficulties, they suffer incredible Hardships and Miseries to accomplish this End, in hopes to please a Good God, and obtain his Favour, which they earnestly Pray for; what Answer can he make them within himself but this; *take the Reward Chance may give you, I do not intermeddle in these Affairs*; he sees others continually doing all manner of Evil, and bringing by their Actions Misery and Destruction among Mankind: What can he say here but this, *if Chance rewards you I shall not punish you, I am not to be concerned.* He sees the just, the innocent and the Beneficent in the Hands of the wicked and violent Oppressor; and when the good are at the Brink of Destruction they pray to him, *thou, O God, art mighty and powerful to save; help us we beseech thee*: He answers, *I cannot help you, 'tis none of my Business nor do I at all regard these things.* How is it possible to believe a wise and an infinitely Good Being can be delighted in this Circumstance; and be utterly unconcern'd what becomes of the Beings and Things he has created; for thus, we must believe him idle and unactive, and that his glorious Attributes of Power, Wisdom and Goodness are no more to be made use of.

In the Third Place. If you say he has decreed some things and left others to the Events of Nature and Free Agency, Which he never alters or interrupts; Still you unGod him, if I may be allow'd the Expression; he has nothing to do; he can cause us neither Good nor Harm; he is no more to be regarded than a lifeless Image, than Dagon, or Baall, or Bell and the Dragon; and as in both the other Suppositions foregoing, that Being which from its Power is most able to Act, from its Wisdom knows best how to act, and from its Goodness would always certainly act best, is in this Opinion supposed to become the most unactive of all Beings and remain everlastingly Idle; an Absurdity, which when considered or but barely seen, cannot be swallowed without doing the greatest Violence to common Reason, and all the Faculties of the Understanding.

We are then necessarily driven into the fourth Supposition, That the Deity sometimes interferes by his particular Providence, and sets aside the Events which would otherwise have been produc'd in the Course of Nature, or by the Free Agency of Men; and this is perfectly agreeable with what we can know of his Attributes and Perfections: But as some may doubt whether 'tis possible there should be such a Thing as free Agency in Creatures; I shall just offer one Short Argument on that Account and proceed to shew how the Duties of Religion necessary follow the Belief of a Providence. You acknowledge that God is infinitely Powerful, Wise and Good, and also a free Agent; and you will not deny that he has communicated to us part of his Wisdom, Power and Goodness; i.e. he has made us in some Degree Wise, potent and good; and is it then impossible for him to communicate any Part of his Freedom, and make us also in some Degree Free? Is not even his *infinite* Power sufficient for this? I should be glad to hear what Reason any Man can give for thinking in that Manner; 'tis sufficient for me to shew tis not impossible, and no Man I think can shew 'tis improbable, but much more might be offer'd to demonstrate clearly that Men are in some Degree free Agents, and accountable for their Actions; however, this I may possibly reserve for another separate Discourse hereafter if I find Occasion.[11]

---

[11] Here Franklin provides a brilliantly simple argument against Calvinism. Calvinists often present the false dichotomy that either God is sovereign or man has a free will, and then by demonstrating the absurdity of God not being sovereign, they triumphantly claim that therefore man's will is not free. Arthur W. Pink famously presented this dichotomy in this manner:

"Two alternatives confront us, and between them we are obliged to choose: either God governs, or He is governed; either God rules, or He is ruled; either God has His way, or men have theirs." (Pink, 51)

Franklin solved this dichotomy by presenting the third option of a sovereign God having the power to give men freedom. His question "Is not even his infinite Power sufficient for this?" places the Calvinist in a quandary. If he answers that God is not powerful enough to give men a free will, then he will have denied God's omnipotence, but if he allows that God could give men free will, then he

Lastly if God does not sometimes interfere by his Providence tis either because he cannot, or because he will not; which of these Positions will you chuse? There is a righteous Nation grievously oppress'd by a cruel Tyrant, they earnestly intreat God to deliver them; If you say he cannot, you deny his infinite Power, which [you] at first acknowledg'd; if you say he will not, you must directly deny his infinite Goodness. You are then of necessity oblig'd to allow, that 'tis highly reasonable to believe a Providence because tis highly absurd to believe otherwise.

Now if tis unreasonable to suppose it out of the Power of the Deity to help and favour us particularly or that we are out of his Hearing or Notice or that Good Actions do not procure more of his Favour than ill Ones. Then I conclude, that believing a Providence we have the Foundation of all true Religion; for we should love and revere that Deity for his Goodness and thank him for his Benefits; we should adore him for his Wisdom, fear him for his Power, and pray to him for his Favour and Protection; and this Religion will be a Powerful Regulater of our Actions, give us Peace and Tranquility within our own Minds, and render us Benevolent, Useful and Beneficial to others.

Self Denial not the Essence of Virtue – Feb 5, 1735

It is commonly asserted, that without *Self-Denial* there is no Virtue, and that the greater the *Self-Denial* the greater the Virtue.

If it were said, that he who cannot deny himself in any Thing he inclines to, tho' he knows it will be to his Hurt, has not the Virtue of *Resolution* or *Fortitude,* it would be intelligible enough; but as it stands it seems obscure or erroneous.

Let us consider some of the Virtues singly.

---

will have admitted that his original dichotomy is false. This was sufficient to convince Franklin to abandon the dichotomy entirely in favor of this third option.

If a Man has no inclination to *wrong* People in his Dealings, if he feels no Temptation to it, and therefore never does it; can it be said that he is not a just Man? If he is a just Man, has he not the Virtue of Justice?

If to a certain Man, idle Diversions have nothing in them that is tempting, and therefore he never relaxes his Application to Business for their Sake; is he not an Industrious Man? Or has he not the Virtue of Industry?

I might in like manner instance in all the rest of the Virtues: But to make the Thing short, As it is certain, that the more we strive against the Temptation to any Vice, and practise the contrary Virtue, the weaker will that Temptation be, and the stronger will be that Habit; 'till at length the Temptation has no Force, or entirely vanishes: Does it follow from thence, that in our Endeavours to overcome Vice, we grow continually less and less Virtuous; till at length we have no Virtue at all?

If Self-Denial be the Essence of Virtue, then it follows, that the Man who is naturally temperate, just, &c. is not virtuous; but that in order to be virtuous, he must, in spight of his natural Inclinations, wrong his Neighbours, and eat and drink, &c. to excess.

But perhaps it may be said, that by the Word *Virtue* in the above Assertion, is meant, *Merit*; and so it should stand thus; Without Self-Denial there is no Merit; and the greater the Self-Denial the greater the Merit.

The Self-denial here meant, must be when our Inclinations are towards Vice, or else it would still be Nonsense.

By Merit is understood, Desert; and when we say a Man merits, we mean that he deserves Praise or Reward.

We do not pretend to merit any thing of God, for he is above our Services; and the Benefits he confers on us, are the Effects of his Goodness and Bounty.

All our Merit then is with regard to one another, and from one to another.

Taking then the Assertion as it last stands,

If a Man does me a Service from a natural benevolent Inclination, does he deserve less of me than another who does me the like Kindness against his Inclination?

If I have two Journeymen, one naturally industrious, the other idle, but both perform a Days Work equally good, ought I to give the latter the most Wages?

Indeed, lazy Workmen are commonly observ'd to be more extravagant in their Demands than the Industrious; for if they have not more for their Work, they cannot live so well: But tho' it be true to a Proverb, *That Lazy Folks take the most Pains,* does it follow that they deserve the most Money?

If you were to employ Servants in Affairs of Trust, would you not bid more for one you knew was naturally honest, than for one naturally roguish, but who had lately acted honestly? For Currents whose natural Channel is damm'd up, (till the new Course is by Time worn sufficiently deep and become natural,) are apt to break their Banks. If one Servant is more valuable than another, has he not more Merit than the other? And yet this is not on Account of Superior Self-denial.

Is a Patriot not praise-worthy, if Publick Spirit is natural to him?

Is a Pacing-Horse less valuable for being a natural Pacer?

Nor in my Opinion has any Man less Merit for having in general natural virtuous Inclinations.

The Truth is, that Temperance, Justice, Charity, &c. are Virtues, whether practis'd with or against our Inclinations; and the Man who practises them, merits our Love and Esteem: And Self-denial is neither good nor bad, but as 'tis apply'd: He that denies a Vicious Inclination is Virtuous in proportion to his Resolution, but the most perfect Virtue is above all Temptation, such as the Virtue of the Saints in Heaven: And he who does a foolish, indecent or wicked Thing, meerly because 'tis contrary to his Inclination, (like some mad Enthusiasts I have read of, who ran about naked, under the Notion of taking up the Cross) is not practising the reasonable Science of Virtue, but is lunatick.

Autobiography

About the Year 1734. there arrived among us from Ireland, a young Presbyterian Preacher named Hemphill, who delivered with a good Voice, and apparently extempore, most excellent Discourses, which drew together considerable Numbers of different Persuasions, who join'd in admiring them. Among the rest I became one of his constant Hearers, his Sermons pleasing me, as they had little of the dogmatical kind, but inculcated strongly the Practice of Virtue, or what in the religious Stile are called Good Works. Those however, of our Congregation, who considered themselves as orthodox Presbyterians, disapprov'd his Doctrine, and were join'd by most of the old Clergy, who arraign'd him of Heterodoxy before the Synod, in order to have him silenc'd. I became his zealous Partisan, and contributed all I could to raise a Party in his Favour; and we combated for him a while with some Hopes of Success. There was much Scribbling pro and con upon the Occasion; and finding that tho' an elegant Preacher he was but a poor Writer, I lent him my Pen and wrote for him two or three Pamphlets, and one Piece in the Gazette of April 1735. Those Pamphlets, as is generally the Case with controversial Writings, tho' eagerly read at the time, were soon out of Vogue, and I question whether a single Copy of them now exists.[12]

---

[12] Fortunately, Franklin was mistaken in thinking that none of his defenses of Hemphill survived. In fact, all three of his pamphlets as well as the article from the Gazette are included in this book.

During the Contest an unlucky Occurrence hurt his Cause exceedingly. One of our Adversaries having heard him preach a Sermon that was much admired, thought he had somewhere read that Sermon before, or at least a part of it. On Search he found that Part quoted at length in one of the British Reviews, from a Discourse of Dr. Forster's. This Detection gave many of our Party Disgust, who accordingly abandoned his Cause, and occasion'd our more speedy Discomfiture in the Synod. I stuck by him however, as I rather approv'd his giving us good Sermons compos'd by others, than bad ones of his own Manufacture; tho' the latter was the Practice of our common Teachers. He afterwards acknowledg'd to me that none of those he preach'd were his own; adding that his Memory was such as enabled him to retain and repeat any Sermon after one Reading only. On our Defeat he left us, in search elsewhere of better Fortune, and I quitted the Congregation, never joining it after, tho' I continu'd many Years my Subscription for the Support of its Ministers.

Dialogue Between Two Presbyterians – Apr. 10, 1735

Mr. Franklin,

You are desired by several of your Readers to print the following Dialogue. *It is between Two of the Presbyterian Meeting in this City. We cannot tell whether it may not be contrary to your Sentiments, but hope, if it should, you will not refuse publishing it on that Account: nor shall we be offended if you print any thing in Answer to it. We are yours, &c.*

A.B.C.D.

S. Good Morrow! I am glad to find you well and abroad; for not having seen you at Meeting lately, I concluded you were indispos'd.

T. *Tis true I have not been much at Meeting lately, but that was not occasion'd by any Indisposition. In short, I stay at home, or else go to Church, because I do not like Mr. H. your new-fangled Preacher.*

S. I am sorry we should differ in Opinion upon any Account; but let us reason the Point calmly; what Offence does Mr. H. give you?

T. *Tis his Preaching disturbs me: He talks of nothing but the Duties of Morality: I do not love to hear so much of Morality: I am sure it will carry no Man to Heaven, and I do not think it fit to be preached in a Christian Congregation.*

S. I suppose you think no Doctrine fit to be preached in a Christian Congregation, but such as Christ and his Apostles used to preach.[13]

T. *To be sure I think so.*

S. I do not conceive then how you can dislike the Preaching of Morality, when you consider, that Morality made the principal Part of their Preaching as well as of Mr. H's. What is Christ's Sermon on the Mount but an excellent moral Discourse, towards the End of which, (as foreseeing that People might in time come to depend more upon their *Faith* in him, than upon *Good Works,* for their Salvation) he tells the Hearers plainly, that their saying to him, *Lord, Lord,* (that is, professing themselves his Disciples or *Christians*) should give them no Title to Salvation, but their *Doing* the Will of his Father; and that tho' they have prophesied in his Name, yet he will declare to them, as Neglecters of Morality, that he never knew them.[14]

---

[13] Most scholars attribute the words of S. to Franklin himself. We know that Franklin wrote the entire dialogue because of his reference to it in his autobiography as the "one Piece in the Gazette of April 1735" which he wrote in Hemphill's defense. And although scholars generally focus on the doctrinal errors presented by S., it is important to note that this dialogue marks a significant move on the part of Franklin to embrace religious terminology. For example, this article is the earliest record we have of Franklin using the term "Christ" as we see here.

[14] This paragraph marks the first recorded instance of Franklin relying on Scripture as authoritative. In all of his previous writings on religion, Franklin expressed his own opinion of the relationship between God and man without any reference to Scripture. We know that he knew the Bible, for he tells us in his

T. But what do you understand by that Expression of Christ's, Doing the Will of my Father?

S. I understand it to be the Will of God, that we should live virtuous, upright, and good-doing Lives; as the Prophet understood it, when he said, *What doth the Lord require of thee, O Man, but to do justly, love Mercy, and walk humbly with the Lord thy God.*[15]

T. But is not Faith recommended in the New Testament as well as Morality?

S. Tis true, it is. Faith is recommended as a Means of producing Morality: Our Saviour[16] was a Teacher of Morality or Virtue, and they that were deficient and desired to be taught, ought first to *believe* in him as an able and faithful Teacher. Thus Faith would be a Means of producing Morality, and Morality of Salvation. But that from such Faith alone Salvation may be expected, appears to me to be neither a Christian Doctrine nor a reasonable one. And I should as soon expect, that my bare Believing Mr. Grew to be an excellent Teacher of the Mathematicks, would make me a Mathematician, as that Believing in Christ would of it self make a Man a Christian.[17]

---

autobiography that he was raised in a Christian home and that he received biblical training in the hope that he would someday be a preacher. Franklin knew what the Bible had to say about his topics, he simply ignored it because, as he put it, "Revelation had indeed no weight with me as such." In the "Dialogue" however, the character S., whom most scholars recognize as conveying Franklin's opinion, frequently cited Scripture as the sole support for his claims.

[15] This is a direct quote of Micah 6:8, and it marks the first time that Franklin quoted Scripture in support of any of his arguments. Throughout the "Dialogue" S. quotes a total of nine passages of Scripture in support of his position.

[16] This is the first recorded instance of Franklin referring to Jesus Christ as the Savior.

[17] If the arguments of S are an accurate conveyance of Franklin's thoughts, then it is obvious from this paragraph that Franklin was not a Christian when he wrote the "Dialogue."

T. *Perhaps you may think, that tho' Faith alone cannot save a Man, Morality or Virtue alone, may.*

S. Morality or Virtue is the End, Faith only a Means to obtain that End: And if the End be obtained, it is no matter by what Means. What think you of these Sayings of Christ, when he was reproached for conversing chiefly with gross Sinners, *The whole,* says he, *need not a Physician, but they that are sick;* and, *I come not to call the Righteous, but Sinners, to Repentance:*[18] Does not this imply, that there were good Men, who, without Faith in him, were in a State of Salvation? And moreover, did he not say of Nathanael, while he was yet an Unbeliever in him, and thought no Good could possibly come out of Nazareth, *Behold an Israelite indeed, in whom there is no Guile!*[19] that is, *behold a virtuous upright Man.* Faith in Christ, however, may be and is of great Use to produce a good Life, but that it can conduce nothing towards Salvation where it does not conduce to Virtue, is, I suppose, plain from the Instance of the Devils, who are far from being Infidels, *they believe,* says the Scripture, *and tremble.* There were some indeed, even in the Apostles' Days, that set a great Value upon Faith, distinct from Good Works, they meerly idolized it, and thought that a Man ever so righteous could not be saved without it: But one of the Apostles, to show his Dislike of such Notions, tells them, that not only those heinous Sins of Theft, Murder, and Blasphemy, but even *Idleness,* or the Neglect of a Man's Business, was more pernicious than meer harmless Infidelity, *He that neglects to provide for them of his own House,* says he, *is Worse than an Infidel.*[20] St. James, in his second Chapter, is very zealous against these Cryers-up of Faith, and maintains that Faith without Virtue is useless, *Wilt thou know, O vain Man,* says he, *that Faith without Works is dead;*[21] and, *shew me your Faith without*

---

[18] Mark 2:17

[19] John 1:47

[20] I Timothy 5:8

[21] James 2:20

your Works, and I will shew you mine by my Works.[22] Our Saviour, when describing the last Judgment, and declaring what shall give Admission into Bliss, or exclude from it, says nothing of *Faith* but what he says against it, that is, that those who cry *Lord, Lord,* and profess to have *believed* in his Name, have no Favour to expect on that Account;[23] but declares that 'tis the Practice, or the omitting the Practice of the Duties of Morality, *Feeding the Hungry, cloathing the Naked, visiting the Sick,* &c.[24] in short, 'tis the Doing or not Doing all the Good that lies in our Power, that will render us the Heirs of Happiness or Misery.

T. *But if Faith is of great Use to produce a good Life, why does not Mr. H. preach up Faith as well as Morality?*

S. Perhaps it may [be] this, that as the good Physician suits his Physick to the Disease he finds in the Patient, so Mr. H. may possibly think, that though Faith in Christ be properly first preach'd to Heathens and such as are ignorant of the Gospel, yet since he knows that we have been baptized in the Name of Christ, and educated in his Religion, and call'd after his Name, it may not be so immediately necessary to preach *Faith* to us who abound in it, as *Morality* in which we are evidently deficient:[25] For our late Want of

---

[22] James 2:18

[23] Matthew 7:21

[24] Matthew 25:31-46

[25] In his responses to the trial of Hemphill, Franklin abandons the argument that salvation comes from works, and focuses instead on this argument that it is more important to preach to Christians about the morality that they lack than about the faith which they already posses. This shift in Franklin's argument is completely overlooked by most scholars. They latch on to Franklin's earlier statement about works in the "Dialogue" and ignore the fact that this piece marks the last time that Franklin ever wrote of earning salvation through good works. In the rest of his defenses of Hemphill, Franklin presents a properly Christian view of the relationship between faith and works.

Charity to each other, our Heart-burnings and Bickerings are notorious. St. James says, *Where Envying and Strife is, there is Confusion and every evil Work:*[26] and where Confusion and every evil Work is, *Morality* and Good-will to Men, can, I think, be no unsuitable Doctrine. But surely *Morality* can do us no harm. Upon a Supposition that we all have Faith in Christ already, as I think we have, where can be the Damage of being exhorted to Good Works? Is Virtue Heresy; and Universal Benevolence False Doctrine, that any of us should keep away from Meeting because it is preached there?

T. *Well, I do not like it, and I hope we shall not long be troubled with it. A Commission of the Synod will sit in a short Time, and try this Sort of Preaching.*

S. I am glad to hear that the Synod are to take it into Consideration. There are Men of unquestionable Good Sense as well as Piety among them, and I doubt not but they will, by their Decision, deliver our Profession from the satyrical Reflection, which a few uneasy People of our Congregation have of late given Occasion for, to wit, That the Presbyterians are going to persecute, silence and condemn a good Preacher, for exhorting them to be honest and charitable to one another and the rest of Mankind.

T. *If Mr. H. is a Presbyterian Teacher, he ought to preach as Presbyterians use to preach; or else he may justly be condemn'd and silenc'd by our Church Authority. We ought to abide by the Westminster Confession of Faith; and he that does not, ought not to preach in our Meetings.*

S. The Apostacy of the Church from the Primitive Simplicity of the Gospel, came on by Degrees; and do you think that the Reformation was of a sudden perfect, and that the first Reformers knew at once all that was right or wrong in Religion? Did not Luther at first preach only against selling of Pardons, allowing all the other

---

[26] James 3:16

Practices of the Romish Church for good? He afterwards went further, and Calvin, some think, yet further. The Church of England made a Stop, and fix'd her Faith and Doctrine by 39 Articles; with which the Presbyterians not satisfied, went yet farther; but being too self-confident to think, that as their Fathers were mistaken in some Things, they also might be in some others; and fancying themselves infallible in *their* interpretations, they also ty'd themselves down by the Westminster Confession. But has not a Synod that meets in King George the Second's Reign, as much Right to interpret Scripture, as one that met in Oliver's Time? And if any Doctrine then maintain'd is, or shall hereafter be found not altogether orthodox, why must we be for ever confin'd to that, or to any, Confession?[27]

T. *But if the Majority of the Synod be against any Innovation, they may justly hinder the Innovator from Preaching.*

S. That is as much as to say, if the Majority of the Preachers be in the wrong, they may justly hinder any Man from setting the People right; for a *Majority* may be in the wrong as well as the *Minority,* and frequently are. In the beginning of the Reformation, the *Majority* was vastly against the Reformers, and continues so to this Day; and, if, according to your Opinion, they had a Right to silence the *Minority,* I am sure the *Minority* ought to have been silent. But tell me, if the Presbyterians in this Country, being charitably enclin'd, should send a Missionary into Turky, to propagate the Gospel, would it not be unreasonable in the Turks to prohibit his Preaching?

---

[27] Here Franklin presents an excellent argument against the creedal churches. He reasoned that any church which claimed that a previously held creed was wrong must accept the possibility that their own creed could be in error too. He then argued that if it is possible for a church's creed to be in error, then that church has no authority to forbid its pastors from preaching contrary to that creed. The reference to "Oliver's Time" was a reminder to the Presbyterians that, when they were the dominant religious group in England less than 100 years earlier with the rise of Oliver Cromwell, they had abolished the Episcopacy along with the Act of Uniformity thereby creating a state of religious freedom in which all doctrines had been permitted to be preached.

T. *It would, to be sure, because he comes to them for their good.*

S. And if the Turks, believing us in the wrong, as we think them, should out of the same charitable Disposition, send a Missionary to preach Mahometanism to us, ought we not in the same manner to give him free Liberty of preaching his Doctrine?

T. *It may be so; but what would you infer from that?*

S. I would only infer, that if it would be thought reasonable to suffer a Turk to preach among us a Doctrine diametrically opposite to Christianity, it cannot be reasonable to silence one of our own Preachers, for preaching a Doctrine exactly agreeable to Christianity, only because he does not perhaps zealously propagate all the Doctrines of an old Confession.[28] And upon the whole, though the *Majority* of the Synod should not in all respects approve of Mr. H.'s Doctrine, I do not however think they will find it proper to condemn him. We have justly deny'd the Infallibility of the Pope and his Councils and Synods in their Interpretations of Scripture, and can we modestly claim *Infallibility* for our selves or our Synods in our way of Interpreting? Peace, Unity and Virtue in any Church are more to be regarded than Orthodoxy. In the present weak State of humane Nature, surrounded as we are on all sides with Ignorance and Error, it little becomes poor fallible Man to be positive and dogmatical in his Opinions. No Point of Faith is so plain, as that *Morality* is our Duty, for all Sides agree in that. A virtuous Heretick shall be saved before a wicked Christian: for there is no such Thing as voluntary Error.[29] Therefore, since 'tis an Uncertainty till we get

---

[28] Franklin presented this argument for tolerance immediately upon the heels of reminding the Presbyterians of their former passion for religious liberty.

[29] The first part of this sentence has often been quoted by scholars as if it were a summation of Franklin's lifelong position on morality. John Fea said as much when he wrote:

"Franklin's religious beliefs were less about Christian doctrine and more about virtue ... Franklin made this clear when he argued that a 'virtuous Heretick shall be saved before a wicked Christian.'" (Fea, 221)

to Heaven what true Orthodoxy in all points is, and since our Congregation is rather too small to be divided, I hope this Misunderstanding will soon be got over, and that we shall as heretofore unite again in mutual *Christian Charity.*

T. *I wish we may. I'll consider of what you've said, and wish you well.*

S. Farewell.

Observations of the Proceedings against Mr. Hemphill – July, 1735

The Commission of the Synod having published what they thought proper of their Proceedings in Hemphill's Tryal, it is therefore thought expedient to give a true Narrative of the whole Affair, in order to clear his Character from the false Aspersions which have been cast upon it, and to convince the World how unjustly some Men will act, when they have their own private Ends in View.

We have seen already in the "Dialogue" that Franklin held to a works based salvation at this point in his life, but I do not believe that this is what he is referring to in this sentence. What Fea has overlooked in his statement is the simple fact that Franklin himself provided an explanation which disagrees with the view held by most scholars regarding this comparison between virtuous heretics and wicked Christians.

According to Franklin, a virtuous heretic will be saved before a wicked Christian because "there is no such Thing as voluntary Error." In the seventeenth and eighteenth centuries, the term "heresy" was commonly defined as "a voluntary error against that which God hath revealed." (Chillingworth, 393) Franklin probably thought that this definition was illogical since the strict definition of the word "error" refers to an involuntary mistake. In any case, by denying the existence of a voluntary error, Franklin was claiming that there really was no such thing as heresy and, thus, that those Christians who had been condemned as heretics were still just as much Christians as those who had not. Having dispensed with the charge of heresy, Franklin could then return to the philosophy of a works based salvation which he later abandoned as we shall soon see.

The Commission promis'd Hemphill a Copy of the Minutes as soon as they could be transcrib'd; which Promise if they had comply'd with, this *Answer* might have been published before the Printer was taken sick, whose Illness unexpectedly continuing six or seven Weeks has thus long retarded its Publication.

Some Observations, &c.

It will be necessary by way of Introduction, to give a brief Account of the first Cause which gave Rise to the unchristian Treatment which Mr. Hemphill has met with since he came to America.

This was a Letter which Mr. Vance, a Presbyterian Minister in the North of Ireland, sent to his Brother-in-law J. Kilpatrick in Pennsylvania, to the prejudice of Hemphill's Character, of which Letter more hereafter. The Difference between Vance and Hemphill arose thus; Vance having preach'd at a neighbouring Congregation call'd Burt near London-derry, Hemphill soon after preach'd in the same Place and upon the same Subject. Some of those who heard Hemphill's Sermon, told Vance that his Sermon was oppos'd by Hemphill; and altho' neither Vance nor Hemphill were acquainted with each other, nor had they ever heard one another preach, yet this inflam'd Vance's Zeal to that degree, that he took all the care in his Power to defame Hemphill, calling him a vile Heretick, and said that no christian Minister should allow him to preach in his Pulpit, and that he would have him suspended next Synod. The Synod meeting soon after, Vance thought proper to invite Hemphill to a private Conference in order to accomodate the Affair in a christian manner; and accordingly both met, with four other Ministers, viz. Messrs. Ross, Ferguson, Donaldson and Harvey. It was there propos'd by one of the Ministers, that both Sermons should be preach'd before the Synod, which Hemphill agreed to, but Vance would not, altho' he had traduced him in so vile a manner. At length Vance freely own'd he had reported Things of Hemphill which he himself did not believe, that he believ'd Hemphill was wronged, that he was sorry for it, and would use all the means in his Power to inform his Neighbours that Hemphill was very ill used.

Notwithstanding this solemn Promise, Vance acted with more Malice and Envy than ever; and being accused in a second Conference by Hemphill, when two of the aforesaid Ministers were present, that he not only reported Lies of him, but also violated the solemn Promise he had made at the Synod; he absolutely deny'd that he had said any thing to Hemphill's Disadvantage since their last Meeting at the Synod; this he did upon the Word of a christian Minister, and with uplifted Hands, altho' it could have been sufficiently prov'd against him. And Vance having further an Opportunity of stopping Hemphill's Ordination, being present when his Name was publish'd in the Synod in the usual manner, "desiring if any Member knew any Cause why Hemphill should not be ordain'd, they would tell it to the Synod"; this one would think was the most proper time and place for Vance to have told what he knew of Hemphill, and which without doubt he would have been very fond of, had there been any Truth in what he reported of him before, or afterwards wrote to America. And here I'm amaz'd that Vance could find so many Men in these Parts of his own Principles, who will not only venture to violate the peculiar Duties of Christianity, but even every thing that is human. One would think, that neither Vance, nor those who are the Executioners of his religious Vengeance in America, can be ignorant of that noble moral Precept of *doing as they would be done by.*[30]

In the Letter which Vance sent to J. Kilpatrick, he tells him, that there is a Preacher, Hemphill by name, gone over to Pennsylvania, who is a vile Heretick, a Preacher of Morality, and giving him all the invidious Names that Malice could invent, he desires him to prevent his Settlement in America if possible; at the same time desiring that his Name may not be made use of; from whence it may justly be concluded, that it was not a Regard for Christianity, but Malice, that was his Motive in writing so scandalous a Letter, and none but those of his own Stamp would have given any Credit to it.

---

[30] Matthew 7:12

When Kilpatrick received said Letter, he took a particular care to publish it; he went to the neighbouring Congregations, reading it as often as he could find Hearers, and showing it to the Ministers, who copied after Vance's Example; for soon after, Hemphill was represented by several Ministers to be a *New-Light Man,* a *Deist,* one who preach'd nothing but *Morality,* a Missionary sent from Ireland to corrupt the Faith once delivered to the Saints; in short, he was every thing a persecuting Spirit could invent; altho' neither they nor Vance had ever heard him preach, nor did they know at that Time but he was as full of Enthusiasm and a persecuting Zeal as themselves.

But this was not all, for they made use of all the means they were capable of, to excite the People of New-London in Chester County, where Hemphill had preach'd two Sermons, to prosecute and give Evidence against him for some Heresy or other, and prevail'd upon two Men for that purpose; upon which Hemphill being summoned by the Presbytery of New-Castle, he appear'd and was acquitted, to the great Grief of several of the Members, who since endeavoured to have another Presbytery call'd, in order to suspend him; nay some of them consulted the Records of the Church of Scotland, in order to find a Precedent for deposing him before the Sentence of Suspension.

I should inform my Reader, when Mr. Hemphill came to Philadelphia, immediately after his Arrival in Pennsylvania, Mr. Andrews invited him to preach in his Pulpit once a day, and even told him, that if the Congregation of Philadelphia should chance to be pleased with his Preaching, Mr. Andrews would leave the Place to himself: But some time after this, Mr. Andrews, moved it seems by Envy at hearing Hemphill's Preaching universally applauded, and observing the large Audiences when he preached, thought fit to go from House to House among his Congregation, declaring Hemphill to be a Preacher of erroneous Doctrine, calling him *Deist, Socinian,* and the like, and was pleased to be very angry with those who could not agree with him in his Notions of Hemphill and his Sermons.

Articles *to be presented to the Consideration of the Reverend*

Commis-

"1. That Christianity is nothing else but a Revival or new Edition of the Laws and Precepts of Nature, except two positive Precepts and worshipping of God by a Mediator. Text, Rom. 8:18.

"2. Whether the Sentiments some had of his Opinion about the new Creature from his Sermon on Gal. 6:15, were well grounded, I shall not determine: But his saying in that Sermon that the Sacrament of the Lord's Supper is only a Means to promote a good and pious Life, and afterwards denying any Communion in it, is what I don't agree to. I was also not satisfied at his speaking against the need of spiritual Pangs in order to Conversion.

"3. In his Sermon on Acts 24:25, there were many Things that I was displeased with. He appeared to me and others as declaiming with great Earnestness against the Doctrine of Christ's Merits and Satisfaction, as a Doctrine that represented God as stern and inexorable, and fit only for Tyrants to impose and Slaves to obey. There were also some complained of, as if they made a Charm of the Word *Christ* in their preaching, thereby working up their Hearers to Enthusiasm.

"4. Preaching upon Mark 16:16, he described Saving Faith to be nothing else but an Assent to or Persuasion of the Truth of the Doctrines of the Gospel on rational Grounds. He also said, that the Mysteries mentioned in the Epistles concerned only those Times in which they were wrote, and not us. And that Faith and Obedience are the same Thing.

"5. In his Sermon on Acts 10:34, 35, he appeared to me and others as designing to open the Door of the Church wide enough to admit all honest Heathens, as such, into it, upon a supposition that Cornelius was a Heathen when Peter was sent to him.

"6. In his Sermon on Psalm 41:4, *Lord heal my Soul,* &c. when an Account was given how our Souls came to be distempered, no Distemper by original Sin, as I heard, was mentioned, but only such

Distempers and Diseases as are contracted by evil Practices, and the want of a due Government of our Passions and Affections by Reason; which Passions and Affections were declared right and sound or good in themselves, and made or put into us so by God. And when he came to speak of the Cure of those Distempers and Maladies, there was no mention made (as I remember) of Prayer or the Blood or Spirit of Christ, or any thing said of him; but the whole Cure seemed to me by what he said, to be performed by ourselves. He had also a peculiar Notion, as I took it, about Hell, in the Application, which the perusal of the Sermon will discover.

"7. Preaching upon Eph. 3:8, after having brought again his Account wherein the Nature of Christianity consists, namely in a Revival or new Edition of the Law of Nature, he went on to run down (as I understood him) the Protestant Doctrine of Justification by Faith, saying, among other Things, to this Effect, that what the Apostle says of that Doctrine, concerned new converted Heathens and not us. And to make this good, he set up St. James against St. Paul, saying, is not the Authority of St. James as good as the Authority of St. Paul?

"*Lastly,* In his Prayer he constantly omits to pray for any Church either Catholick or particular, or any Ministers of it, but only for Mankind in general. It is also common with him in his prayers, and sometimes in his Sermons, to say that Reason is our Rule, and was given us for a Rule.

"Some other things might be mentioned, that were displeasing to many when spoken, which, whether there will be any Notice taken of them in the Process I know not, and so say nothing of 'em here.

"If I am mistaken in any of the above-mentioned particulars, I shall be abundantly more ready to retract than I was to accuse.

"April 7. 1735.

J. Andrews."

How trifling some of these Accusations are, may be left to the Observation of every Reader; and how groundless the rest are will appear when we come to the particular Consideration of them; which before we enter upon, I shall endeavour to give a true and faithful Account of the Proceedings of this reverend Commission, and if in any thing I deviate from the Truth, I may be contradicted by those who were present during the whole Tryal.

After the Articles were read, Mr. Hemphill objected to Messrs. Thompson and Gillespie, as not being proper Persons to be of the Number of his Judges, by reason that they had condemn'd him already; having declar'd their Sentiments that he was guilty of preaching great Errors; and that they had done this without any personal Acquaintance with him, nor had they ever heard him preach. This was clearly made to appear with relation to Thompson, by several Gentlemen who had seen his Letters. What concern'd Gillespie had been so notorious, that Hemphill referr'd it to himself, whether he had not upon a particular Occasion, before many People, asserted that Mr. Hemphill was a New-Light Man, and other Words importing that he was guilty of preaching Errors? Mr. Gillespie made answer, that he did not remember that he ever said any such thing. In Charity we are to suppose that he had forgot it; but the Allegation was nevertheless true, as can be incontestably prov'd. However, neither of these Objections were allow'd to have any Weight with the Commission.

Then Mr. Hemphill being requested to deliver up his Sermons for their Perusal, denied to do it for these Reasons, viz. 1st, It was contrary to the common Rights of Mankind, no Man being obliged to furnish Matter of Accusation against himself. 2dly, It was contrary to the Usage of the Church of Scotland, from whence they pretend to take a Pattern of their Church Government. 3dly, He was inform'd from all Hands that his Cause was prejudg'd, that there was a strange Spirit of Bitterness rais'd up against him among the People by the Ministers, and that there was little Probability of obtaining a fair and impartial Decision in his Case. And how just these Reasons were, the Sequel of this will plainly show. Upon his Refusal to deliver up his Notes, tho' they acknowledged they had no

Right to insist upon it, yet they were charitable enough to make Suggestions, that Hemphill's Guilt was the Occasion of his not delivering up his Sermons. How becoming such a Conduct as this was, in Judges who had not as yet heard any thing more of the Cause than barely the reading of the Charges, let the Reader judge. Sure in a civil Case such Judges would not deserve the Character of very impartial ones; however, it is very necessary to make Allowances for some Clergymen.

In answer to what they alledge of his Promise; Hemphill declar'd he had let Mr. Andrews know in private Conversation, being inform'd by him that he intended to draw up a Charge against him, that if he would call at his House, he would act so friendly as to show him his Notes, in order to set him right in any Part, if he should be wrong; which Andrews never thought proper to do: And two Gentlemen that were present, declared, That some little time after this Conversation had with Andrews, Hemphill had told 'em separately the Story in the same manner. And as to the Evidences produc'd to prove the Promise, he alledges that they mistook him when he told this Story, it being well known to many Gentlemen that are his Friends, that he had ever since the Information he had receiv'd of the unfair Usage he was like to meet with, resolv'd not to show his Notes; in which Resolution he was strengthen'd by their Advice. Further, if Mr. Andrews had depended upon such a Promise of Hemphill's, as he declar'd he did, (giving it as a Reason for the Weakness and Imperfection of his Charges) he must have depended upon that Promise long before he himself said it was made, for the Charges antecedent to the Promise are much more imperfectly drawn up, than those consequent upon it; which in my humble Opinion, plainly proves that Andrews had no Dependance on any such Promise, neither did he expect that the Notes would be given to the Commission, but only made use of it as an Excuse for the Nonsense and Inconsistencies with which these Charges are stuffed.

After this, the Commission proceeded to hear such Evidence as was brought before 'em, the Credibility and Faithfulness of which they say *they had no Reason to object against,* which can't but be very surprizing to all Persons present at the Tryal. The main Evidence, or rather, to make use of the Moderator's own Words, the *plumb* Evidence, deposed that he heard Mr. Hemphill in his Sermon say, *That to preach up Christ's Merits and Satisfaction, his Death and Sufferings, was to preach up a Charm,* with many other Things equally absurd as false. This Man's Evidence exceedingly surprized all the Members of the Congregation then present, who then positively declared that no such Words had been utter'd; and forty People could have been adduced to contradict his Testimony; but this they were told by the Commission was admitting of negative Evidence; nor could they by any means prevail so far as to have Leave to set the Matter in its true Light, by declaring the Truth; tho' sundry Persons remember'd the very Words of the Sentence in which the Word *Charm* was contain'd; and the Commission was told, that Mr. Andrews's Charge corroborated what they had to say. And when nothing would prevail with them, a Gentleman of the Congregation appealed to the Accuser, who had brought this Evidence, Whether he did not believe that what that Evidence said was untrue? To which, to the great Surprize of many, he was forced to make this disingenuous Reply, *That he was not obliged to answer the Question.* This Answer, together with his adducing a Person to depose a thing that he knew was false, has stagger'd many People who formerly had received a good Opinion of his Integrity. And to give you a Sample of the Spirit that was then predominant, one of the Ministers, and who was one of Hemphill's Judges too, justified this vile Action of Andrews in Conversation afterwards; he call'd it, *an innocent Wile,* and said, *there was no harm in admitting a false Evidence in order to force the Accused to confess the Truth.* This needs no Remark; for I can't help thinking the bare reading of it is sufficient to fill the Mind of every candid Reader with Horror!

There were several other Evidences produced, particularly one who declared, that the Accused said in his Sermon, *there were no Mysteries in Christianity.* This, together with several other things, was offer'd to be invalidated by the Testimony of a great many ingenious Persons then present; but it was that time absolutely refused, as admitting negative Evidence: Notwithstanding it was urged to 'em, that their Duty was to find out Truth, and that good End ought not to be impeded by any Quirks or Evasions; and surely that Affair of negative Evidence deserved no better Name. It was urged likewise, that it might be any of their own Cases, that one or two of the most ignorant Members of their Congregations, might accuse 'em in the like manner, and if the Testimony of the rest could not be allow'd to invalidate it, they might be brought to the Circumstances of Hemphill, and condemned upon very false Evidence; and that such a Method of Proceedure would destroy all Safety both in Church and State. All this and much more was said, but to no purpose. True indeed it is, after they had adjourn'd, being somewhat abated from the Heat they were in the Evening before, and reflecting how this Conduct of theirs would be censured by the World, they agreed to let Hemphill adduce Evidences, to invalidate the Depositions given in against him: But in order to render their Indulgence ineffectual, they peremptorily refus'd to let him have a Copy of them. Which Action of theirs was a strange Piece of Mockery; for how can any Man invalidate the Testimony of another without knowing what it is; especially where there were so many Evidences, and where it is in Relation to Words spoken, which was then the Case.

And here I shall conclude this Head, by observing, if they gave any Credit to the Sermons upon which they afterwards condemned him; and which they were pleas'd to declare they believ'd to be genuine, and read to 'em as they were preached, they had then the highest Reason to object to the Credibility and Faithfulness of the Evidence; seeing the Sermons plainly prov'd most of the Evidences to be false: Nor can these reverend Gentlemen make it appear, that either Andrews's Charges or Evidences were justly founded on these Sermons they heard read. But this will more fully appear in the Sequel of these Papers.

Having spent the remaining Part of the Week in examining the Evidences, they then adjourn'd to Monday, the Moderator and Mr. Cross being appointed to preach on Sunday; tho' at that time the Affair of Mr. Hemphill was still under consideration, and he being the next Day to offer what he thought proper in his Defence, yet, I say, these two charitable Men, these impartial Judges, were pleased to deliver such Sermons as plainly convinc'd all indifferent Persons,

65

that they had condemned Hemphill before they left their own Homes: Their Discourses were calculated to exasperate the People against him, to represent him as a Preacher of erroneous Doctrine, a Seducer, &c. And lest they should not be understood against whom their Discourses were levelled, they cautioned the Hearers against Preachers who *deny'd the Merits and Satisfaction of Christ,* which was one of the Crimes upon which Hemphill was falsly accus'd, and afterwards unjustly condemn'd. How proper such Sermons as these were in the Time of this Tryal, how consistent with Christian Moderation or with their own Reputations as Men, or what Justice was to be expected from such Judges, let the Reader imagine. They have indeed upon this Occasion given such Impressions of themselves as will not be very soon forgotten in Philadelphia.

Mr. Hemphill by this time perceiving that he was not to expect any fair Usage, from Men who upon all Occasions gave such evident Proofs of their Bitterness against him, had Thoughts of taking his Leave of them, without saying any thing further in his own Defence: But at length, out of a Regard to his own Reputation, and to clear himself from the Aspersions thrown upon him by the Evidences, and the uncharitable Invectives deliver'd in the Sermons abovementioned; he determin'd to make the Commission of the Synod an Offer of publickly Reading of his Sermons to 'em; which Offer of his, after some short Time, they accepted of: And this publick Method he chose to take, that the World might be convinced how far he had been injured in his Reputation, and what little Reason he had given for the unchristian Usage he afterwards met with. His Sermons were then read, which for the Strain of Christian Charity that run thro' the whole of them, and their constantly urging the Necessity of a holy Life and Conversation in order to our final Acceptance with God, were approved of by People of all Persuasions; and I believe I may venture to affirm, that few People present discover'd the Heresies that seemed so plain and obvious afterwards to the Commission of the Synod and Correspondents.

After the Sermons were read over, and such Extracts taken out of them as any Member of the Commission thought proper, they then proceeded to desire Hemphill to appear before 'em the next Day, to offer what he had to say in his own Defence. But what Meaning they had in this, no one but they can devise. Hemphill at first imagined, they intended to have examined him the next Day, upon the Extracts they had taken from his Notes, and to have shown him in what Sense they thought them worthy of Censure, and have heard him to the several Points; but herein he was greatly mistaken.

And here I can't help being fill'd with Amazement, to see what Lengths the crafty Malice of some, and the hot distemper'd Zeal of others will carry them! The Day following Hemphill appear'd before the Commission of the Synod, and was then prepared to answer any Objections made to the Doctrines he had preach'd, or to have explained his Words where they might have been misunderstood; but to his very great Surprize, they refused to let him know what in particular they objected to, nor would they by any means point out to him, in what part of the Extracts they had taken, they had deemed him to be erroneous; altho' they had told him when he read the first Sermon, that he should have an Opportunity to vindicate every part they would object against; but this was promis'd with a View to end a Dispute between the Moderator and Hemphill. Indeed some of them contended that he had no Right to explain his own Words; tho' that was offered to them only for their own Satisfaction, and it was not expected that the Explications should have any further Weight with them than what the natural Construction of the Words would bear, and this was declared to them at the same time. This Point was afterwards given up by 'em, but in Words only; for when he was told he might explain his own Words, they at the same time refused to let him know what part of the Extracts wanted explaining, or in their Opinion contained Errors. No, a more just Method of Proceeding would not have been conducive to the End they had in View; the malicious, or to give it the most charitable Name it can bear, their mistaken Manner of taking down Parts of his Sermons, and the false Glosses they were pleased to put upon 'em, would then have been manifest to the World. The Truth of which Assertion will plainly appear to the Reader in the Sequel of this; where he may perceive, that in some Places they have falsly recited his Words, in others taken only Parts of Sentences, and left out the remaining Parts which would have cleared up their Objections, and render'd ridiculous the pretended Heresies for which they condemned him. If they had at that time in the face of the World, declared in what they judged him to be erroneous, and produced Authority from Scripture to support their Opinions, and *then* given him an Opportunity to offer what he thought proper in his own Defence; they then surely would have acted a more Christian and justifiable Part, and would not have brought such a Reproach on themselves and their Profession as they have done.

And here I am sorry, that I am obliged to say, that they have no Pattern for their Proceedings, but that hellish Tribunal the *Inquisition,* who rake up all the vile Evidences, and extort all the Confessions they can from the wretched Object of their Rage, and without allowing him any Means of invalidating the Evidence, or convincing 'em of their own Mistakes, they assemble together in secret, and proceed to Judgment. No Precedent from the Church of Scotland will warrant these their Proceedings; for when any Affair of this kind is laid before their Judicatures, they debate amongst themselves publickly, and the Members of which it is compos'd do separately give Reasons for their Opinions, and point out what they take to be subversive of the Gospel of Christ, and their well known Confession of Faith; and give an Opportunity to the Person accused to answer their several Objections, and to take all just Methods of clearing himself: And this is done in order to demonstrate to the World, the Sincerity and Candour of their Actions, and upon what Motives they have proceeded. These Gentlemen on the contrary, only took Extracts out of Hemphill's Sermons, and without acquainting him or any other Person of their Sentiments in relation to 'em, or publickly declaring in what manner they understood 'em, they assembled together in secret, refusing to admit any Persons to be present at any of their Debates (if they had any) and proceeded to devise Reasons for their condemning of him. This indeed took them several Days; for as they could not give good Reasons for their so doing, it was necessary to invent some plausible ones: which I shall here transcribe from the *Extract of their Minutes,* in order to answer them one after another.

Extract page 6.

"The Commission proceeded to consider the Affair of Mr. Hemphill, in order to form a Judgment, and accordingly determined to take each Article of the Charge distinctly, and to compare them with the Extracts of his Sermons; and upon mature Consideration of the first Article, we find that agreeable to the first Charge brought in against him, viz. That Christianity, which he calls the second Revelation of God's Will agreeable to the first, is by him asserted to be only an Illustration and Improvement of the Law of Nature, with the Addition of some few positive Things, such as the two Sacraments, and our going to God and making our approaches to him in the Name and Mediation of his Son Jesus Christ. And what, in our Apprehension, further supports this Charge, is what he asserts when he is professedly treating of such Things as are more purely and properly Christian; after an Enumeration of several Particulars, he has these Expressions, viz. *This is no more than to live and act according to our Nature, and to have the Government of our selves in our own Hands.* And this is further confirmed by an Extract of his Sermon on Mark 16: 16, wherein he asserts, That *the Gospel is, as to its ultimate End and most essential Parts, implanted in our very Nature and Reason;* which Description of Christianity we judge to be inconsistent with our well-known Confession of Faith, and subversive of the Gospel of Christ."

Allowing freely that Hemphill deliver'd such a Description of Christianity as this, he nevertheless denies the Assertion of these Gentlemen, that it is inconsistent with their Confession of Faith, and more especially he denies that it is subversive of the Gospel of Christ. What he means in his Account of Christianity, is, that our Saviour's Design in coming into the World, was to restore Mankind to the State of Perfection in which Adam was at first created, and that all those Laws which he has given us are agreeable to that original Law, as having such a natural Tendency to our present Ease and Quiet, that they carry their own Reward, tho' there were nothing to reward our Obedience or punish our Disobedience in another Life; and that to this very End he has given us some few positive Precepts, such as the two Sacraments, and going to God and making our Approaches to him in the Name and thro' the Mediation of his Son Jesus Christ; and that all those Duties are inforced by new and stronger Motives than either the Light of Nature or the Jewish Religion could furnish us with.

This, I say, is so far from being subversive of the Gospel, that the opposite Opinion is destructive both of the Gospel, and all the Notions we have of the moral Perfections of God, and the disinterested Love and Benevolence which appears throughout his whole Conduct towards Mankind. I would desire these Gentlemen to point out to the World those Duties which are not included in his Description of Christianity. 'Tis surprizing to me, that Men who call themselves Christians, and more especially those who pretend to preach Christianity to others, should say that a God of infinite Perfections would make any thing our Duty, that has not a natural Tendency to our Happiness; and if to our Happiness, then it is agreeable to our Nature, since a Desire of Happiness is a natural Principle which all Mankind are endued with.[31]

And in order to make the World believe the Justice of their Censure, they have perverted and altered the very Words of Hemphill's Sermon. They declare in their Minutes that he says, *the Gospel is, as to its ultimate End and most essential Parts,* &c. These two Words they have falsly added, viz: *Gospel* and *End,* which changes the Meaning of the Whole. What Hemphill has in his Sermon is this, "That the Doctrines absolutely necessary to be believed, are so very plain and nigh unto us, that they are, as to their ultimate and most essential Parts implanted in our very Nature and Reason, and more

---

[31] Here Franklin expresses his agreement with Hemphill's claim that Christ came into this world for the express purpose of restoring mankind to a state of perfection from which he had fallen. He also argues that the duties which God requires of Christians are such that they all produce happiness in this life. Franklin presents this as if it should be common sense to every Christian, and indeed it should be, for the Bible assures us in Psalm 1:1-2:

"Blessed is the man that walketh not in the counsel of the ungodly, nor standeth in the way of sinners, nor sitteth in the seat of the scornful. But his delight is in the law of the LORD; and in his law doth he meditate day and night."

And Jesus Himself assured His disciples that "If ye know these things, happy are ye if ye do them." (John 13:17)

distinctly and authoritatively delivered in the Discourses of our Saviour, and in the Writings of the Apostles." That is, Those Doctrines delivered by our Saviour and the Apostles, which are absolutely necessary to be believed, are so very plain, that the meanest Capacities, may easily understand 'em, they being so reconcilable to our Reason, and so agreeable to our Nature, as having such a Tendency even to our present Happiness; and this he illustrated from our Saviour's Sermons upon the Mount, which are so very plain, that every impartial Man who reads 'em, may easily reconcile to his Reason, as being wisely calculated to serve that noble End of Man's Happiness. Now let any impartial Reader consider what a poor State these Men have brought themselves to, that they are forced, in order to answer their own base Views, to change the very Meaning of the Paragraph, by adding some Words, and leaving out others. If what they have inserted in the Minutes were true, with what immediately follows in the same Paragraph, the whole would amount to this, *that the Gospel was contained in the Gospel*,[32] which would not have been Sense, neither did he ever preach any such thing; but the Words in Truth were as they are inserted above.

And if these Reverend Gentlemen were as well acquainted with what they call their *well-known* Confession of Faith as they pretend to be, they would not have found Hemphill's Sermons inconsistent with it; he will undertake to prove that all his Discourses are agreeable to the *fundamental* Articles of it, which was all he declared to at his Admittance into the Synod: And surely they would not offer to condemn him for differing with them about extra-essentials.

Extract page 7.

---

[32] When the Synod's erroneous quotation of "the Gospel is, as to its ultimate End and most essential Parts" is combined with Hemphill's phrase, "delivered in the Discourses of our Saviour, and in the Writings of the Apostles," the end result is essentially: "The Gospel was contained in the Gospel." This, as Franklin noted, is nothing more than a tautology and, thus, is evidence that the Synod's quotation was flawed.

"*2dly.* As to the second Article which concerns the new Creature or Conversion, upon mature Consideration, we find by the Extract of Mr. Hemphill's Sermon on Gal. 6: 15, that he denies the necessity of Conversion to those that are born in the Church, and are not degenerated into vitious Practice; particularly in these Words, viz. *Such as are born of Christian Parents, and brought up in a Christian Country, cannot be so properly called new Creatures, when compared with themselves, because they were always what they are, except the progress and improvement which they daily make in Virtue;* which Doctrine we judge to be contrary to the sacred Scriptures and to our Confession of Faith."

With a Design to amuse the World, they assert, that they have acted upon mature Consideration; whereas nothing but Envy and Malice could move 'em to act so unjustly as they have done. In the Extract taken out of Hemphill's Sermon, they have omitted to insert those Parts of it in their Minutes, that would have explained the rest, and only inserted the middle of a Paragraph; the whole runs thus, "Altho' that Change was most visible in the first Conversion of Heathens to Christianity, or of wicked Professors of Christianity to a Conversion becoming the Gospel of Christ, yet the Effects of Christianity truly believed and duly practiced, is the same in those who were neither Heathens nor wicked Christians, but are born of Christain Parents, brought up in a christian Country, and had the Benefit of a virtuous Education, and were never engaged in vicious Practices; such as these, I say, tho' they can't so properly be call'd new Creatures, when compared with themselves, because they were always what they are, except the Progress and Improvement which they daily make in Virtue; yet when compar'd with others they may be so call'd; they are new Creatures, different Men and of another Sort, from those who either never heard of the Gospel of Christ, or never firmly believed and practiced it; so that still the Design of Christianity is the same, to make us new Creatures, quite other Men from what we should have been without the Gospel, to cure the Corruption and Depravity of Human Nature, and restore it to the Image of the Divine Nature in which Man was at first created, and from which by Transgression he fell."

And even suppose nothing had followed to clear what they have inserted in the Minutes, 'tis surprizing to me that those Gentlemen should look upon Mankind, to be so very weak and ignorant, as to be persuaded to believe, that it contradicted the sacred Scriptures. I would advise these Reverend Gentlemen impartially to read the Scriptures, and they will find that it is said, *the Day begins in an insensible Dawn, and the Path of the Just shines more and more unto a perfect Day,*[33] that is, Men don't become very good or very bad in an Instant, both vicious and virtuous Habits being acquired by Length of Time and repeated Acts. And the Kingdom of Heaven, that is Christianity, is compar'd to *Leaven hid in so many Measures of Meal,*[34] to a *Grain of Mustard Seed,* to a *Field sown with Corn,* &c.[35] all which Things do not obtain their several Effects in an Instant, or any particular Time we can fix on: We can't say, that the Leaven wrought just that Moment, or that the Mustard Seed shot up into a Tree that very Minute, or that the Corn appear'd above-ground at that very Instant. And then we are told, that there are some *converted from the very Womb,* and that *little Children are qualified for Heaven,*[36] which is the same thing. Now if all these Texts of Scripture are true, how is it possible their Conversion should be so sensible either to themselves or others, as that of Heathens or wicked Christians? I have said, it cannot; which is all that can be justly founded upon the Extract of the Sermon they have condemn'd. I may add, that whoever preaches up the absolute necessity of spiritual *Pangs* and Convulsions in those whose

---

[33] Proverbs 4:18

[34] Matthew 13:24-33

[35] The section from "the Day begins in an insensible dawn" until the "&c.," is a quotation of Benjamin Ibbot's sermon on "The New Creature." (Ibbot, 45) Ibbot was a well known clergyman in the Church of England. He was a chaplain to George I and an assistant to Dr. Samuel Clarke, and he was appointed by the Archbishop to preach a course of sermons for Boyle's Lectures. The sermon which Franklin quoted was part of a collection of thirty sermons that were printed in London while Franklin was there as a young man. (Chalmers, 221-222)

[36] Franklin may have been referring to Galatians 1:15 and Matthew 19:14.

Education has been in the Ways of Piety and Vertue, and who therefore are not to pass from a State of Sin to a State of Holiness, but to go on and improve in the State wherein they already are, represent Christianity to be unworthy of its divine Author.[37]

---

[37] Both Franklin and Hemphill have been unjustifiably maligned over their statements regarding the conversion of little children. The Synod claimed that Hemphill was preaching against the need for children of Christian parents to receive the salvation of Christ. And Frazer said of Franklin that:

"Among the charges that Franklin admitted were accurate were that Hemphill taught (1) that people born in Christian families who led moral lives did not need to be converted." (Frazer, *Religious Beliefs,* 143)

What Hemphill actually said, however, was that children who become Christians at an early age will not appear to experience as great a change in their lives as someone who comes to Christ as an adult. And Franklin makes the same argument in Hemphill's defense. He does not claim that Christian children have no need of salvation, but rather that they have no need of the "pangs and convulsions" that many ministers of that time argued were necessary in order to be truly converted.

In addition to this, it is interesting to note that if this charge against Hemphill had been correct: if he had been guilty of claiming that children born in the church have no need of conversion in order to become Christians, then Hemphill would have been guilty of adhering to the Westminster Confession and not of violating it as the Synod claimed. According to the Westminster Confession,

"Not only those that do actually profess Faith in, and Obedience unto Christ, but also the Infants of one or both Parents, are to be baptized." (Bryce, 317)

The "Directory for the Publick Worship of God" which stands alongside the confession as an equal part of the Westminster Standards contains this explanation of the baptism of infants:

"the Seed and Posterity of the Faithful, born within the Church, have, by their Birth, Interest in the Covenant, and the Right to the Seal of it, and to the outward Priviledges of the Church, under the Gospel ... Children, by Baptism, are solemnly received in to the Bosom of the visible Church, distinguished from the World, and them that are without, and united with Believers ... they are Christians and foederally holy before Baptism, and therefore are they baptized." (Bryce, 221)

Extract, page 8.

"The Commission reassuming the third Article of Accusation against Mr. Hemphill, and considering it with all seriousness and impartiality that we are capable of, we cannot but judge that the most plain and obvious scope of the Extract of the Sermon now before us appears subversive of the true and proper Satisfaction of Christ (notwithstanding of any Sound or Orthodox Expressions made use of by him, particularly in that summary of Principles delivered to the Commission, taken from his Sermon on Mark 16: 16) inasmuch as the said Paragraph, wherein he professedly takes while he amply insists upon Christ, as a King and Law-giver, giving the best System of Laws, he takes no Notice of his making Satisfaction to the Justice of God, but once barely mentions him as a Saviour, which any Socinian in the World might do. And this will be more clearly evident if it be considered what he says in the same Paragraph, wherein he speaks of those who maintain that God doth demand a full Satisfaction for the Offences of Sinners, as exalting the Glory of Christ as a kind condescending Saviour, to the dishonour of the supreme unlimited Goodness of the Creator and Father of the Universe, representing him as stern and inexorable, expressing no indulgence to his guilty Creatures; which will be further evident from what is expressed towards the close of the same Sermon, inference the Second, viz. *To explain and press the eternal Laws of Morality is not only a truly Christian, but beyond*

Lemay claimed that "Presbyterians believed that a new birth was necessary for conversion," (Lemay, 2: 235) but this is not entirely true. It seems apparent that the Synod in Philadelphia held to the necessity of a new birth, but this is certainly not what the Westminster Assembly considered to be orthodox. According to the Presbyterians of that time, the children of believers were Christians by virtue of their first birth and had no need of a second.

This illustrates the flaw in relying on confessions and creeds in order to determine who is and who is not a Christian, and it is why Franklin later writes of the necessity of relying solely on the words of Scripture in such determinations.

It should also be noted that Franklin here referred to the Author of Christianity as being divine. This is a direct admission that Jesus Christ was not merely a man.

Comparison the most useful Method of Preaching. And also by what he speaks in his Sermon on Acts 10: 34, 35, viz. *That God hath no Regard to any thing but Mans inward merits and deserts.* And also in the same Sermon it is said, *it cannot be deny'd but that they* (viz. good Works performed by the Light of Nature) *put Men in God's Way, reconcile him to them, and whatever else is wanting, dispose him to reveal even that unto them;* and tho' some Gentlemen, to whose Evidence we give an intire Credit, declared that it was his Manner in his publick Prayer, to give Thanks to God for sending his own Son Jesus Christ into the World to redeem poor lost Mankind; the Attonement he has made for the Sins of Mankind; and that he ends his Prayers by saying, *all petitioned for is upon the Account, and for the Sake of Jesus Christ;* yet we cannot think these or any such Expressions can justify his declaiming against this Doctrine in many Places of his Sermons."

The former Part of this Minute relates to the Merits and Satisfaction of Christ, as they word it; if they mean by that the Doctrine of Christ's Satisfaction, as held by Protestants, if Hemphill endeavoured to subvert That, he will not only be condemned by them, but by all good Christians.[38] This is a very heavy Charge, and surely ought to be well made out, before any Minister should be deemed guilty of it. In this Case I can't help believing that every impartial Reader will be convinced, that this was done purely to blacken the Man; and here introduced in order to deceive the World, well knowing there are a sort of People who think no Usage can be too bad for such as they deem Hereticks, by whom the Commission imagined they should be applauded, let other Parts of their Conduct in this Affair be never so unjust, could they but once persuade 'em that he was guilty of opposing this important Doctrine of

---

[38] This is an extremely important statement from Franklin that is ignored by every historian I have read. Most historians view Franklin's defense of Hemphill as evidence that Franklin rejected the core doctrines of Christianity, but here we find Franklin himself saying that if Hemphill denied "the Doctrine of Christ's Satisfaction, as held by all Protestants," then he should be condemned "by all good Christians." This bold statement stands as strong evidence that Franklin agreed with the doctrine of Christ's satisfaction for our sins.

Christianity, which by all Christians is esteem'd a Fundamental Article of Belief:[39] Except this one Article, every thing for which they have been pleased to censure him, truly considered, will, I make no doubt, redound more to his Praise and Reputation, than to his Discredit; and that the Generality of the World, instead of censuring him, will rather condemn them for holding Doctrines full of Uncharitableness, and giving People unworthy and dishonourable Notions of the supreme Being. They therefore thought it absolutely necessary to condemn him upon this Point, which they could not have been guilty of doing, if Reason, Justice or Charity had had any Weight with them. In order to support what I have said, I shall now give the Reader the Paragraph upon which the Censure is grounded.

"To preach Christ is universally allowed to be the Duty of every christian Minister, but what does that mean? 'Tis not to use his Name as a *Charm,* to work up the Hearers to a warm Pitch of Enthusiasm, without any Foundation in Reason to support it: 'Tis not to make his Person or his Offices incomprehensible: 'Tis not to exalt his Glory as a kind condescending Saviour, to the Dishonour of the unlimited Goodness of the Creator and Father of the Universe, who is represented as stern and inexorable, expressing no Indulgence to his guilty Creatures, but demanding full and rigorous

---

[39] As if the former statement were not convincing enough, Franklin again emphasizes that the doctrine of Christ's satisfaction for our sins is a vitally important component of Christianity and a "Fundamental Article of Belief."

Fea argues in his book that:

"In the end, Franklin's religion – both his stated views on orthodox Christianity and the American philosophy he helped to define – seldom fits comfortably with the teachings of Christianity. Franklin rejected most Christian doctrines in favor of a religion of virtue." (Fea, 227)

It is important to note that Fea makes very few references to Franklin's pamphlets defending Hemphill. His analysis of this period of Franklin's life focuses almost exclusively on the words of S. in Franklin's "Dialogue." Beginning here in the "Observations," however, Franklin presents a very different view of Christian doctrine than that which was argued by S.

Satisfaction for their Offences: 'Tis not to encourage undue and presumptuous Reliances on his Merits and Satisfaction to the Contempt of Virtue and Good Works. No, but to represent him as a Law-giver as well as a Saviour, as a Preacher of Righteousness, as one who hath given us the most noble and compleat System of Morals inforced by the most substantial and worthy Motives; and shows that the whole Scheme of our Redemption is *a Doctrine according to Godliness*."

Mr. Hemphill is here preaching against the Antinomians, who hold, that Christ's Merits and Satisfaction will save us, without our performing Good Works, which they say are unnecessary, and some of them even hold to be sinful; because, say they, to believe that Good Works or a holy Life is necessary in order to our Acceptance with God, is depreciating the Sufferings of Christ, who is sufficient without our Compliance; and therefore they never look upon him as a Lawgiver, but only in their mistaken Notion of a Saviour. This is the most impious Doctrine that ever was broached, and it is the Duty of every christian Minister to explode such Errors, which have a natural Tendency to make Men act as if Christ came into the World to patronize Vice, and allow Men to live as they please. Surely they who preach up Christ in this manner, do Dishonour both to the Father and the Son. [40] If the Reader will consider the Paragraph, he will find the whole Meaning of it to be this, We are not to preach up Christ so as to dishonour God the Father, nor are we to make such undue Reliances upon his Merits, as to neglect Good Works; but we are to look upon him in both Characters of Saviour and Lawgiver; that if we expect he has attoned for our Sins, we must sincerely endeavour to obey his Laws. [41] I am afraid, that it is the Antinomian

---

[40] Not only did Franklin accept and defend the doctrine of Christ's satisfaction for our sins, but he also expressed his acceptance of the doctrine that Jesus is the Son of God.

[41] Here Franklin makes a very clear departure from the works based salvation which he advocated in the "Dialogue." By this point, he has come to recognize that good works are to follow our faith in Christ. He recognizes that Christ is both our Savior and our Lawgiver, and he presents our responsibilities to this fact

Doctrine of Christ's Merits and Satisfaction, which they call the true and proper One, with whose Principles these Gentlemen seem to be too much tinctured. However that be, I shall leave the World to judge how fond these Men were to condemn Hemphill, when they ground their Censure upon his taking *no Notice* of Satisfaction made to the Justice of God; and if this be a just Method of judging Men's Sermons, there is no Preacher safe; even the soundest that ever preach'd, may be proved guilty of all the Heresies that have ever been in the World; seeing a Man's *omitting* any particular Doctrine proves his *denying* of it. In order to show that his Words were wrested, and that there is no Probability he should mean any such Thing as they have falsly fathered upon him, I shall here subjoin an Extract taken from his Sermon on Mark 16: 16, which he calls *a Summary of the Principles necessary for a Christian to believe,* and which they promised to insert in their Minutes, viz. "That there is one God the Father and Lord of all Things: That he sent his eternal Son, who was the Brightness of his Glory, and the express Image of his Person, both to condemn Sin in the Flesh, and also to obtain Pardon for it, by the shedding of his own Blood; and that to this end, the Son of God freely and willingly left the Bosom of the Father, was incarnate and made in the Likeness of Man, became subject to all the Infirmities and Frailties of Human Nature, Sin only excepted; preached and declared the Will of his Father to Mankind, died for our Sins upon the Cross, rose the third Day from the Dead, ascended up into Heaven and sate down on the right Hand of God, where he is continually making Intercession for us." And another Extract which

---

in the proper order. First we expect Christ to have atoned for our sins, and because of this, we endeavor to obey His Laws.

This is perfectly consistent with the teaching of Scripture in the second chapter of James where we read that "faith, if it hath not works, is dead, being alone" (vs. 17) and that "by works a man is justified, and not by faith only." (vs. 24) James is not arguing that salvation comes through works, but rather that a faith which is not accompanied by good works is incapable of producing salvation. Such faith is said to be dead and of no greater value than the faith of demons. (vs. 19) Franklin was acting in agreement with this passage when he condemned the antinomians – not for relying on faith for their salvation but for relying on a faith that failed to produce good works.

they likewise promised to insert, viz. "This is the Design of the Death of Christ, and the Redemption purchased for us by his Blood; for he gave himself for us, that he might redeem us from all Iniquity, and purify unto himself a People zealous of Good Works." In both these, this Doctrine is owned in express Words; and what will put it beyond Dispute with all unprejudiced Men, is, that Mr. Hemphill constantly in his Prayers gave Thanks to God for sending his Son into the World, to redeem poor lost Mankind, and for the Atonement made for their Sins. Now how is it probable he should preach, or what End could he have in preaching against a Doctrine which he so solemnly own'd in his Addresses to God every Day? Would it not be giving himself the Lie in the Face of the World? Would it not be prevaricating both with God and Man?

Now let the Reader judge, after so much positive Evidence of his acknowledging the Doctrines of Christ's Merits and Satisfaction, all which was laid before the Commission, how charitable, how just and reasonable these Men were when they condemned him. And what makes the Judgment in this Case more surprizing, especially when they say they had not one dissenting Vote in their whole Transactions, is, that one of the Ministers, the supposed Compiler of the Minutes, and one of the chief Managers in the whole Tryal, being shewn the very Paragraph upon which they pretend to ground their Censure concerning the Satisfaction of Christ, by a Gentleman in Philadelphia, he after Perusal declared his Sentiments in this Manner, *For my part, I do not know what other People may think of it, I can't see any Heresy in it, it is all very right.* This Man surely wanted either Courage or Honesty afterwards, when he did not dissent from the rest. Where they say that Hemphill declaims against that Doctrine in many places of his Sermon, few People will believe them, for they have given so many Samples of their Disposition (especially where they put down Words which they had not from his Extracts, and leave out Parts of Sentences necessary to have been inserted in order to explain the rest) that if there were these *many Places,* they would have pointed out at least some of them, and not have set down those that are nothing to the purpose: For Example, *To explain and press the eternal Laws of Morality, is not only a truly christian, but beyond comparison the most useful Method of*

Preaching. And because the whole would not have answered their Ends, they have omitted the explaining part which immediately followed, viz. *in this I include the enforceing the Rules of Virtue by all the peculiar Motives which the christian Religion suggests, making all its Doctrines subservient to Holiness.* Which I say is the End and Design of the christian Scheme, for Christ gave himself for us that he might redeem us from all Iniquity, and purify to himself a peculiar People zealous of Good-Works.[42] And there is scarcely a Chapter in the whole Gospels or Epistles from which this Doctrine can't be prov'd.[43] And the next Extract they produce, viz: *God hath no Regard to any thing but Mens inward Merit and Desert,* is in my humble Opinion as little to the purpose as the other. I would ask these reverend Gentlemen, Does God regard Man at all? The Answer I suppose will be, That he does, but that it is upon the Account of Christ's Merits; which I shall grant them, and allow it to be the Merits and Satisfaction of Christ that purchased such easy and plain Conditions of Happiness; but still it is our Compliance with these Conditions that I call inward Merit and Desert which God regards in us. For to say that God regards Men for any thing else besides Goodness and Virtue, is such a Notion as makes all Men both virtuous and vicious capable of being equally regarded by him, and consequently there is no Difference between Virtue and Vice.[44] And the Apostle Peter is, with Hemphill, condemn'd by these Men for a Heretick, in saying, that *God is no Respecter of Persons, but in every Nation he that feareth him and worketh Righteousness is*

---

[42] Titus 2:14

[43] This is yet another evidence that Franklin had changed his view of the relationship between works and faith. In the "Dialogue," he clearly argued that salvation came through good works, but here he quotes the words of Scripture to prove that good works are to follow our redemption by Christ.

[44] In this segment Franklin is not discussing salvation but rather the favor and consideration which God chooses to show to men. On the question of whether God has any regard for man at all, Franklin answers that God has regard toward men as they comply with the conditions that He set forth.

accepted of him.[45] I shall make no more Remarks upon this Minute, but conclude with saying, If these Gentlemen had regarded their own Honour, (not to talk of the Honour of Christianity, which breathes such a Spirit of Benevolence, Justice and Charity through the whole of it) they would not have condemned Hemphill upon a single Expression, supposing there had been any such; but would have compared the whole Extracts of his Sermons in order to understand his Meaning, which is common in every such Case, where Men are impartial and desirous to find out the Truth; but this is inconsistent with a Spirit of Persecution, with which these Gentlemen were possessed.

Extract, page 9.

"4*thly.* As to the fourth Article, viz. The Description of saving Faith in his Sermon on Mark 16: 16. We acknowledge that saving Faith doth include (as Mr. Hemphill asserts) a firm Perswasion of Mind of the Truths of the Gospel upon good and rational Grounds, and producing proper and suitable Effects; yet we cannot but apprehend that this is too general a Description of saving Faith, as not explicitly mentioning our receiving of Christ upon the Terms of the Gospel, which is so essential an act or ingredient of the Faith which is unto Salvation, that without it our Faith will be vain and ineffectual; and so the Description may be apt dangerously to mislead Persons in this important Article, and incourage them to trust to a naked assent to the Gospel Revelation, especially if this their assent be accompanied with an externally regular Conversation."

---

[45] Acts 10:34-35 – Franklin's use of this passage demonstrates that he is not speaking of good works earning salvation. In this passage, Peter was speaking to Cornelius whom he found to be a virtuous man even though he was not a Christian. After making this comment about Cornelius being accepted of God, Peter then began to preach about the sacrifice of Christ, and it was then that both Cornelius and all those who were with him became Christians. The good works of Cornelius had brought him the favor of God but not salvation. His salvation was solely the result of his acceptance of the sacrifice of Christ. Franklin addresses this further in his reply to the fifth article.

I am at a Loss what could move these Gentlemen (unless it was to shew their Learning) to censure Hemphill's Description of Saving Faith as being too general, when at the same time they have given a more general one; but in their Illustration they seem not to have understood either of them; where they say, that it has a Tendency to make Men rely upon a bare Assent to the Truths of the Gospel; which is impossible; for how can such a Faith, in the Description of which Good Works are expressly mentioned, be a Means to lead Men from Good Works.

Extract page 10.

"5*thly*. As to the fifth Article of the Charge, respecting the Salvation of Heathens while they continue such, we judge it abundantly supported by the Extracts of his Sermon on Acts 10: 34, 35. Wherein he evidently contradicts the Necessity of Divine Revelation, and asserts the sufficiency of the Light of Nature to bring us to Salvation; particularly in these Expressions, viz. *They who have no other Knowledge of God and their Duty, but what the Light of Nature teacheth them, no Law for the Government of their Actions but the Law of Reason and Conscience, will be accepted if they live up to the Light they have, and govern their Actions accordingly:* And further he asserts, *That Cornelius, who,* as he affirms, *had neither imbraced the Jewish nor Christian Religion, was for this accepted of God and highly Favoured.*"

In this 5th Article, Mr. Hemphill is censured as denying the necessity of a divine Revelation, from these Words: "They who have no other Knowledge of God and their Duty, but what the Light of Nature teaches, no Law for the Government of their Actions but the Law of Reason and Conscience, will be accepted of God if they live up to the Light which they have, and govern their Actions accordingly." But they have omitted the latter part of the Paragraph which explains the former, viz. "This was the Case of Cornelius, who worshipped God and did Good to Men, he pray'd to God always and gave much Alms to the People, and this he did from the meer Light of Nature, not having embraced either the Jewish or Christian Religion; for this he was accepted of God, and had a farther Revelation of his Will. So that tho' it may be disputed how far such Righteousness as this, such Good Works as these, are of themselves available for Salvation, yet it can't be denied but that they put Men in God's Way, reconcile him to 'em, and whatever else is wanting dispose him to reveal even that unto them."

Now from the whole of the Extract, (part of which they left out, for what End I shall leave the World to judge) I believe no unprejudiced Person can see a just Foundation of this Censure: For all that they can found it upon, is this, that Hemphill maintains it was the Good Works of Cornelius, (a Heathen) which disposed God to give him a miraculous Revelation of the Gospel. But to corroborate their Censure, they assert a downright Falshood, viz. That Hemphill says it was upon the Account of Cornelius's not having embraced either the Jewish or Christian Religion that he was accepted of God; Whereas in the Extract taken from his Sermon, it is said, it was his praying to God always, and giving much Alms to the People that rendered him acceptable to God. And this is sufficient to show the base Conduct of these Men, who to accomplish their wicked Ends, will not only venture to change the Meaning but the very Words Themselves.

Extract page 11.

"6*thly.* As to that Article of the Charge wherein he is alledged to pervert the Doctrine of Justification by Faith, we find it sufficiently supported by the Extracts from his Sermon on Eph. 3: 8, Wherein he has these Words, viz. *It will not be amiss to consider what the Apostle means when he says that Christians are saved by Faith; it may be well said of them, because it is their Faith that saves them from the Guilt of their Sins committed before their Faith, a Privilege which peculiarly belonged to the first Christians, converted at Years of Discretion from a Life of Sin and impurity; and therefore this first Justification is often inculcated by St. Paul in his Epistles, and attributed to Faith; but this doth not concern those who have been educated and instructed in the Knowledge of the Christian Religion.* And by asserting, towards the close of the said Sermon, *That all Hopes of Happiness, but what are built on purity of Heart and a* *virtuous Life, are, according to the Christian Scheme, vain and delusory, and will certainly end in Disappointment and Confusion;* which Expressions we cannot but look upon as subversive of the Scripture Doctrine of Justification by Faith, tho' we zealously maintain the indispensible Necessity of universal Holiness in order to Salvation."

In this 6th Article they assert, that they find Mr. Andrews's Charge against Hemphill sufficiently supported. What is it that they would not find supported from his Sermons, if Andrews had charged him with it? In this Discourse Hemphill was endeavouring to show the Folly of those who make that first Justification by Faith, which the Apostle mentions, an Encouragement to us, that if we believe even at our Death, tho' we have wilfully persisted in Disobedience to Christ's Commands, we shall be equally entitled to Salvation with those who, as soon as they heard Christianity preached, embraced it, and who therefore had their Faith imputed to them for Righteousness. And I suppose all Christians, Antinomians excepted, will allow this, that Faith will not be imputed for Righteousness to those Men who have been educated in the Christian Religion, and yet have never endeavoured to practice its Precepts; I say that such Men have no Reason to expect that they shall be justified by a bare Faith, as the primitive Christians were, who embraced Christianity as soon as they heard it preached.[46] And then he went on to show,

---

[46] When Edmund Morgan wrote of Franklin's defenses of Hemphill, he summarized Franklin's position on faith and morality as:

"The heathen might be converted to Christianity, but people brought up in Christian morality had no need of any kind of conversion. Nor could they expect to be saved by the righteousness of Christ. They had to earn their own salvation by their own righteousness." (Morgan, 21)

When we actually read the text, however, we find that Franklin differentiates between a "bare faith" and a faith that procures salvation. According to Franklin, there is no hope of salvation for a man who holds to a bare faith in the facts of Christianity and who, at the same time, adamantly refuses to comply with any of the commands of Scripture. Franklin illustrates this fact by comparing those who first learn of Christianity as adults and those who have known the Christian religion from the time that they were born. When the former abandon their

that we may be said to be justified by Faith, because it is impossible we should embrace those Terms offered by Christ for our Salvation and Happiness until we once believe them to be true, or as it is the Means of our Obedience. This, say they, is plainly denying Justification by Faith, and this they confirm from another Part of the Sermon, viz. "that all Hopes of Happiness but what are built on Purity of Heart and a virtuous Life, are, according to the christian Scheme vain and delusory, and will certainly end in Disappointment and Confusion." This they absolutely condemn in Hemphill, altho' they at the same time confess, that they zealously maintain the very same thing; or, in their own orthodox Words, the indispensible necessity of universal Holiness in order to Salvation.

Extract page 12.

"*Ordered,* That our whole Minutes since Monday last be read.

"Upon reading of which we find that we have gone through the several Articles of Charge exhibited against Mr. Hemphill, and tho' we have past over many Particulars, as either not being clearly supported by the Extracts taken out of his Sermons, or not of sufficient Weight to deserve a Censure, yet to our great Grief we cannot but judge, that many of the Articles of most considerable Weight and Importance, are fully supported by said Extracts, as will more clearly appear by our preceeding Minutes, reference thereunto being had: Many of these Doctrines therefore which he hath delivered in these Sermons, we are obliged to declare unsound and dangerous, contrary to the sacred Scriptures and our excellent Confession and Catechisms, having an unhappy tendency to corrupt the Faith once delivered to the Saints, and that such Doctrines

---

previous beliefs and accept the truth of the gospel, their faith is immediately demonstrated to be a saving faith because of the change that it produces. However, when those of the latter group give a bare assent to the truth of the gospel while living a life contrary to that truth, their faith is demonstrated to be a dead faith that is incapable of saving them from the wrath to come. This is the relationship between faith and works that Franklin endorses here, and he will continue to hold to this same view throughout the course of his life.

should be delivered by Mr. Hemphill is the more surprizing to us, when we consider that the said Mr. Hemphill solemnly declared, last September, before the Synod, his Assent to the Westminster Confession, and adopted it as the Confession of his Faith."

Having gone thro' the several Charges exhibited by Andrews, they declare with great Solemnity, that it was their great Grief to find so many of these Charges justly grounded upon the Extracts of the Sermons. I must confess they are the best Judges of their own Grief; yet it appears to me and many others, that their great Grief was because Andrews's Charges were not more justly founded upon the Sermons; which plainly appears from the whole Trial. And then they are not ashamed to say, *We are obliged to declare many of these Doctrines unsound and dangerous, contrary to the sacred Scriptures and our most excellent Confession.* If there be any Meaning in this, it must be, that they were obliged to it, as they designed to defend Andrews's Character, tho' never so unjustly. I shall give these Gentlemen my Word, that 'tis as surprizing to me, as it was to them, that they should affirm that Hemphill solemnly declared last September before the Synod, his Assent to the Westminster Confession of Faith; whereas it was only to the *fundamental Articles* of it that he declared, and not the Whole of it; and it seems very hard that they should make this Book the Standard and Test, when at the same time they own'd to him, that *they knew not how many fundamental Articles were in it.* He himself is sufficiently satisfied, that he has not preached any thing contrary to his Declaration at the Synod, and he offered to the Commission, that he would reconcile all his Doctrines to the Confession as he had adopted it, provided they would but point out to him the Parts they thought he had contradicted. But this would not have answered the Ends they had in View, and therefore they refus'd it. I shall only add, that many of these reverend Gentlemen, who are now so zealous for the Confession, that they seem to give it the Preference to the Holy Scriptures, were of late Years more indifferent than Hemphill has yet appear'd to be; and altho' they then agreed, that there were some Articles in it of no great Moment whether Men believed 'em or not, nay some publickly declared they did not understand many of 'em, (which I sincerely believe was very true) yet they would now make 'em all Fundamentals, in order to serve a Turn.

Extract page 13.

"And now we are come to the Conclusion of this weighty Affair, we cannot but observe, with the utmost Gratitude to Divine Providence, that all our Consultations have been carried on with an undisturbed Unanimity, such a remarkable Harmony and good Agreement has subsisted among us, that in the whole Transaction we have not had one dissenting Vote."

And here they conclude this weighty Affair, with acknowledging their utmost Gratitude to divine Providence for their Unanimity. This I suppose they mention as an Argument of the Justice of their Censure: But this will likewise prove that the Spanish Inquisition is in the right, which is as unanimous in all its Transactions as the Commission. The Reverend Inquisitors go to Prayer, they call upon God to direct them in every [one] of their Censures (altho' they have unanimously determined to condemn all who are so unfortunate as to be call'd before them) and, I am sorry to say it, all this is too applicable to the present Case: For these Reverend Gentlemen came to Philadelphia with the same Spirit, proceeded in the same manner, and have gone as far in proportion to their Power as ever the Inquisition went.

I shall conclude with an Extract out of the *Layman's Sermon,* and therewith take my Leave of the Reverend Commission. It is as follows,

"What adds to this Evil and Insolence, this Cruelty on the Score of Opinion, and makes it still more provoking and intolerable, is, that it is all perpetrated in the Name of Christ, of the meek Jesus, and said to be for his Church and Cause: A Declaration so impudent and incredible, that it could only be made by Men who wanted Shame, to Men who had no Eyes. It is as false as the Gospel is true, nor could a Revelation which inspired or warranted any Degree of Bitterness or Cruelty, ever have come from God, or from any but the

Antagonist of God and Enemy of Man, from Hypocrites reigning, that is, tyrannizing in the Name of the Lord.

"And all Persecution is Popery, and every Degree of it, even the smallest Degree, is an Advance towards the Inquisition: As negative Penalties are the first Degree, so Death and Burning is the last and highest: All the other Steps are but natural Gradations following the first Degree, and introducing the last: For the smallest implies the necessity of a greater where the former fails, and consequently of the greatest of all, which is the Inquisition."

A Letter to a Friend in the Country – Sep. 22, 1735

It is sufficiently known to all the thinking Part of Mandkind, how difficult it is to alter Opinions long and universally receiv'd. The Prejudices of Education, Custom and Example, are generally very strong; it may therefore seem, in a manner, needless to publish any Thing contrary to such long imbib'd and generally receiv'd Opinions. It were, however, much to be wish'd, that Men would consider how glorious a Conquest they make, when they shake off all manner of Prejudice, and bring themselves to think *freely, fairly,* and *honestly.*

This is to think and act like Men; 'tis a Privilege common to Mankind; 'tis the only way to promote the Interests of Truth and Liberty in the World; and surely, none but Slaves and Lovers of Dominion and Darkness can be out of humour at it; nor would any Man, or any Set of Men, pretend to hinder others from a free impartial Enquiry into Matters of Religion especially, if they had not some sinister Designs in so doing.

My Brethren of the Laity, as it is to you that this Letter is address'd, and chiefly for your Sakes that I take the Liberty of Publishing it, it is hop'd you'll seriously consider the Contents of it. The Generality of the Clergy were always too fond of Power to quit their Pretensions to it, by any thing that was ever yet said by particular Persons; but my Brethren, how soon should we humble their Pride, did we all heartily and unanimously join in asserting our own natural

Rights and Liberties in Opposition to their unrighteous Claims. Besides, we could make use of more prevailing Arguments than any that have been yet advanc'd, I mean such as oppose their temporal Interests. It is impossible they could long stand against the united Force of so powerful Antagonists. Truth manag'd by the Laity in Opposition to them and their temporal Interests, would do much. Their pretending to be the Directors of Men's Consciences, and Embassadors of the meek and lowly Jesus, ('twere greatly to be wish'd they study'd more to imitate so perfect a Model of Meekness and Humility, and pretended less to a Power that belongs not to 'em) and their assuming such like fine Titles, ought not to frighten us out of a good Cause, *The glorious Cause of Christian Liberty.* It is very probable, indeed, that according to their laudable Custom, they will make very free with the Characters of those that oppose their Schemes, and like sound, orthodox Divines, call them Hereticks, unsound in the Faith, and so on; but there is no Argument in such kind of Language, nor will it ever persuade. And we ought to value such ridiculous Epithets just as little as St. Paul did, Acts 24:14,[47] since instead of a Reproach, they may be our greatest Glory and Honour. Such kind of Treatment was always look'd upon to be a strong Argument either of a bad Cause or a weak side. That it is our Duty to make a vigorous Opposition to them, is plain from these two Considerations: *First,* that when and wherever Men blindly submitted themselves to the Impositions of Priests, whether Popish, Presbyterian or Episcopal, &c. Ignorance and Error, Bigotry, Enthusiasm and Superstition, more or less, and in Proportion to such Submission, most certainly ensu'd, And *Secondly,* That all the Persecutions, Cruelties, Mischiefs and Disturbances, that ever yet happen'd in the Church, took their rise from the usurp'd Power and Authority of her lawless Sons. Let us then to the utmost of our Power endeavour to preserve and maintain Truth, Common Sense, universal Charity, and brotherly Love, Peace and Tranquility, as recommended in the Gospel of Jesus, in this our infant and growing Nation, by steadily opposing those, whose Measures tend to nothing

---

[47] "But this I confess unto thee, that after the way which they call heresy, so worship I the God of my fathers, believing all things which are written in the law and in the prophets:"

less than utterly to subvert and destroy all. Nothing, in all Probability, can prevent our being a very flourishing and happy People, but our suffering the Clergy to get upon our Backs, and ride us, as they do their Horses, where they please.

I shall make no other Apology to the Author, or any one else, who may think it unfair to publish what was only a private Letter to my self, than this, viz. that I believ'd it might be useful.

Your affectionate Brother, and hearty Well-wisher,

A Layman

A Letter, &c.[48]

Sir,

It is somewhat surprizing, that a Sermon, which you tell me in yours is said to be preach'd here by a Stranger, (whom you believe to be your humble Servant) should make so great a Noise already, as you speak of, especially at the Distance you live from Philadelphia. As I have no Reason to induce me to conceal it, I own I did give a Discourse, in the sermonizing way, upon the Subject you mention.

You say, the Representation made of it in your Part of the Country, has given Occasion to much Speculation, not only among some of

---

[48] There are some historians who claim that the body of this letter may not have been written by Franklin, but Lemay points out that:

"The preface to the pamphlet, titled 'The Publisher ['B. Franklin'] to his Lay-Readers,' which is signed 'A Layman,' is obviously by Franklin. The same voice recurs in the 'sermon,' and the unusual opinions expressed in the preface are repeated there. The postscript continues the same voice and opinions." (Lemay, 2: 247)

Lemay then proceeds to compare the contents of the letter with Franklin's other writings and demonstrates that there is very little reason, if any, to doubt that Franklin is the author of the entire letter.

the Clergy of the Presbyterian Denomination, but many of the Priest-ridden Laity, who, it seems are put into a Pannick, and much alarm'd at the suppos'd Tendency of it. I would not willingly offend any; but some People's being offended at important Truths, ought not to hinder their being urg'd and inculcated. All I have to say about the Load of hard Names which you tell me they begin already to heap upon me, is, that their Reproaches, however inveterate, cannot at all hurt me; nor can they affect me any farther than to excite Pity and Compassion towards the Authors of them. I am not much surpriz'd at the Conduct of a certain Set of Clergy, especially since Calumny and Reproach, where they could not command the civil Sword, were (for want of Argument) always the Weapons with which they fought, whenever their exorbitant Claims to Power and Authority were oppos'd. I most heartily wish them a better temper. Christianity teaches us *to bless them that curse us, to pray for them that despitefully use and persecute us.*[49] And I think indeed, the Names of the aforesaid Persons ought to be given in, to all well-dispos'd Christian Congregations in the Province, to be publickly pray'd for every Sabbath.

As I was always a Lover of Truth and Christian Liberty, my only Design in the Discourse was to promote the Interests of both.

I had almost forgot to tell you, that (if we may believe Report) a Gentleman of this City, in a Sermon which he preached here not long ago, out of his great and abundant Zeal for Orthodoxy and the Safety of the Church, suggested to his Audience, that there were some Preachers lately come into this Country, who might be Jesuits, (a most surprizing Discovery!) and whose Credentials, for that Reason, ought to be enquir'd into. Some of those that heard him, say it was very easy, by the Tenor and Strain of his Discourse, to apprehend who were pointed at in the Insinuation; and think the Probability of their Conjecture greatly strengthen'd, by the vast Care, godly Pains, and pious Industry made use of by this

---

[49] Matthew 5:44

wonderfully charitable Son of the Church, to hinder Mr. H—p—ll, whose Story you know, from getting a Place to preach in.

How well founded the Charge of *Jesuitism* is, where this Reverend and worthy Gentleman (if Report be true) would fix it, is not difficult to apprehend: Some are ill-natur'd enough to suggest, the Charge may much more justly, be laid elsewhere, and that the Occasion of his Clamours is his Fear of losing some of his Parishioners. How strangely censorious the World is grown!

Your Advice to print the Sermon in my own Defence, as you call it, is what I do not at all relish, nor can I comply with for very obvious Reasons. Yet upon the Supposition which you make of my refusing this; since you insist upon it as the only Evidence I can give of that Esteem and Regard which I always profess'd for you, I so far comply with your Desire, as to send you some loose Hints of what was advanc'd in that Sermon. And as I only write this Letter for the Perusal of a Friend, so I hope you will excuse Want of Method and Exactness in it, which I really resolve to be no way sollicitous about, nor shall I strictly confine myself to the Method, or Manner of Expression made use of in the Sermon, lest we turn too grave upon it. Without any farther Preamble, then, let us come to the Point. After the Formalities of an Introduction and Textual Explication, which I shan't trouble you with, the Question Propos'd to be consider'd was,

Whether it be lawful to impose any other Term of Communion, Christian or Ministerial, than the Belief of the Holy Scriptures? Or, *Whether a Man that professes to believe the Holy Scriptures, and the Christian Scheme of Religion as contain'd in them, ought not to be admitted to Christian and Ministerial Communion, if no Reason can be alledg'd against him in other respects, why he should not?*

The general Method in which it was propos'd to manage this Point, was to consider the principal Arguments offer'd by those who contend for other Terms of Communion than the Belief of the holy Scriptures, &c. and to endeavour to shew their Weakness.

The first Argument examin'd was this:

A Thing agreed on by almost all Christian Churches, of all Denominations: A Thing universally practic'd in the early Times of Christianity, &c. ought not to be abolish'd without the strongest Reasons. For tho' it be acknowledg'd that even the greatest Unanimity of the Christian Church in general, does not amount to a full Proof of the Truth of any Position, or the Reasonableness of any Custom or Practice, yet it must be confess'd, that the said Unanimity forms at least a very strong Presumption in Behalf of the Position asserted, or the Practice establish'd. Now for the Point in question, we have Antiquity, Unanimity, and the Practice of the Church Time out of mind.

Answer.

As there is no great Stress laid upon this Argument, since it is confess'd that Antiquity, Unanimity, &c. cannot amount to a full Proof, and do at best but form a strong Presumption, so I might without much Prejudice to that Cause that I here contend for, *The Cause of* Liberty, leave said Argument wholly unanswer'd; but to evince that the Cause of Liberty in this Case, seems to have the Advantage on all sides, let it be observ'd that the Custom contended for is not Apostolical. We see nothing of it in the Holy Scriptures; nay the very contrary may most probably be deduc'd from several Passages. When the Eunuch, when Cornelius, when Three Thousand Souls at once, were converted, there is not the least Hint, that any of the Articles of Faith now stiffly maintain'd by some Sects of Christians as essential ones, and esteem'd by others not necessary, and altogether rejected by others as erroneous, were impos'd as Terms of Communion, or even mention'd at all. It rather appears, that nothing more was required of these new Converts, but that they should acknowledge Jesus Christ to be the Messiah promised by the Prophets, the Son of God; and that they should to the best of their Power, act agreeable to his Precepts, and obey his Laws.[50] And

---

[50] This seems to be a reference to John Locke's *Reasonableness of Christianity*. The goal of Locke's book was to prove that the only thing necessary to be

believed in order to make one a Christian is that Jesus is the Messiah which was promised in the Old Testament. Locke asked his readers:

"Can there be any thing plainer, than that the asserting to this proposition, that Jesus was the Messiah, was that which distinguished the believers from the unbelievers?" (Locke, 25)

And Locke further taught that the thing which distinguishes the faith of Christians from that of non-Christians is the fact that it is accompanied by repentance from a life of sin and toward a life of good works. For he wrote in one place that:

"Though the devils believed, yet they could not be saved by the covenant of grace; because they performed not the other condition required in it, altogether as necessary to be performed as this of believing: and that is repentance." (Locke, 103)

In fact, Locke seems to have had exactly the same view of the relationship between faith and works as Franklin expressed in his defense of Hemphill. Franklin argued that those who claimed to have faith while not producing good works were trusting in a faith that could not save them, and Locke argued in his *Reasonableness of Christianity* that:

"These two, faith and repentance, i.e. believing Jesus to be the Messiah, and a good life, are the indispensable conditions of the new covenant, to be performed by all those who would obtain eternal life." (Locke, 105)

And he wrote still further that:

"If they believed him to be the Messiah, their King, but would not obey his laws, and would not have him to reign over them; they were but the greater rebels; and God would not justify them for a faith that did but increase their guilt, and oppose diametrically the kingdom and design of the Messiah ... that faith without works, i.e. the works of sincere obedience to the law and will of Christ, is not sufficient for our justification, St. James shows at large, chap. ii " (Locke, 111)

Thus, it is evident that Franklin and Locke shared the same view of the relationship between faith and works. They both claimed that the only faith necessary for one to become a Christian is a belief in Jesus Christ as the promised Messiah of the Old Testament, and they both viewed a life of good works as a necessary evidence of genuine faith.

inform them of all the metaphysical Notions, nice Distinctions, which are now brought into our Confessions of Faith as necessary Articles. Had infinite Wisdom thought it any way necessary, or useful, to frame long Confessions of Faith, or to establish numerous Tests of Orthodoxy, as is now done in most Christian Churches, is to be suppos'd, that neither our Saviour nor his Apostles would have left any such thing in their Writings; especially if it be consider'd that many Things are wrote, which in point of Importance are not to be compar'd to the Necessity or Usefulness of Creeds contended for by the Imposers of them?

In the two or three first Centuries of Christianity, those acquainted with the History of those Times, tell us, they can find no Signs, no Footsteps of such Confessions of Faith, or Tests of Orthodoxy. The Creed commonly called the Apostles' Creed, is on all hands allow'd to be an ancient Piece; it is suppos'd by some, to be compos'd in the Beginning of the third Century; and this is the utmost Antiquity that the Learn'd will allow it. This Creed, however, is rather for than against the Principle here contended for: And indeed it is very observable, that it is couch'd in so loose a Manner, with respect to the Points chiefly controverted among Christians, that it is highly probable it was fram'd on purpose with that remarkable Latitude, in order to let into the Church all such as in general sincerely believe the Holy Scriptures, tho' with respect to many metaphysical Speculations, they should widely differ from other Christians, or, if you will, from the far greatest Number of the Members of the Catholick Church. This having in all Probability been the prudent Practice of the two first Centuries, the Framers of this Creed thought it proper not to recede much from that discreet Proceeding, whatever it was that induc'd them to make the said Creed, and engag'd afterwards the Church to receive and impose it. Upon the whole, The Practice of the Apostles, and of the purest Ages of Christianity, with respect to the Matter in Debate, seeming to be on the Side of *Liberty* in this Case, a good deal of Advantage might be taken from it; but having Arguments to offer which I think of much greater Weight, I will infer nothing from the aforesaid Observations, but that they are more than sufficient to remove the first Difficulty alledg'd. What has been done since those primitive Times, may be

look'd upon as a general Corruption,[51] and the Authority of the
Church in this Case is of no greater Force, than it was in respect to

---

[51] Franklin makes several references to the corruptions of Christianity throughout
his long life, and Gregg Frazer claims in both his book and his lectures that
Franklin's use of this term is a reference to the works of Joseph Priestley who
published a book entitled *An History of the Corruptions of Christianity* in 1782. As
Frazer put it in his book:

"Adams, Jefferson and Franklin showed the influence of Priestley with their
frequent references to 'the corruptions of Christianity' or to 'corrupting changes'
or 'corruptions' in the doctrines of Jesus." (Frazer, *Religious Beliefs*, 28)

But surely the astute reader can see that Franklin's reference to the corruptions
of Christianity in this instance could not possibly be a reference to Priestley's
book. Franklin wrote his *Letter to a Friend* in 1735, nearly fifty years before
Priestley's book was published. In fact, at the time that Franklin published this
letter, Joseph Priestley was barely two years old.

Throughout most of the seventeenth century, the phrase "corruptions of
Christianity" and its variants were used primarily in reference to the unscriptural
teachings of any given sect of Christianity and, more often than not, of the
doctrines of the Catholic church. That is precisely how this term was used by
John Tillotson, the Archbishop of Canterbury and one of Franklin's favorite
authors. In a sermon entitled "The Protestant Religion Vindicated from the
Charge of Singularity and Novelty" which Tillotson preached on April2, 1680, he
had this to say of the Catholic church:

"But now the Church of Rome hath innovated in the Christian Religion, and made
several Additions to it; and greatly corrupted it both in the Doctrines and
Practices of it; And these Additions and Corruptions are their Religion, as it is
distinct from ours; and both because they are Corruptions and Novelties we have
rejected them: And our rejection of these is our Reformation." (Tillotson, 286)

But Tillotson was not the only one to refer to the corruptions of Christianity in
this manner. William Sherlock did so as well when he referred to the Protestant
religion as "nothing else but the Christian Religion, purged from the Corruptions
and Innovations of Popery." (Sherlock, 2) And several years prior to Tillotson's
sermon, Richard Baxter also made reference to the corruptions of Christianity
when he wrote:

"But if any Sects have been since tempted to any additions, enlargements, or
corruptions, its nothing to the disparagement of Christ, who never promised,

the many Abuses which our Reformers have successfully oppos'd: Nor indeed can our happy Reformation from Popery and Religious Slavery be defended upon any other Principle than what is here asserted.

Another Argument consider'd was this;

Every Society, say Creed-Imposers, *has a Right to make such Laws as seem necessary for its Support and Welfare: The very Nature of a Society requires, nay supposes this; else it would lie open to all kinds of Enemies; there would be no Provision, no Remedy against the Intrusion of Adversaries, that might destroy its very Vitals; in a Word, no Means to keep them off, or turn them out. And why of all imaginable Societies, a Christian one alone should be depriv'd of such a Right, is not to be accounted for. It is acknowledg'd,* say they, *that in a christian Civil Society, penal Laws may be justly made, to punish even to Death notorious Transgressors of the Rules of Morality; now, either you must suppose that all speculative Matters of Religion are indifferent, or, in other Words, that there are no Articles of Faith necessary to Salvation; or else you must own, that such Persons as obstinately refuse to believe such necessary Articles, may lawfully, nay ought to be excluded that christian Society, wherein the said Articles are receiv'd as essential to Christianity.*

Answer.

The Parallel that is so frequently drawn between a Society consider'd meerly as civil, or as concern'd only in Temporals, is very lame, or rather, it is no Parallel at all. A civil Society may

---

that no man should ever abuse his Word, and that he would keep all the world from adding or corrupting it." (R. Baxter, *Reasons*, 430)

In spite of Frazer's attempts to equate Franklin's use of this phrase with Priestley, It is obvious that Franklin's usage was more in line with Tillotson's, since he afterward references the "many Abuses which our Reformers have successfully oppos'd."

lawfully indeed make what Laws it pleases for its Defence, Preservation and Welfare; It is not accountable for such Laws to any superior earthly Power; it has no other Master here besides the Consent of the Plurality, or the Will of one or more whom the Plurality has appointed to act for the Good of the whole Body. But a christian Society has no manner of Right to make any Laws that may any how infringe upon the Laws already made by our common King Jesus;[52] or that may in any Measure encroach upon the Rights and Privileges of his Subjects. Our King is absent, he has left us a System of Laws which is on all Hands own'd to be perfect and compleat (and for that Reason, no Occasion for new Laws) and they that acknowledge him for their King and Head, and believe that System to contain his Will in full, and seem resolv'd to act accordingly, are upon that very Account to be admitted Members of the Christian Society or Church. For this our spiritual King has not deputed any one to be here on Earth his Vicegerent, or to interpret that Will as he pleases, and impose that Interpretation on any. Every Subject is equal to any other Subject; their Concerns have nothing to do with this World; every one is accountable for his Belief to Christ alone. Let no Man then presume to judge of another Master's Servant.[53] One Man's Salvation does not interfere with the Salvation of another Man, and therefore every Man is to be left at Liberty to work it out by what Method he thinks best.[54]

---

[52] Here again, we see Franklin identifying himself as a Christian. He does not argue that Christians have no right to exceed the authority of their King Jesus but rather that of "our King Jesus."

[53] Romans 14:4

[54] Lemay writes of this paragraph that:

"Franklin's statement denied any theological reason for organized religions to exist, though they could still have communal and social functions." (Lemay, 2: 249)

But that is not at all what Franklin is saying here. What Franklin actually claims is that the laws which govern Christian societies are given to us in the Bible, and no Christian has the authority to require another Christian to conform to a different

Speculative Points are not indifferent, but then their Necessity or Importance varies; it increases or diminishes according to the various Circumstances and Capacities of those to whom they are proposed. Those Articles of Faith which the Society is pleas'd to declare to be essential, or necessary to Salvation, may not appear so to this or t'other Man, altho' he acknowledge Jesus Christ to be his Redeemer or spiritual Monarch: Now the Society's insisting upon the Essentiality or Necessity of such Articles, does not add to them one Grain of Importance with respect to this or t'other Man's spiritual Welfare.

If Jesus Christ has not most distinctly and positively pronounc'd that such and such a speculative Point, understood so and so and not otherwise, is necessary to Salvation; then the Society's peremptorily pronouncing and imposing the Belief of it, according to its own Interpretation, as a Term of Christian or Ministerial Communion, seems plainly to be an unjustifiable assuming of a Power that belongs to Christ alone, a Tyrannical Treating as a Rebel, a Man whom perhaps Jesus Christ himself loves as one of his most faithful Subjects, and a manifest Infringement upon the most sacred Laws of christian Charity.

The Words *obstinate, obstinately,* and the like, are of no Force here; God alone knows whether a Man that refuses to believe such or such a speculative Point, be guilty of *Obstinacy* or no. What seems to Men to be the Effect of Obstinacy, may in reality be the noble Result of a steady Sincerity, and a real Love of Truth.

Here perhaps it will be said, that by this Scheme all manner of Power and Authority is taken away from the Church, even with

---

set of laws. According to Franklin, anyone who claims to be a follower of Jesus Christ and who submits himself to the teachings of the Bible should be accepted as a Christian. The church does not have the authority to proclaim that adherence to a particular creed is necessary. That authority belongs solely to the King of Christianity, Jesus Christ, and He has not delegated it to anyone else. To claim that this is an argument against organized religion, Lemay is forced to ignore much of the paragraphs which follow.

respect to Matters of Indifferency, as suppose Settling the outward Modes and Circumstances of Worship. And it is very true, indeed; I know no proper Legislative Authority she is invested with, no Power to make Laws which Christ has not already made, and impose those Laws as Terms of Communion.

The Church, according to the very Notion of our Antagonists, must be resolv'd into the Majority. By the by it may happen, that a Blockhead, or a wicked Man may have the Casting Vote, for establishing this or that Rite or Ceremony, or this or that Doctrine. A very comfortable Thing indeed, that Terms of Communion should be impos'd by the Decision of such a Man! A mistaken, I had almost said a ridiculous Notion of Unity, is the Spring of all those tyrannical Pretences which occasion the Dispute before us. Some of our Adversaries seem to think it essential, or at least highly useful to the Interests of Christianity; that there should be not only an Unity of Opinion, but an outward Uniformity in Worship, (and indeed, as to Worship, as well as Opinion, an outward Uniformity is all that the most absolute Church Authority can effect; for as to the secret Thoughts and Sentiments it cannot reach them) whereas in reality such an Uniformity is neither the One nor the Other. And if it be of some Advantage, I cannot help thinking, that allowing Christians as much Liberty as is here contended for, is the likeliest Means to produce that very Unity, or Uniformity, so much recommended. The Reason is plain; many a Man who justly and with Indignation rejects an erroneous Opinion, or an insignificant Rite, which the Church or Religious Society would impose upon him as a Term of Christian Communion, that is, as a Thing essential to the Being or at least to the Purity of Christianity, would let People quietly go on in such an Opinion if it were not of an evil Tendency, and join with them in the insignificant Rite if it were left to his Choice.

In abundance of Things in Life, but most peculiarly in Religion, a rational Creature may easily be led, but will not be driven. And tho' a Thing be in itself of little Consequence, yet the Making or Declaring it essential, renders it highly prejudicial to Religion; and therefore out of a discreet Zeal, not any Obstinacy, a good Man may reject and oppose it, because enforc'd as material: Whereas if look'd upon and left as what it really is, he would scarcely mind it, much less would he scruple to comply.

But suppose that an outward Uniformity could be introduc'd into the Catholick Church, yet at least an inward Unity, a Unity of Affection, which is infinitely preferable, would in all Probability soon spring from Liberty. Truth having then full Room to play, would soon diffuse it self, and settle in almost every Man's Breast, at least with respect to Matters of Importance in Religion.

On the other Hand, that same Liberty would probably soon lead People to lay aside all impertinent Practices, and cause them perfectly to forget, or at least hardly to think it worth while Disputing about a Number of metaphysical useless Points, which the Spirit of Pride and a Love of Power and Authority on one side, and Impatience of spiritual Servitude on the other, turn into so many Engines of Contention and War.

Here it may be farther ask'd; Must there not be some Form of Worship? Must not that be agreed on? Must it not be carried by the Majority either of the whole Church, or of those who are appointed to preside in it, and settle such Matters? Yes. Well what then? Why if there be in the Church some refractory Person, who not liking the Form of Worship, or, if you will, the Confession of Faith agreed on, What must be done with him? Why truly, just nothing.[55]

If a Man thinks your Worship inconsistent with the Purity of Christianity, or your Confession of Faith subversive of some fundamental Tenets, and that you (i.e. the Church in general, or the acknowledg'd Rulers of it) on the other Hand, be convinc'd that all your Tenets or Rites, or some of them, which are rejected by that

---

[55] Here Franklin explicitly refutes Lemay's charge that he is arguing against organized religion. When considering the question of whether churches should be organized around particular confessions of faith, Franklin answered, yes. Every church should have a confession of faith that the majority of the body agrees on, but they should not make agreement with that confession of faith a requirement for salvation.

Man, are either necessary, or so highly useful, that the Salvation of others would be endanger'd, or that their Instruction and Edification cannot so well be carried on without them; then indeed (and not perhaps in any other Case; for it were better to erase out of your Creed twenty uncertain Tenets, which, if true, have little or no Influence on the Conduct of Men; and abolish twenty trivial Formalities in publick Worship, than to offend one single weak Brother, and move him to separate from you) then indeed, I say, you may retain such Tenets, and keep up the Practice of such external Acts of Devotion: For surely you, i.e. a Number of Men, have the same Liberty to think and act in Religion as that one Man has.

But then, what will authorize you, or the Church to impose these your Tenets and Forms upon him as Terms of Communion? You cannot say he is not a Christian, for he solemnly professes to believe the holy Scriptures. Let him alone as to his Belief. Nay, hear him patiently if he be willing to preach to you; for he *may* be in the right; and as to publick Worship, why should you hinder him from joining with you if he pleases? He certainly is or may be (and that *May be* is equivalent to a Certainty with respect to our Duty to him) I say, he is, or *may be,* a true Christian, and as such I think one may defie all the World to show from Scripture or Reason, that Jesus Christ, the sole King and Governor of the Christian Church, allows any Man, or any Set of Men, or any Nation, to refuse him Admittance to all the Advantages and Comforts of Christian, and consequently Ministerial Communion.[56]

---

[56] Of this section, Lemay again writes that it reveals:

"the radical relativism of Franklin - an extraordinary attitude in colonial America, embraced only by Franklin." (Lemay, 2: 250)

In reality, Franklin's arguments in this section are neither radical nor relativistic. Franklin is merely repeating an argument that had been voiced by the English dissenters for more than a century. Remember that Franklin was raised in a family of dissenters, and this argumentation would have been very familiar to him. Perhaps the most well known expression of this "radical relativism," as Lemay calls it, can be found in John Locke's essay, "A Letter Concerning Toleration" where we read:

To make Judging of a Man's Soundness in the Faith, who professes himself a Christian, to make that, I say, a Matter of Prudence, and to invest any Set of Men with a Power of thus Judging, and Censuring and Excommunicating according to their Determinations, is prodigiously odd among Protestants. It seems the Assertors of such Maxims do not consider that they make such Judges just so many *Popes.*

As to those Texts of Scripture which are sometimes adduc'd to prove such an Authority in the Church, they are, in my humble Opinion, just nothing to the purpose. That we ought to pay a certain Respect and Civility to such Persons as are apppointed to teach

---

"Whosoever requires those things in order to ecclesiastical communion, which Christ does not require in order to life eternal, he may, perhaps, indeed constitute a society accommodated to his own opinion and his own advantage; but how that can be called the Church of Christ which is established upon laws that are not His, and which excludes such persons from its communion as He will one day receive into the Kingdom of Heaven, I understand not." (Locke, 15)

Locke, of course, was an Englishman, but Franklin can hardly be said to be the only American of his time who embraced Locke's view of toleration. In fact, James Wilson who, like Franklin, was one of only six men to sign both the Declaration of Independence and the Constitution, made the following statement in the introduction to his *Lectures on Law*:

"The doctrine of toleration in matters of religion, reasonable though it certainly is, has not been long known or acknowledged. For its reception and establishment ... the world has been thought to owe much to the inestimable writings of the celebrated Locke." (Wilson, 4-5)

But then Wilson continues by asking why Locke should receive all the credit when he was actually preceded by so many men in America such as Lord Baltimore who established religious freedom in Maryland, William Penn who established the same in Pennsylvania and many others who practiced this philosophy both before and after Locke wrote his famous essay. And in the same list with Lord Baltimore and William Penn, Wilson also includes the name of Benjamin Franklin.

others, to preside in the Church,[57] and to take Care that Things be done decently and in order,[58] is not, I believe, deny'd by any body; and that is all that can be fairly infer'd from some of those Passages of Scripture. And it appears too, that the rest of the said Passages are applicable only to the Apostles, or to those Pastors who in the Apostolical Times were endued with the Gifts of the Holy Ghost. And really, common Observation shews us, that you stiff Maintainers of Church-Authority, are as far, if not farther, than any other Men, from being bless'd with those heavenly Qualifications.

Another Argument consider'd was this;

Private Judgment in Matters of Religion, will surely be allow'd of by Creed-Opposers; *Now, if every Man may judge for himself, then he may join with such other Men as think as he does. They may form a Society, and separate themselves from all others, who in their Way of Thinking maintain pernicious Errors. They may reject any Teacher that entertains erroneous Notions in Points which they look upon as essential. It were very hard truly,* say Creed-Imposers, *that Men should not have the Liberty of chusing their Teachers. If a Man that offers to be a Minister or Teacher, refuse to subscribe the* Confesson of Faith *receiv'd in that Society into which he would be introduc'd as a Teacher, that Society has reason to think that that Man entertains and might broach Heretical Doctrines; and if they have a Right to reject him, 'twould be very imprudent to admit him. And those Proceedings,* say they, *can by no Means be stiled Persecution, or any thing like it. The Man thus excluded Christian or Ministerial Communion, does not thereby suffer in his Person, Interest or Reputation; far be it from us,* say they, to make use of Gibbets, Tortures, &c. nay to do a Man any Harm for Heretical Principles, that have no Tendency to subvert the civil Society. Nor do we imagine, that a Man's being excluded Communion with this or that Christian Society, can affect his spiritual Concerns. We do not judge of the State of his Conscience, much less do we pronounce

---

[57] I Thessalonians 5:12-13

[58] I Corinthians 14:40

Damnation. &c. Therefore there is here no placing our selves in the Judgment-Seat of Christ, there is no usurping an Authority that belongs to him alone, &c.

Answer.

How from the Right of private Judgment (and as to that Right, we had as good give up at once, our Reason, our Religion and all, as part with it) how from that Right, I say, it is infer'd, that you may refuse a Man Christian or Ministerial Communion, upon Account of his differing from you in Matters disputable, I confess I am utterly at a Loss to see. Before I proceed, I must observe, that by Matters disputable amongst Christians, I mean all such as are or may be controverted. Perhaps it will be said, that a Man may dispute even the Truth of Christianity itself, reject Christ, look upon him as an Impostor, &c. Well, what then? Why, say they, must even that Man be admitted into Christian Communion with us? The Answer is obvious: That Man does not at all pretend to Communion, for he declares himself no Christian; he denies the Truth of Christianity in general. We don't exclude him, he excludes himself. But this is altogether out of the Question: For the Person here suppos'd, is one that professes to believe the Holy Scriptures, or who declares himself a Christian. But to return.

The Right of private Judgment seems to me most fairly and evidently to lead us to a Consequence directly opposite to the one that was deduc'd. If I allow my self the Privilege of private Judgment, surely I cannot without Injustice deny it to another. I happen to differ widely from this or that Man, concerning this or that Speculative Point; I should certainly think it very rash in him to declare I am no Christian; since I am conscious I believe in Christ,[59] and exert my best Endeavours to understand his Will aright, and

---

[59] I have never seen a single historian comment on this sentence. Many have referenced and quoted from Franklin's "Letter to a Friend in the Country" as evidence that Franklin held to a one opinion or another in the area of religion, but never have I witnessed a single historian referring to this statement in order to discuss whether or not Franklin was a Christian.

strictly to follow it. By that grand Law of Christianity, *whatsoever ye would that Men should do unto you, do ye likewise unto them,*[60] I ought not to pass on him that Judgment, which I should think very presumptuous as well as uncharitable in him. Now, the Case between a whole Society and one Man, is exactly the same as between Man and Man; the Number of Persons on one side, and their Fewness on the other, does not make any Alteration in it.

Shall We refuse that Man Communion with us Christians, who perhaps is deem'd by the Almighty himself a good Christian? What Authority have we for doing so? Infinite Wisdom has not thought it proper to appoint any infallible Interpreters of his Reveal'd Will, and to impose this Interpretation of theirs as a Term of Communion. And if he has not, how come any Set of Men to pretend to a Power of determining the Sense of the Holy Scriptures for others? Why should I pretend to impose my Sense of the Scriptures, or of any part of them, upon you, any more than you yours upon me? and since a Pretence to Infallibility is absurd, these Interpretations may in many Instances be wrong, and when this is the Case (as it is much to be fear'd, it but too often happens) Error and Falshood is impos'd instead of Truth.

But suppose nothing but Truths be impos'd, it can never answer the End intended. The Man on whom they are impos'd is either convinc'd of, and consequently believes them, or he is not, and consequently does not believe them. If he be convinc'd, there is no Occasion for such Imposition at all, it is altogether unnecessary and foolish. If he be not, this Method will never clear up his Understanding; will never set the Evidences, by which those suppos'd Truths are supported, in a Light which shall convince him. He may play the Hypocrite indeed, *'dissemble and speak a Language foreign to his Heart'* (I wish there was less Ground for suspecting it to be too often the Case) nor, can I conceive any other End that can be answer'd by the Imposition of Creeds and Confessions. At best, if a Man pretends to believe the Truth of such

---

[60] Luke 6: 31

and such Propositions or Articles, the Evidences of which he does not see, but meerly upon the Authority of other Men like himself, or because they tell him they are true, his Faith can be no other than human, not divine, or rather indeed it is altogether a blind implicit Faith. The only Way to convince a Man of his Errors, is to address his Understanding. One solid Argument will do more than all the human Creeds and Confessions in the Universe; and if a Man once clearly sees the Truth of any Proposition or Article, his assent necessarily follows, and in all Cases of this Nature his Assent will be in Proportion to Evidence perceiv'd.

And as to Ministerial Communion, does it not at first View appear extreamly odd, not to say whimsical, to deny it to a Man of Piety and Virtue, Learning and good Sense. These are the only Qualifications, that I know of, necessary to entitle him to it.

Suppose he differs much from the Sentiments of the Church, or Society to whom he offers his Ministry, if these Differences in Opinion do not affect his Christianity, what Reason can be assign'd for rejecting him? Why, he may, say you, preach dangerous Doctrines; that is, Doctrines which you now think dangerous; but those very Doctrines, for what you know at present, may prove vastly conducive to the Interests of Religion in general, and Christianity in particular. Take Care that you do not obstruct the Propagation of Truth, by rejecting a Man, who is perhaps a very wise and good Man. What are you afraid of? Let him be heard; and if he cannot convince you that you are in the Wrong, retain your present Notions. If you have the Truth on your Side, his unsuccessful Attacks upon it, will rather root it deeper in your Mind, than shake it. Trust your self to Reason and to God's kind Providence; but never do any Thing that may hinder the Discovery of any useful and important Truth. You say, you may be led into Error, but if you be sincerely persuaded an erroneous Opinion is a true one, do you imagine our good and just God will punish you for it? No, surely; or else what would become of all Mankind. Sincerity is the Touchstone. 'Tis that will decide our future Condition.[61] The Justness of our Reasonings, in all Instances, we cannot absolutely answer for; but we can know whether we be sincere in our Enquiries and Searches after, or Love for any Truth, whereby we suppose God's Glory, and the Good of our Fellow-Creatures may be promoted. Nor can I think it too bold to say, that it were better for a Man to fall into many Errors, by earnestly and sincerely endeavouring to find out Truth, than accidentally to stumble upon it.

It were hard, say they, *that we should not have the Liberty of chusing our Teachers; and what if we will not receive any but such as do in the Main believe as we do, what Injury or Wrong is done to them? Are we in Duty bound to receive any one that desires it?*

In answer to this, let it be observ'd, that I do assert our own spiritual Liberty, and that our Fellow-Creatures, by allowing every Man qualified according to the Scripture Rules, to teach, and we our selves to mind and consider what he takes to be Truth. No Man ought to resign his Liberty: Let him make Choice of his Minister as his Judgment and Conscience direct him. The Circumstances of the World require that some Men be establish'd among us constantly to do the Functions of a Minister, and they are maintain'd for that purpose. Now as a Maintenance can be afforded only to a certain Number of such constant Ministers, so People are necessitated to single out some Persons among those that pretend to that Office. It is very proper to prefer a Man of Learning and good Sense, to one that is known to be an ignorant Person. Discretion, Good Nature, and an exemplary Life, are chiefly to be minded: But to reject a Man in other Respects preferable, to reject him, I say, because he does not

---

[61] Some readers may be tempted to use this statement as evidence that Franklin still held to a works based salvation. However, Franklin is not claiming here that sincerity is what makes one a Christian. Rather, he is arguing that sincerity is what will determine the final condition of those who are already Christians. This is likely a reference to what is referred to in Scripture as the judgment seat of Christ. According to II Corinthians 5:10 and I Corinthians 3:11-15, every Christian will be judged by God in order to determine the extent of his reward in Heaven, and Franklin is most likely referring to this judgment when he speaks of sincerity being the deciding factor.

in the Whole believe as we do, is to declare we will not upon any Account, or for any Reason, alter our Opinions whatever they be. It is to declare that we are infallibly in the right: It is to profess we will not be taught any material Truth but what we know and are persuaded of already. How absurd would it not be to say to a Man, *Sir, we acknowledge you to be a very learned and diligent Person, we believe you know a vast deal more than the Generality of Christians; upon these Accounts we pitch upon you to be our Teacher or Minister, with this one little Proviso, that you will teach us nothing but such and such Truths which we perfectly know and are fully convinc'd of.* As ridiculous as this appears to be, 'tis exactly the Case before us.

But, say they, *that learn'd Person whom we make choice of, and who submits himself to the Laws of our Society, may adorn, illustrate, and set those Truths in a clearer Light,* &c. But yet the Absurdity still remains as to the most material Points; and in a Word, I cannot see how a fix'd Resolution to remain invariably in the Belief of such and such Articles, can be freed from the heavy Imputation of either a Pretence to Infallibility, or a wilful Blindness. Neither can I see what great Occasion there is for a Teacher at all, except it be to save Parents and Masters the Trouble of Instructing their Children and Servants. It looks prodigiously odd that any should think That an Act of Christian Liberty which in reality appears the very contrary. To confine our selves to listen only to such Teachers as are sworn to tell us nothing but what we do sufficiently know and believe, is actually to forsake our Liberty, to fetter our Understandings, and limit ourselves to a poor, slavish, narrow Circle of Thought.

Allow me here to observe by the by, that it were greatly to be wish'd that we had Teachers among us, who could live independently of the Gratuities and Voluntary Contributions of the People, who upon Occasion would give us the Fruits of their studious Piety. Any Man in easy Circumstances, that had a competent Share of Learning, and a fair Character in the World, should at first Request be with Gratitude admitted into the Number of our Teachers. It is easy to see what Advantages might probably flow from his Instructions. But to proceed.

As to the Wrong done to a Man who is deny'd Communion with a Society of Christians, tho' he declares his Belief of the Holy Scriptures, it is obvious that the Thing is not so harmless as our Creed-Imposers alledge. How afflicting must it not be to a Man who is conscious of his sincere Affection to Christianity, and consequently for all those that profess it, to be look'd upon by his Brethren as a Heretick and Infidel. &c. Thus in the first Place he suffers in his Reputation. 'Tis well known how the Generality of Men, shun, dread, and even hate a Person branded with Heresy by the Rulers of a Church or spiritual Society. No Advantages, no Places of publick Trust and Honour or Profit, no temporal Favours to be expected for him wherever they can prevent it. Thus he suffers in his Worldly Circumstances. Poverty, Contempt, Aspersion often pursue him, and destroy his Health and Constitution: Thus our suppos'd Heretic suffers in his very Person. Now you may call this what you will; but if it be not Persecution, it is something so very like it, that for my own Part I confess, it shocks all my Notions, Sentiments and Affections of Humanity and Christian Charity to a very high Degree. So also as to a Teacher; a Man may have spent his Substance and Youth to fit himself for the Ministry, if he be rejected when there is nothing against him but his refusing to subscribe Creeds which perhaps he does not well understand, or in the Belief whereof he cannot rest entirely satisfied, or if he refuses if for some other Reason, it is or may be a very great Disappointment. Then follows the general Odium that constantly pursues a poor Soul once call'd a Heretick. The Case is yet worse with a Man that has been a Minister for some Time, and who in his Search after Truth having dropt into an Opinion deem'd erroneous, is so ingenuous and fond of doing what he thinks advantageous to Mankind, as to confess or declare the Alteration of his Sentiments. The Case is worse indeed, for he is immediately depriv'd of Office and Benefice, and may, for ought I know, he and his Family, go and starve on a Dunghill with his fine Discoveries. And is this then their Separating themselves from such a Man, (as they mildly express it) is their Refusing him Christian or Ministerial Communion, so inconsiderable, so easy, so harmless a Thing? Who is it that does not see how inconsistent it is with Christian Charity? And tho' these Men tell us, they would not be for making use of Racks, Tortures, Gibbets, Death, &c. yet it is plain that if they have a Right to make Use of the lowest Degrees of Persecution, or to lay a Man under any Restraints for religious Speculations; they have a Right to proceed to higher degrees, if the lowest don't answer the End, and so to go on to the highest that even a Spanish Inquisition cou'd invent, if nothing less will do.[62] O rare Protestants! It is well observ'd by an ingenious Gentleman, that *whoever would convince by Stripes and Terror, proclaims open War against Christianity and Common Sense, against the Peace of Society and the Happiness of Mankind. Persecution,* says he, *for any Opinion whatsoever, justifies Persecution for any Opinion in the World; and every Persecutor is liable to be persecuted, upon his own Principles, by every Man upon Earth of a different Opinion and more Strength. What dismal Butcheries would such a cruel Spirit raise!* But to proceed.

To alledge that a Person truly heretical can by no means deserve the Name of a true Christian, would not be to the Purpose; for the very Point in question is, Whether a Person that believes the Holy

---

[62] In this paragraph, Franklin presents a situation that is completely foreign to the modern American mindset. At this time period, the charge of heresy was not merely an expression of strong disagreement as it is so often used today. Rather, it was an effectual banishment of the one receiving the charge. To be branded a heretic in modern times has little effect on a man's livelihood. He can simply leave the church in which he received that condemnation and find another church that is more accepting of his opinions. Franklin reminds us, however, that in his day, this was not the case. A man branded as a heretic then was immediately ostracized from society. The people of the community would refuse to conduct business with him out of fear that they would be labeled as sympathizers with his doctrines, and so the heretic and his family were condemned to a future of pure subsistence farming.

This is the result that Franklin is arguing against. He is not asking the church of his day to employ heretics as ministers. He is criticizing the church for its use of societal persecution to force men to outwardly conform to a creed with which they do not agree.

Scriptures, and that differs from the Generality of Christians only in Points determined and interpreted by Creed-makers and not by Christ, be undoubtedly a Heretick or no. Or even, Whether real Errors in Matters not most distinctly and evidently declar'd essential by Christ and his Apostles, but afterwards denominated such by Creed-Makers, do constitute a Man a Heretick, or blot out of him the noble Character of a sincere and real Christian. Now in this Case to declare against that Man what Christ or his Apostles have not declar'd, is demonstrably, as was observ'd before, to usurp his Authority, and venture to act in direct Opposition to his Design and Will. Who can deny, that to say as the Romanists do, *We are certainly in the Right, and Heretics cannot plead the same,* is grossly to beg the Question? And in a Word, to deny Christian or Ministerial Communion with a Man only because he does not think as we do, is evidently to make a moral Impossibility a Term of such Communion. How injurious this to the Spirit and Design of the Christian Scheme of Religion, which breathes forth nothing but Concord and Harmony: How injurious to the great and benevolent Author of it, who is all Love, Truth, Meekness and Charity! It is, I say, to make a moral Impossibility a Term of Christian or Ministerial Communion. For as long as Men are made by God himself, of different Constitutions, Capacities, Genius's, &c. and since in his all-wise Providence he affords them very different, very various Opportunities of Education, Instruction and Example, a Difference in Opinion is inevitable. Besides a Man's Sentiments are not in his own Power; Conviction is the necessary Result or Effect of Proof and Evidence; and where the Proof does not appear sufficient, a Man cannot believe or assent to the suppos'd Truth of any Proposition if he would. But to proceed to the Consideration of another Argument offer'd by our Creed-Imposers.

The strange Mixture of various and jarring Opinions, the Confusion which it is imagined would inevitably, upon the Principles here asserted, rush into the Church of Christ, is the grand Difficulty often objected and insisted upon.

Answer.

Indeed if Creeds were a sure Means to form and preserve the Unity of the Church; if they could prevent that Confusion, that Anarchy which it is suppos'd would be introduc'd upon the Scheme of *Liberty* in this Case, then truly our Creed-Imposers would have an Advantage much to be regarded: But it seems, indeed, that Creeds and Confessions are so far from bringing into or keeping up in the Catholick Church,[63] that Unity, that Concord and Harmony which we ought all most earnestly to wish and pray for, that they have been one of the chief Causes of the cruel Divisions whereby the Church has been as it were rent and torn into so many Parties or Sects, and do still as much or more than any Thing else, contribute to perpetuate and heighten Feuds, Animosities and Dissensions; so that as long as such a Use of them as is here oppos'd, remains in Force, there will be little or no Hopes of a Coalition or Re-Union of the Christian Sects into one Body.

In fact, the Catholick Church of Christ (and this must be granted, except you confine the Catholicism of the Church to this or that particular Sect, and will not allow any other Sect to belong to the Church Universal, which I believe no thinking Person will do) the Catholick Church of Christ, I say, actually groans under all those mighty Inconveniences aforesaid; and in fact, all the Creeds and Confessions now extant do not in the least mend the Matter. Things, with respect to a strange Mixture of Opinions, Confusion, Anarchy, &c. cannot be worse than they are. Even in this City we have half a Dozen, for aught I know half a Score, different Sects; and were the Hearts of Men to be at once opened to our View, we should perhaps see a thousand Diversities more. Many a Man who in Appearance is of this or that Profession, entertains many Notions quite opposite to it, or to the Notions of others of the same Denomination. Creeds or Confessions may perhaps bring upon some small Christian Societies, an external Show, an outside Appearance of Unanimity in religious Sentiments. And this is the very best Effect they can produce. A poor, an inconsiderable, a bad one indeed! so that the

---

[63] This is not a reference to the Roman Catholic Church, but rather Franklin is using the word "catholic" in its proper sense as a synonym for universal. When he speaks of the "Catholick Church," he is referring to the collected body of all Christian churches.

Scheme here contended for can do no Harm but what by the opposite one is sufficiently done already, and remains utterly unremedy'd. Fact is against the Advocates for Creeds and Confessions, but they have nothing against the other Party in the present Argument but Conjecture. Besides do we not plainly see that the greatest Absurdities and Falshoods are supported by this goodly Method of imposing Creeds and Confessions: Such as Cringings, Bowings, Mortifications, Penances, Transubstantiations, praying to Saints and Angels, Indulgences, Persecution or playing the Devil for God's Sake, &c. and if the Church has a Power of imposing at all, she has a Power of imposing every thing she looks upon to be Truth, and consequently the aforesaid Impertinences, if she in her great Wisdom thinks proper to do so. And can any Man in his Senses imagine that to be a proper Method of promoting the Interests of Truth in the World, which will as certainly propagate Falshood, Superstition, Absurdity, Cruelty, &c?[64]

---

[64] Franklin here gives a scathing denunciation of the Roman Catholic Church. He refers to its doctrines as "the greatest Absurdities and Falsehoods," as "Impertinences" and as the propagation of "Falsehood, Superstition, Absurdity, Cruelty, &c." There is no doubt that Franklin harbored a strong disagreement with the teachings of the Roman Catholics.

It is remarkable then, that so many historians say of Franklin that he was in favor of any religion that produced good works among its adherents. John Fea writes:

"Franklin's religious beliefs were less about Christian doctrine and more about virtue – moral behavior that serves the public good ... Ultimately, Franklin believed that true religion could be found in any denomination that promoted the 'Duties of morality' which he defined as feeding the hungry, clothing the naked, visiting the sick, and, in general, 'Doing all the good that lies in our Power.'" (Fea, 221-222)

But this is not consistent with Franklin's view of the Catholic Church. He disagreed with this church on doctrinal grounds and not on the morality of its members. In his view, the Catholic Church was teaching "Absurdities and Falsehoods" in their doctrines of "Cringings, Bowings, Mortifications, Penances, Transubstantiations, praying to Saints and Angels, Indulgences, Persecution or playing the Devil for God's Sake, &c." Persecution is the only item in Franklin's list which would have an effect on the morals of society. The rest are purely

It is readily granted, that according to the common Proverb, *As many Men as many Minds,* so in all probability, very great would still be the Diversity of Opinion, should Creeds and Confessions be abolish'd. But then first, there would be among Christians a full Liberty of declaring their Minds or Opinions to one another both in publick and private. And secondly Heresy, that huge Bugbear would no more frighten People, would no more kindle among us the hellish Fires of furious Zeal and Party Bigotry. We might peaceably, and without the least Breach upon Brotherly Love, differ in our religious Speculations as we do in Astronomy or any other Part of natural Philosophy. Those two invaluable Blessings, full Liberty and universal Peace would in all likelyhood make the Ways of Truth so easy, that the greater Number of Christians would even come to think alike in many Cases in which they now widely differ. And, in a Word, that mighty Diversity of Opinions look'd upon as such a horrid and monstrous Thing, (and such indeed it is, when it carries along with it the Venom and Claws of religious Animosity, Tyranny and Persecution) that mighty Diversity of Opinions, I say, would be look'd upon as a harmless, innocent Thing, if Men would bring it under the amiable Power of mutual Love and Forbearance. Let the Church but enjoy Unity in Point of reciprocal Benevolence, make all the various Members of it one Body by the Bonds of Charity and mutual Forbearance, and then let them differ as much as you will in their Speculations, it will not occasion any thing like Confusion or Anarchy. Whereas imposing this or that System of Articles, this or that Rite or Ceremony, enslaving People's Minds, excluding them from Christian or Ministerial Communion, in short, unjustly vexing them will hardly ever change their Sentiments; but it will surely tend to turn their Hearts against such Imposers, Enslavers, &c. and Animosities will soon greatly encrease the speculative Differences.

Thus, Sir, you have a random Account of the principal Things advanc'd in that frightful and monstrous Sermon; and a longer one than I at first intended. There are several Things in it, which would require farther Illustration: But I thought it needless, since I write to

---

doctrinal in nature, and Franklin's condemnation of them reveals that he was just as concerned about issues of doctrine as he was about morality.

you, *Verbum Sapienti satis;*[65] besides, I was afraid of tiring you overmuch; and indeed if the Reading of this Scroll tires you as much as the Writing of it has me, you'll be provok'd to commit it to the Flames.[66] I am, Sir, Your most Humble Servant.

Philadel. Aug. 30. 1735.
Postscript.

Allow me here, however, to subjoin, by way of Postscript, some Observations of a very worthy and ingenious Gentleman, concerning the Argument drawn by Creed-Imposers from the Rights of *Private Judgment.* This I add, because in our last Conversation you seem'd not to be altogether satisfied with any Thing I could offer upon this particular Argument. What follows, will, I hope, thoroughly convince you; wherein the Author shews that the Principle of the opposite Party, pursu'd thro' its just and natural Consequences, gives all manner of Encouragement to the Popish Usurpation.

The Principle (of Creed-Imposers) says he, is this, That even where the religious Rights of others are affected by our private Judgments, we must judge for our selves, and are in so doing only maintaining our own just Rights, that are concern'd in these Judgments. The opposite Principle is, That where the religious Rights of others are affected, we ought to rest in the express Decisions of Scripture. I believe this, says the candid Author, is a very fair State of the Controversy. If it be not so, 'tis owing to Mistake and not Design.

Now if we are to pursue our private Judgments, even in those Cases in which the religious Rights of others are affected, *where shall we stop?* Are we not to go as far as our private Judgments direct us, and are not all Men right in doing so? To this Argument, it is no matter, whether the particular Judgments Men form, are just and according to Truth, or not; for Truth consider'd as abstracted from the Discerning of the Mind, is no Rule of Action to any Man, nor can any Thing be Truth to us but as we apprehend it to be so, and *see* the

---

[65] Translation: A word to the wise is sufficient.

[66] This may have been a humorous reference to Jeremiah 36:20-23.

Agreement *between the Ideas* compar'd in our Minds. So that in *receiving* the Truth ourselves, or *imposing* it upon others it must be the *Apprehension* or *Perception* of our Minds that must be our Rule. And this Rule must equally direct Men, whether they are really in the Right, or only *think* themselves so, seeing Truth not known or perceiv'd by the Mind, can be no Rule at all. And so even supposing Men are wrong in their Particular Decisions, yet they are right in following their Judgment, while they continue of it; which is only saying that they are right in not contradicting the Light of their own Minds; and this, I suppose, no body will dispute. Now if all Men are right in following their private Judgments, even where the religious Rights of others are affected, will not this justifie any Encroachments upon our religious Rights, that any Man or body of Men shall judge necessary and just? To apply this to the Popish Usurpations, (which I do to shew the Tendency of the Principle, without intending a Reflection upon any Protestant, as if he approv'd what I know in his Heart he abhors) Pray what has the Popish Church been doing all this while, but pursuing *this very Principle?* Has she not judg'd for herself in all the Creeds she has ever published? Has not she judg'd for herself that she is *infallible?* Has she not as the natural Consequence of this, judg'd *that all Men ought to submit to her?* has she not judg'd for herself *that she ought to use Force?* and *that Hereticks ought not to live at all?* Has she not judg'd for her self *that the Magistrate ought to execute her Sentences?* and *that the Civil Power should wait upon the Ecclesiastick?* These are very wrong Judgments, I own; but yet they are the *Judgments* of *that Church.* They own no Conviction that they are in the Wrong, and no doubt Thousands thro' strong Prejudice believe they are in the right. Well then, they must not contradict the Light of their own Minds, but are right in going on according to it. And here is no Stop. Let a Man or Body of Men be never so far wrong, let him never so much injure the civil or religious Rights of his Fellow-Creatures in following his private Judgment; yet according to this Scheme, while he is of that Judgment he is in the right to follow it. So that no Protestant whatsoever can condemn a Papist, for doing what he does, while he judges he ought to do so. This is so obvious, that I cannot make it more so. Now it is not possible that a Principle should be a good and just one, in Pursuance of which such odious Things can be and have been done.————And this may be applied to all Imposition that ever was in the World, and to all that ever shall be in it. Let Men be never so far in the Wrong, let their Impositions be never so *unscriptural,* while *they have that way of Thinking,* they *do right* in imposing their Errors; there never can be any Security for Truth from such Impositions, and every Church that ever was or shall be, is right in fixing such Terms of Communion, and such Doctrines and Usages, as shall be agreeable *to the Sentiments of such Men as have the greatest Numbers or Interest on their Side, when the Constitution is fram'd, and the publick Confessions compos'd.* So that here we can never have any fix'd Rule or Standard, either for Faith or the Terms of Christian Communion; and a Man that's accepted as a good Christian in one Place, may stand excommunicated in another; while 'tis certain, he is equally the Object of Divine Favour in every Place. In a Word, Private Judgment in this Scheme, is just another Name for *Arbitrary Power,* and no Man can set a Limit to it.

The other Way of Thinking furnishes a very clear Answer to Papists, and all others that are guilty of Imposition, if it be but *a just one,* viz. that their whole Scheme is wrong, for they are wrong in forming Judgments so as to affect the religious Rights of others, other than the express Decisions of Scripture: This cuts the very *Nerves* of all Anti-Christian Authority, and leaves us a fix'd Point to rest at.

A Defense of Mr. Hemphill's Observations – Oct. 30, 1735

When I first read the Rev. Commission's Vindication, I was in doubt with my self, whether I should take any publick Notice of it. I had reason to believe this Part of the World was troubled with Impertinence enough already, and that a Reply would be only affording our Authors a new Occasion for more of it by another Publication. Besides, I had little Reason to hope, that the most obvious Refutation of what our Reverend Authors have said to flatter and deceive their unthinking Readers into an Opinion of their honest Zeal and inflexible Justice, should ever gain one Proselyte from the Dominion of Bigotry and Prejudice.

As for the discerning Part of Men in this Place, especially those who were immediate Witnesses of the Proceedings which gave Rise to this Controversy, they must be own'd to be the most impartial Judges of this Affair; And those who were not present at the Tryal, if they are at all concern'd about the Merits of the Cause, will depend rather upon the Relation of those who attended it, as they are respectively influenc'd by an Opinion of the Veracity and Judgment of the Relater, than upon any Vindication of the Parties themselves.

For these Reasons then, tho' Occasion be taken to address this Part of the World once more about this Affair, yet I shan't undertake a formal Answer to every trifling Impertinence in the Vindication. It were but an ill Complement paid to the intelligent Reader, to pretend helping him to see Absurdities in such *Meridian Lustre,* as our Authors elegantly phrase it. There is good Reason to believe the Opinion of thinking Men, who know the Affair, is not much chang'd by it, and that they entertain much the same Sentiments of the Rev. Commission which they did before. Perhaps the more Pains they have taken, by invented Surmises, wrested Constructions of Hemphill's Words and Actions, and sinister and palpable Prostitutions of Scripture-Phrase, to hang him up, as a Scare-crow to the People, and represent him as a dangerous Innovator; the more Occasion they have given to many to call in question their slavish and arbitrary Principles; and the more they have convinc'd them, even in these remote Parts of the Earth, (where they thought themselves secure) of their Inconsistency to every Thing that is real Virtue, Religion and Christian Liberty. Actions, and the Principles from whence they flow, do mutually illustrate each other; at least we can have no other Way in judging of either, but by comparing them respectively: However it must be own'd, that here the most curious Observers of Men, their various Affections and Desires, in many Instances make erroneous Conclusions; but 'tis evident, that nothing can render such Error or Mistake excusable, but a fair and candid Enquiry, free from all Humour and Interest, and a Consciousness of Honesty in Searching after Truth. Now whether the Authors of the Vindication had this latter more in view, than an Impatience to justify themselves by any Methods they could contrive, not to be too obviously reprehended by the Bulk of their Readers; and to raise a religious Pannick among the People, by pointing out one as professedly disclaiming the most important Doctrines in the Christian Scheme, I would even leave to their own Consciences upon a serious Self-Examination.

But this is not the first Time, that such pretended Defenders of *the Faith once delivered to the Saints,*[67] have us'd the same Artifice, and let loose the popular Rage upon their Adversaries.

A Defender of the Faith, must be own'd a truly great and venerable Character; But I can't forbear quoting the Advice of a great Author, and applying it to the Gentlemen, Members of the Commission, "That since they have of late been so elated by some seeming Advantages which they are ill-suited to bear; they would at least beware of accumulating too hastily, those high Characters, Appellations, and Titles, which may be Tokens perhaps of what they expect hereafter, but which as yet don't answer the real Power and Authority bestowed on them."

If Truth stands in no need of false and deceitful Arts to support it, as our Rev. Authors themselves own; I wonder that they should in the very next Paragraph, use so much Flourish, either to palliate what

---

[67] Jude 3

they were asham'd to own, or to publish a palpable Falsehood. Certainly had they been more honest to have told the Truth, or more ingenious in the Texture of their Inventions, they would not have expos'd themselves so much; I speak with Reference to the Sermons preach'd by Messrs. Cross and Pemberton during the Tryal; which were mention'd by Hemphill, as an Evidence of their having prejudg'd his Cause; Here they say, "they thought they could recommend the great Doctrines of the Gospel to their Hearers, and warn them against destructive Errors, and the prevailing Errors of the Day, without being charg'd with reflecting upon Mr. Hemphill, or accusing him as a guilty Person, and that Mr. Hemphill was neither accus'd nor condemn'd in them." But if these Discourses were not calculated against Hemphill, against whom then? who besides himself had at that time stirr'd up their watchful Zeal? None surely. For they say themselves in the second Page of their Performance, "that they had no Suspicion of being call'd into the Field of Battle, and oblig'd to defend the great Doctrines of the Christian Religion, 'till Complaints were deliver'd in against Mr. Samuel Hemphill, a Minister who arriv'd at Philadelphia the last September." Now if they had been enclin'd to have spoke Truth, they would have said, That Mr. Andrews's long establish'd Character for Virtue and Integrity, was sufficient Evidence of the Truth of any Charge they might have received against Hemphill from him, and that it was high Time to bestir themselves, and exorcise the Demon out of Philadelphia.

What occasion'd, say our Authors, *Hemphill's Removal from his native Country, we know not,* &c. What it was that occasion'd his Removal is not material to enquire. He may return to his native Country, when he will, which is more than a certain Person (and a principal one too) among them dare do. But I forbear——

Page the 5th our Authors say, "Now let the World judge, whether our declaring our selves of an Opinion different from Mr. Hemphill, and refusing to own him as one of our Members, while his Principles were so contrary to ours, gave him any Ground to load us with so many hard Reflections, and represent us as Men fir'd with a persecuting Spirit, and fill'd with Malice and Prejudice against him.

Have not we an undoubted Right to judge for our selves, and to declare what our Opinions are?"

Tho' I believe no body will deny their undoubted Right to declare *their* Opinions, yet 'tis certain that to go farther, and deprive him as far as they can of Liberty to declare *his*; to deprive him of the Exercise of his Ministerial Funcion, and of a Livelihood as far as it depends on it, because his Principles were thought contrary to theirs, gave him a just Occasion to *represent them as Men fir'd with a persecuting Spirit,* since this was Persecution, as far as they could carry it. They farther add "Has not the Commission that Liberty which is common to all Societies, of Judging of the Qualifications of their own Members? Mr. Hemphill is possess'd with the same Right, and may declare Non-Communion with us, if he sees Reason for it." If, by judging of their Members Qualifications, they mean, that they have a Right to censure them, as they have done him, and expel 'em their Society; I think it is clear they have no such Right; for, according to this way of Reasoning, the Spanish Inquisitors may say to a Person they imagine heretical, You, 'tis true, have a Right to judge for your self, to quit our Communion, and declare yourself Protestant; but we have likewise the common and natural Right of Societies, to expel you our civil and ecclesiastical Society, destroy your Reputation, deprive you of your Estate, nay your Life, or in other Words do you all the Mischief we please, notwithstanding your Right of declaring Non-Communion with us. How so? Because we have the Power, and Inclination to do it. Are not these Reasons by which they vindicate themselves every whit as good to justify the Practice of the Inquisition? Neither do, nor can the Synod or Commission give any better, for expelling a Man their Society, branding him with the Name of Heretick, and depriving him of a Livelyhood, as much as lies in their Power, for a meer Difference in Opinion: And after all, out of their great Goodness, declare, they neither gagg his Mouth nor cut off his Hands; or in other Words, allow him Liberty to declare Non-communion with them. A great Favour this! A most extraordinary Act of Grace indeed But how long he would enjoy it, if 'twas in their Power to dispossess him of it, is not difficult to guess, if we may judge of what Men would do by what they have already done. How then were they injur'd by a

Comparison with the Inquisition, when thus they justify themselves by the same Reasons, and copy them as far as they can, or dare do?

How then must we act, say they; have we no Power to suppress Error and advance Truth? Yes, all the Power that any Set of calm, reasonable, just Men can wish for. They may consider his Assertions and Doctrines expose their evil Tendency, if such they have, and combat the Falshood they find in them with Truth, which will ever be the most effectual Way to suppress them and to attempt any other Method of doing it, is much more likely to propagate such suppos'd Errors of false Doctrines, than suppress them: In this free Country where the Understandings of Men are under no civil Restraint, and their Liberties sound and untouch'd, there is nothing more easy than to shew that a Doctrine is false, and of ill Consequence, if it really be so; but if not, no Man, or Set of Men can make it so, by peremptorily declaring it unsound or dangerous, without vouchsafing to shew how or where, as the Commission did at the Beginning of this Affair, and indeed have yet done no better.

Upon the whole, if the controverted Points be false and of ill Consequence, let them be expos'd to the World, if not, the Sentence which the Commission hath pronouc'd against them, will prove their own Condemnation; for, to alledge they may treat any Doctrines they please to call false, and the Believers of them, as they have done Hemphill and his Doctrines, is to give them an unbounded Latitude, an unlimited Power of discouraging and oppressing Truth it self, when it happens to clash with their private Judgment and mercenary selfish Views, as I dare say it will often do. See this Argument farther discuss'd in a late Pamphlet entitled, *A Letter to a Friend in the Country, containing the Substance of a Sermon, &c.*

Page 6. Our Rev. Authors observe, that "in the greatness of his (Hemphill's) Modesty, he takes Care to inform us, *how universally his Sermons were applauded, to what large Audiences he preach'd, and how much (upon their being read in the Synod) they were approv'd by People of all Perswasions, for the Strain of Christian Charity that runs thro' them, &c.*"

This aukward, ill-tim'd, and unjust Raillery is level'd against Hemphill for his being, as they elegantly phrase it, *the Trumpeter of his own Praises;* 'Tis true, he says, his Sermons were applauded, &c. but this they shou'd have omitted [for] their own sakes, for if it be Matter of Fact that they were so approv'd (on being read in the Synod) as they neither do nor can deny, 'tis a very fair and weighty Argument against them, and plainly shews they proceeded against and censur'd what was the avowed Common Sense of all unbias'd and disinterested Judges at the time; and surely we may suppose, he inserted it from some other Motive than meer Vanity, when it was so much to his purpose in helping to strengthen his Argument, and set their candid Proceedings in a fair Light.

Here they also endeavour to lessen Hemphill, by representing him as a Plagiary, and say, *They are apt to think, that if he had honestly given Credit to the several Authors from whom he borrowed much of what de deliver'd, it wou'd have made a considerable Abatement of the Reputation he supposes he gain'd, &c.*

But which of these Gentlemen, or their Brethren, is it, that does give due Credit for what he borrows? Are they beholden to no Author, ancient or modern, for what they know, or what they preach; Why then must we be told, the Ministers ought to have a good Salary, because they are at great Expence in Learning, and in purchasing Books? If they preach from their own natural Fund or by immediate Inspiration, what need have they either of Learning or Books? Yet Books they have, and must have, and by the help of them are their Sermons compos'd: But why then, you will ask, are we entertain'd with such dull, such horrid Stuff, for the most part? 'Tis the want of the *Bongoût* [good Taste] that spoils all. Their Taste is corrupted, and like a bad Stomach will corrupt the best Food in digesting it. They chuse the dullest Authors to read and study, and retail the dullest Parts of those Authors to the Publick. It seems as if they search'd only for Stupidity and Nonsense. If there be in a Book a weak Piece of Reasoning on any Point of Religion, That they remark, and keep it safely to be adopted upon Occasion. If an Author otherwise good has chanc'd to write one Impertinency, 'tis all they retain of him. But when Hemphill had Occasion to borrow, he gave us the best Parts of the best Writers of the Age. Thus the Difference between him and most of his Brethren, in this part of the World, is the same with that between the Bee and the Fly in a Garden. The one wanders from Flower to Flower, and for the use of others collects from the whole the most delightful Honey; while the other (of a quite different Taste) places her Happiness entirely in Filth, Corruption, and Ordure.

Page 6 and 7. We have a lively Instance of their boasted Candor, Truth and Probity, both in their Proceedings at the Trial, and in their Writing of the Vindication. They acknowledge the Charge against 'em for admitting Thompson and Gillespie as Hemphill's Judges, (who, it was alledg'd *had condemn'd him already, having declar'd their Sentiments that he was guilty of preaching great Errors*) wou'd have some Weight in it, were it true; But these Men have the Confidence to say, No Evidence *appear'd to the Commission, that these Gentlemen had prejudg'd his Cause, or declar'd him guilty.* 'Tis true, the Letters written by Thompson cou'd not be produc'd; They were burnt; by whose Instance I know not; But was there therefore (as these Authors are hardy enough to say) No Evidence? Were there not three Gentlemen of undoubted Credit, that declar'd they had seen those Letters? Men of unquestionable Understanding, and therefore capable of giving an Account of what they had read? Did they not evidence, that the whole Tenor of these Letters discover'd a manifest Prejudice in Thompson towards Hemphill? and did they not repeat one Sentence that made it evident to the whole Congregation? If this was not Evidence, I wou'd fain know what Evidence is. But it cou'd not be admitted by our wise Commission as Evidence; and the Case must have been the same with regard to the Words spoken against Hemphill by Gillespie. That Thompson had written in Prejudice of Hemphill, was prov'd; But That Proof, it seems, must pass for nothing, unless the Writing appear'd to the Commission; By the same Rule, if Evidence had been brought of Gillespie's Speaking against Hemphill, it wou'd have signify'd nothing with these righteous Judges, unless Gillespie had been pleas'd to repeat the Words before them. Senseless therefore is the Introduction of their Latin Scrap, *De non entibus et non apparentibus, idem est Judicium.* A Maxim, which if it prov'd what they wou'd have it, wou'd prove that no Fact, how atrocious soever, and witness'd by ever so many credible Persons, shou'd be punish'd unless done in open Court, that the Judges themselves might see it. Extraordinary Doctrine truly! and worthy none but it's reverend Authors; who have giv'n us this Sample that they are able to outdo the Jesuits themselves, in *Subterfuge, Distinction and Evasion.*[68]

And therefore topical Evasions
Of subtil Turns and Shifts of Sense
Serve best with th' Wicked for Pretence,
Such as the learned Jesuits use,
And Presbyterians, for Excuse.   Hud.[69]

But when Hemphill had with so much Justice excepted against these Gentlemen, how mean, how ungentlemanlike, how scandalous, was their earnest Insisting to be continued his Judges! A strong Evidence of that Partiality and Enmity which they deny'd and labour'd to conceal!

I dare venture to say, that, except themselves, there was not a Man so mean in that Congregation, who being call'd upon a Jury, in a common Court, if he had been excepted against by the Prisoner, tho' without cause, but wou'd have thrown up the ungrateful Office with Pleasure, and scorn'd to open his Mouth, or say the least Syllable tending to continue himself in the Place. But the Zeal of having a hand in the Condemnation of a Heretick carried them beyond all other Considerations. The Synod upon the whole unanimously voted them proper Judges; which Unanimity, in the Extract of their Minutes, they ascribe to God as the Work of divine Providence. To make God the Author of a palpable Piece of Injustice, is little better than Blasphemy,[70] and I charge it on 'em as such. And their saying,

---

[68] Once again, we see Franklin's strong distaste for the Roman Catholic Church.

[69] This excerpt is from the satirical poem *Hudibras* by Samuel Butler.

[70] The charge of blasphemy again shows that Franklin was concerned with more than just virtue in the area of religion. Blasphemy is the act of attributing evil to

in the case of Thompson, that there was no Evidence; I charge upon 'em, as a downright Falsehood. Of these two Burthens, I leave them to disengage their Shoulders as well as they can. But

Tis the Temptation of the Devil,
That makes all human Actions evil,
For Saints may do the same thing by
The Spirit in Sincerity
Which other Men are tempted to,
And at the Devil's Instance do.   Hud.

Page 8. of the Vindication, it is said, *Nor was it any Breach of Charity in the Commission, to suppose, that his Persisting in the Refusal,* (of his giving up his Notes) *look'd too much like a Consciousness of his own Guilt, when the first Reason he gave for this his Refusal, was,* that no man was oblig'd to furnish Matter of Accusation against himself. *What was this but a tacit Acknowledgment of his Guilt, otherwise his producing his Notes wou'd have been his best and noblest Defence, and no Accusation against him.*

But however they censure Hemphill for refusing to give up his Notes, it appears from all their Proceedings, that he was in the right to do so, since the worthy, candid and impartial Commission was determin'd to find Heresy enough in them, to condemn him; nor cou'd any thing annex'd to the Paragraphs objected against, (which explain'd or obviated their suppos'd heretical meaning) have any weight at all with them; for elsewhere in their Performance, when they allow that Hemphill in his Sermons and Prayers gave several Proofs of his Orthodoxy; yet, to invalidate this, they charitably insinuate at the same time, that he cloaks his real Sentiments, in order to have the more ample Occasion of doing secret Mischief to the Cause he publickly professes to espouse. A Suspicion truly replete with christian Charity, and in every Respect worthy it's Authors.

God, and we can see that Franklin was just as concerned with this violation of God's character as he was with the immorality of the lie being told.

But say they, they cou'd not allow some Gentlemen to contradict the Evidence against Hemphill, *by affirming that they heard no such Words in his Sermon,* as *their* Evidences said they had heard, because they were a negative Evidence, or cou'd only swear they did not hear such Words; But that was not the case; and here as in other places, their pious Fraud, their sanctify'd Prevarication stands them in great Stead; for at the same time, that those illiterate Evidences were sworn against Hemphill, there were Gentlemen of undoubted Probity and good Sense ready to affirm to the particular Expressions, as they really were deliver'd by Hemphill, the meaning of which widely differ'd from that of those sworn to, by his Accuser's Witness which when Mr. Moderator saw, he stifled the Motion by crying out, He wou'd have no clashing of Evidences so that tho' the Evidence in Hemphill's Favour was beyond Comparison, the least likely to mistake the Expression, (and as much a positive Evidence as the other or any Evidence cou'd be in such a case) yet their appearing for him was Cause sufficient to make the impartial Commission disregard or suppress their Testimony. What was this, but chusing to credit the Evidence against Hemphill at all hazards; to encourage his Accusers, and stifle every Truth that seem'd to make in his Favour?

These Reverend Gentlemen have always made a mighty Noise about a pretended Promise of Hemphill's to produce his Sermons to the Commission; and now they tell us, that *three Gentlemen of undoubted Veracity solemnly declar'd that they heard Hemphill say, he wou'd give up his Notes to the Commission of the Synod, if requir'd.* Two of these Gentlemen of undoubted Veracity, were the Rev. Mr. Tenant, and one of his Sons, of whose Evidence having taken particular Notice, I shall beg leave to set it in its true Light.

Mr. Tenant the Father was ask'd What he knew of the Affair? (the Clerk being ready to write down what he shou'd say) and he answer'd thus, *Being with Mr. Hemphill, I ask'd him, if he thought he shou'd be willing, when the Commission met, to shew them his Notes, if requir'd; and he answer'd,* Yes. The Clerk minuted it thus, *I ask'd him, if when the Commission met, he wou'd shew them his Notes, if requir'd; and he answer'd,* he wou'd.

Thus by a *Hocus Pocus* slight of hand in the management of this Evidence, they converted an Opinion of Hemphill's of what he might be willing to do some Months afterwards, into an absolute Promise of what he really wou'd do. And thus alter'd and wrapt up, the Rev. Witnesses took their solemn Affirmation to the Truth of what the Clerk had written.

For if the Devil to serve his turn
Can tell truth, why the Saints shou'd scorn,
When it serves theirs to swear or lye,
I think there's little reason why.   Hud.

But, as they pretend, It was the glorious Cause of Christ and his Church, and in behalf of *the Faith once delivered to the Saints,* and who can doubt, after what one of the Commission has said concerning *innocent Wiles,* but that in such a Cause, 'tis lawful to say or swear any thing.

However, since the Vindicators declare their Abhorrence of the Principles of that unknown Member of theirs, who thinks any Method of promoting a good Cause, innocent and lawful; I imagine it not improper to inform them who he is, if it were only to see how far their Abhorrence will carry them in their Dealings with him, and whether their Zeal against Impiety be equal to their Zeal for Orthodoxy. The Rev. Gentleman's Name therefore is Nath. Hubbel.

I pass by, and leave to the Observation of every Reader, what sad Work the Vindicators, *Page* 10, make on't, when they wou'd justify Andrews upon the Charge of adducing a false Evidence. Vain is their Endeavour to wipe out the indelible Stain he has fix'd upon his Character by his Conduct in that Affair. They flounder and wallow in his Quagmire, and cover themselves with that Dirt, which before belong'd to him alone; bringing as a Proof of his Innocence, That, which in the strongest Manner confirms his Guilt; Since it shews that he knew the Truth at the same time, that he procur'd a Witness to swear the direct contrary. But to proceed,

In this Page, They put the Trial on the Credit of Hemphill's Notes, and yet out of their usual Good-nature and Charity, suppose that Evidence true, which is utterly falsify'd by his Notes, and rather believe he had delivered some Heresy from the Pulpit omitted in his Notes, than mistrust the Memory or Integrity of a crazy, weak, furious and partial Evidence. Behold the Men and their Impartiality! Lo the Desire they profess to have of seeing him vindicated from every Article of Accusation!

They farther insinuate that Hemphill had no right to expect their particular Objections to the Extracts, and for this reason, because they were there, not as his Accusers, but Judges; and tell us, that their *sincere Design was to give him full Opportunity of explaining his Sense, defending his Doctrines, &c.*

I shall not now dispute what was their sincere Design, which, I believe, is by this time very evident to every impartial and discerning Man, nor whether they came there with an Intent to judge or condemn him, tho' the latter plainly appear'd to all By-standers. But they ask, *how* they *cou'd point out his Errors to him, before they found him guilty of any; how* they *cou'd acquaint him with the Censures they thought him worthy of, before they had concluded him censurable, &c.*

I wou'd gladly have seen these Gentlemen, when they were writing this; they must certainly have been in great pain to keep Countenance, with all their saint-like Assurance, when they assert a thing so ridiculous, false and absurd; for, Who mark'd out the several Passages objected against in Hemphill's Sermons? I suppose the Commission. What did they mark 'em out for? They thought them not Orthodox; or did they mark 'em at random without understanding their Meaning, or without meaning any thing themselves. I believe they'll hardly allow this to be the Case, tho' one wou'd almost think it was, from reading their Minutes and the Extracts. I take it then for granted that the Extracts were made by the Commission, because they were thought Heterodox: Now with what Face can they say that they cou'd not shew him his Error because they had not discover'd it, when they themselves had cull'd out those Passages from his Sermons, as containing the most flagrant Heterodoxy and Error. Is not this then a vile, canting, false, prevaricating Excuse? For who were they that ought to have shewn the Errors and Falsehoods of the Doctrines contain'd in the Extracts? Certainly those Men who had made the Extracts, and thought 'em unsound and erroneous. And did not they, by making them, shew themselves the Supporters of Andrews's Charge, and the Abettors of the Accusation? For to prove the Charge on Hemphill was properly the Business of his Accuser, (Andrews) but lest the Accuser shou'd not be able sufficiently to support and make out the Impeachment, the *merciful* and *impartial* Judges took it upon themselves. *Behold that Spirit that wou'd have rejoic'd to see Hemphill vindicate himself; and brought them there, as merciful Judges, not Supporters of the Accuser!*

Nor can they by any Means extricate themselves out of this Difficulty, by alledging they gave him an Opportunity of vindicating himself from the Charge, and explaining what he meant in the Extracts; For, was it to be suppos'd that Hemphill, who did not think them faulty, shou'd happen to pitch upon every particular Article in the Extracts, which they consider'd as objectionable? And to put him upon a general Explanation was to impose a tedious, and indeed a useless Task; for he who had an Opinion of the Extracts, and their Tendency, quite different from the Commission, was very likely in such a Number of them to expatiate sometimes, where *They* wou'd think it needless, or entirely omit what they thought most heterodox. For, as he neither meant to preach, nor thought he had preach'd any dangerous Error, he cou'd not of himself find out where it lay, to explain it, or defend himself upon it, till they who were convinc'd he had done it, wou'd shew him where and how he had done so, and in what Sense they understood him; and this was absolutely the Business of the Commission.

Their Endeavours to justify Cross, p. 39, for changing his Sentiments, and condemning for Heresy, what but a day or two before he acquitted, need not be much insisted on. I shall only say, 'tis strange a Gentleman of his acute Penetration cou'd not 'till after much Consideration discover Heresy in a Paragraph, that shock'd an illiterate Evidence at the first Hearing, and oblig'd him to run out of the Church in the midst of it. But they have, methinks, giv'n up the Point entirely, in blaming the Philadelphia Gentleman for publishing what was spoken in private Conversation, since this is a tacit Acknowledgment that Cross then spoke his true Sentiments in *Confidence,* however he intended to act in Publick. But who, 'till now, cou'd have imagin'd, that the Sentiments of a Minister of the Gospel, deliver'd to one of the Laity upon a Matter of Religion, ought by all Means to have been kept a Secret?

Let us now consider a little their Remarks on Hemphill's Observations upon the Articles of Accusation exhibited against him in their Minutes.

It is a very melancholy and affecting Consideration to find any, who pretend they *are set for the Defence of the Gospel,* taking so much Pains (tho' perhaps ignorantly) to propagate Doctrines tending to promote Enthusiasm, Demonism, and Immorality in the World. This may be look'd upon to be a very heavy Charge upon the Authors of the Pamphlet now before me; yet the Charge is so easily made good, that it looks like an Affront to the Reason and a distrusting the Common Sense of Men to be at any trouble in doing it. But before I come to a particular Examination of the Accusations, &c. it is necessary to consider briefly the main End and Design of the christian Scheme of Religion, which our Authors seem, by their Performance, not at all to understand.[71]

---

[71] Fea claims that Franklin's defense of Hemphill illustrates "Franklin's distinction between true religion and Christian orthodoxy." (Fea, 220) If this is true, then we should expect to discover the clearest example of this distinction in this section where Franklin lays out what he perceives to be "the main End and Design of the christian Scheme of Religion." But Fea does not reference this section at all. All of his quotations of Franklin's defense of Hemphill are taken from the "Dialogue Between Two Presbyterians." Had Fea consulted this section, he would have noted that Franklin recognized no distinction at all between Christianity and true religion.

It is well observ'd by an ingenious Writer, "That the common Mistake to which the Folly and Superstition of Men, in all Ages, has led them, is to over-value things of lesser Importance in Religion in comparison with greater; to substitute the Means in Place of the End; or rest on these as in themselves sufficient. Now if in any case the Worth and Excellency of Means lies in their Subserviency to the End, whence they derive their Value, there can hardly be a grosser Blunder in Practice, than to substitute the Means in place of the End; or to use them otherwise than with Regard, and in Subserviency to it. But if we once justly fix the main End of the christian Institution; a due Regard to that will lead us to a right understanding of the comparative Worth and Excellency of the several things contain'd in it; will direct us what we ought chiefly to be concern'd about, and shou'd have in view, in our use of all the Means Christianity points out to us."

Now the surest way to find out the End and Design of the Christian Revelation, or what View the Author of it had in coming into the World, is, to consult the Revelation itself.[72] And he himself (the

---

[72] This is the same approach taken by John Locke in his *Reasonableness of Christianity*, and it is an approach that Franklin's detractors (both ancient and modern) fail to consider. Franklin's purpose in this section is not to argue over the truth of Christian doctrines but rather to identify the ultimate goal of those doctrines. To accomplish this, he ignores the competing arguments of philosophers and focuses solely on the Revelation of Scripture.

This remarkable change in Franklins approach to theological studies has been completely ignored by other historians. Franklin wrote of his earlier view that, "Revelation had indeed no weight with me as such," and now we find him relying on that same Revelation as the sole foundation of his argument.

It is also important to note that when Franklin refers to the Author of Christianity having a purpose "in coming into the world," he is indicating a belief that Jesus Christ was more than just a man. Men do not make plans and develop purposes before they are born. Thus, to recognize that Christ did create a plan and a purpose before His birth is to recognize that He existed as something other than a man before He came to earth. This reveals that, while Franklin may have had some doubts about the deity of Christ, those doubts were not of the sort that caused him to view Christ as a mere man.

great and glorious Author) tells us, *he came to call Sinners to Repentance;*[73] that is, not only to a hearty Concern for Sin, but to an actual Amendment and Reformation of what was amiss in their Conduct. And Jesus Christ, the Redeemer of Mankind, elsewhere gives us a full and comprehensive View of the Whole of our Religion, and of the main End and Design of the christian Scheme, when he says, *thou shalt love the Lord thy God with all thy heart, and with all thy Soul, and with all thy Mind, and thy Neighbour, as thyself,*[74] and he plainly tells us, that these are the most necessary and essential parts of God's Law, when he adds, *on these two Commandments hang all the Law and the Prophets.*[75] "These are what Nature and eternal Reason teach us; and these are the two great moral Precepts, which the Revelations the Almighty has made to Mankind, are design'd to explain and enforce." Moreover St. Paul in his First Epistle to Timothy expressly tells us, that *the End of the Commandment,* (i.e. of the christian Institution) *is Charity,*[76] or Love, (as the original word might as well, or better, be translated here, and in several other Places) i.e. Love to God, and Love to Mankind.

It wou'd be needless to quote any more Texts of Scripture to this Purpose; they are to be found in almost every Page of the New Testament. So that upon the whole, it may justly be concluded, that the main Design and ultimate End of the christian Revelation, or of Christ's coming into the World, was to promote the Practice of Piety, Goodness, Virtue, and Universal Righteousness among Mankind, or the Practice of the moral Duties both with Respect to God and Man, and by these Means to make us happy here and hereafter. All the Precepts, Promises, Threatnings, positive Institutions, Faith in Jesus Christ, and all the Peculiarities and

---

[73] Luke 5.32

[74] Luke 10:27

[75] Matthew 22:40

[76] I Timothy 1:5

Discoveries in this Revelation tend to this End; and if God gives a Revelation to Mankind at all, it is this, and this only that can make it worthy of him.[77]

Now that natural Religion, or that the Laws of our Nature oblige us to the highest Degrees of Love to God, and in consequence of this Love to our almighty Maker, to pay him all the Homage, Worship and Adoration we are capable of, and to do every thing we know he requires; and that the same Laws oblige us to the Love of Mankind, and in consequence of this Love, as well as of our Love to God, (because he requires these things of us) to do good Offices to, and promote the general Welfare and Happiness of our Fellow-creatures: That the Laws of our Nature, I say, oblige us to these things, even the Rev. Vindicators themselves, will hardly be altogether so absurd as to deny, since they acknowledge, p. 20, of their learn'd Performance, the christian Revelation *to be agreeable to our Nature.*

---

[77] It is easy to miss what Franklin is saying in this paragraph if we do not keep in mind the intent that he presented in the previous two paragraphs. This is amply illustrated by Lemay's analysis of: "In other words, Franklin made religion merely ethics." (Lemay, 2: 256) But Franklin is not claiming to give the extent of Christianity as would be the case if he had said that the Christian religion extends only to a system of ethics. Rather, he is claiming to have discovered the ultimate goal toward which those who follow Christ are carried. Franklin correctly notes that the ultimate goal of Christianity and of Christ Himself is to bring men to a position of righteousness.

Of course, there are many Christians who disagree with Franklin's conclusion, but those who stop to consider his argument in sufficient detail will recognize that it is biblically accurate. For example, most Christians would object to Franklin's claim that our "Faith in Jesus Christ" is merely the means by which we are brought to the end of being righteous, but consider for a moment the question of why Christ's death was necessary in the first place. Was it not because all men are sinners and none possess the level of righteousness that is necessary for fellowship with God? (Romans 3:10) If this is the reason that Christ's death was necessary, then does it not follow that His death procures for us the righteousness which we could not obtain on our own? (I Peter 2:24) Thus, Christ's death and our faith in His sacrifice are the means by which God has chosen to bring us back to a position of righteousness. (II Corinthians 5:21) This is the essence of salvation; Christ died for our sins so that we might live in His righteousness. (I Peter 2:24)

136

By what Accident such an Acknowledgment slipt from their Pen is not easy to guess; I imagine it to be a Mistake of the Printer; if not, how consistent it is with other parts of their wise Scheme is obvious to the lowest Capacity.

What Hemphill means *by the first Revelation which God made to us by the Light of Nature,* is the Knowledge, and our Obligations to the Practice of the Laws of Morality, which are discoverable by the Light of Nature; or by reflecting upon the human Frame, and considering it's natural Propensities, Instincts, and Principles of Action, and the genuine Tendencies of them.

Now, that to promote the Practice of the great Laws of Morality and Virtue both with Respect to God and Man, is the main End and Design of the christian Revelation has been already prov'd from the Revelation itself. And indeed as just now hinted at, it is obvious to the Reason of every thinking Person, that, if God almighty gives a Revelation at all, it must be for this End; nor is the Truth of the christian Revelation, or of any other that ever was made, to be defended upon any other Footing. But quitting these things; if the above Observations be true, then where lies the Absurdity of Hemphill's asserting,

Article I.

That *Christianity,* [as to it's most essential and necessary Parts,] *is plainly Nothing else, but a second Revelation of God's Will founded upon the first Revelation, which God made to us by the Light of Nature.* Let it not be pretended, that these Words, [*as to it's most essential and necessary parts,*] are here added to get over a Difficulty; for, it is plain even from the Extracts themselves, mangl'd as they are, that this is his Meaning; Nor can any Mortals upon Earth be suppos'd stupid enough, (our Authors, and the Rev. Commission excepted) to understand what he says otherwise. Where lies the Absurdity of his saying, that *this second Revelation of God's Will is agreeable to the first, and is an Illustration and Improvement of the Law of Nature, with the Addition of some positive Things, such as two Sacraments, and going to God and making our*

Approaches to him, in the Name and Mediation of his Son Jesus Christ; and so of the rest of the Propositions under this Article. These Gentlemen surely, wou'dn't take upon them to say that the contrary Propositions are true and orthodox; for Instance, That this second Revelation of God's Will, is *not* agreeable to the first, nor is it an Illustration and Improvement of the Law of Nature, &c. If what Hemphill has asserted be false, this must be true. But, whether they look upon what he has advanc'd, to be true or false, they do not directly say, only in general find Fault with it.[78]

---

[78] I am at a complete loss to explain how historian Elizabeth Dunn could summarize these four paragraphs as:

"Design in nature provided sufficient guidance and evidence of mankind's obligation to worship God, love their fellow creatures, and strive for morality. Revelation, while not contradictory, was also not necessary for the teaching of right religion. As for the truth of Biblical writings, Franklin avoided casting doubt on the sacredness of Scripture, but neither did he endorse it." (Dunn, 515-516)

Perhaps she neglected to read Franklin's admission just a few pages earlier that the Jesus Christ is "the great and glorious Author" of the Bible. Or perhaps she failed to understand that Franklin was referring to Christ as being more than just a man when he wrote of the "View the Author of it had in coming into the World." Surely, if she had read and understood these statements, she would have viewed them as an endorsement of the sacredness of Scripture.

But to claim that Franklin here argues against the necessity of revelation in understanding true religion is beyond preposterous. Franklin specifically agreed with Hemphill's claim that the Christian revelation is an:

"*Improvement* of the Law of Nature, with the *Addition* of some positive Things, such as two Sacraments, and going to God and making our Approaches to him, in the Name and Mediation of his Son Jesus Christ." (emphasis mine)

If the revelation contained in the Bible is an improvement of the law of nature, then it follows that this revelation contains things in it that are not to be found in the law of nature alone and that this revelation is necessary in order to properly teach "right religion." How Dunn could come to the opposite conclusion that Franklin thought revelation to be wholly unnecessary is beyond my comprehension.

What they say, is this, p. 16, *What farther serves to illustrate the meaning of all this,* [of what Hemphill has said] (I wish *they* had plainly told us how they understand him) *is his consideration of these things, which are properly christian, wherein Christianity, as being an Improvement of natural Religion, carries our Duty higher than Men generally thought themselves oblig'd to by the Light of Nature. Among all which Peculiars of Christianity,* say they, *wherein (if in any thing) it is distinguish'd from the Law of Nature, we hear not one word of Faith in Jesus Christ, of the Necessity of our Interest in the Benefits of his Redemption, of Justification by his Righteousness, or of Sanctification by his holy Spirit; nor one Word of any thing but what we find urg'd by the Heathen Moralists from the same Sort of Arguments.*

Surely these Gentlemen must have a strong Itch for wrangling, and be greatly inclin'd to Suspicion and *evil Surmises.* Does it follow from Hemphill's not mentioning *Faith in Jesus Christ* among the Instances which he gave of the Peculiarities of Christianity, that therefore he does not look upon *Faith in Jesus Christ* to be a *Peculiar* of it? Besides does he not expressly mention (as in the Extracts themselves) our *going to God, and making our Approaches to him in the Name and Mediation of his Son Jesus Christ,* as an Addition [i.e. a Peculiar] *of this Second Revelation of God's Will* [i.e. of Christianity?] Now can any one imagine that Hemphill, or any one else, that is a Christian, wou'd thus make his Approaches to God without believing in Jesus Christ? But to proceed,

Has Hemphill any where deny'd the Benefits of our Redemption by Christ,[79] or the Assistances of the holy Spirit to all good Men in the Work of their Sanctification? 'Tis possible indeed he may not understand these things, as these Gentlemen do; and since they have not explain'd what they mean by them, nothing more need be here said about 'em, but that it is certain, they were intended, as Means, to promote the great End and Design of the christian Revelation, viz. The Practice of Piety and Virtue; and if this End be not answer'd by

---

[79] Note that Franklin refers to "our Redemption" thereby identifying himself as one of those who have been redeemed by Christ.

the Peculiarities of the christian Revelation, they can be of no Advantage to us with Respect to our Acceptance with God. But again,

What do these mysterious Authors mean here, by these Words, *Justification by his (Christ's) Righteousness,* or as they elsewhere call it *his imputed Righteousness to justify us in the Sight of God?* Do they mean, that the Almighty transfers the personal and perfect Righteousness of Christ to Men, or that he infuses it into them, and looks upon it, as the same thing with their own actual Obedience to his Law, and that in him they fulfil the Law?

Such a Notion is abominably ridiculous and absurd in itself;[80] and is so far from being a Peculiar of Christianity, that the holy Scripture is absolutely a Stranger to it; Nor does the Notion tend to any thing less than the utter Subversion of Religion in general, and Christianity in particular. To prove this, I shall here transcribe the

---

[80] Franklin's comments here on imputed righteousness along with his comments on imputed guilt a few pages later have proven to be the most misunderstood statements of his entire life. Most historians view Franklin's comments regarding imputed righteousness as a simple rejection of the Christian doctrine of justification by faith. Christensen provides an excellent example of this when he summarizes Franklin's view as follows:

"Do they mean that we need only Christ's righteousness and none of our own? If so, then their doctrine is a perversion of the gospel ... and worst of all, it destroys the motives to a virtuous life, for with someone else's merit already assured us, we need not fear punishment nor hope for something better beyond us." (Christensen, 437)

Notice that Christensen frames the argument as a contrast between justification by faith and justification by works, but this is not what Franklin has in mind at all. When we read the excerpt from Boyse that Franklin quoted, we can see that Franklin is not objecting to the doctrine of justification *by* faith but, rather, to the doctrine of justification *before* faith.

Reasonings of a Pious and learn'd Divine, the late Rev. Mr. Boyse of Dublin in Ireland.[81]

"First," says he, "This Scheme [of imputed Righteousness] renders Christ's Satisfaction to the Justice of God, by offering up himself as our expiatory Sacrifice, needless and superfluous.

"The divine Law never subjects any to Punishment, who are regarded and accepted by God any Way as perfect Fulfillers of it. They may have transgress'd it in their *natural Persons;* but if another by God's own Appointment, is constituted their legal Proxy, and his sinless Obedience to the Law be in God's Account, and by an Act of strict Imputation made their personal Obedience, then after such an Act of Imputation, no Sins commited by them in their *natural Persons,* can be any longer charg'd upon them as *theirs;* and as a noted Writer (tho' no profess'd Antinomian) speaks, as to the Elect, *there was never any Guilt upon them in the Judgment of God.* And this shews the Confusion that those run into, who supposing Christ to be in the strictest sense our *Surety,* assert him to have both discharg'd our Debt of *perfect Obedience,* and our Debt of *Punishment too. Whereas he that has fully discharg'd the Debt of Obedience by another, as a legal Surety, can never be liable to the Debt of Punishment. For the Penalty of a Law never extends to any that are justify'd as perfect Fulfillers of it by one that God himself has constituted their legal Proxy, made his sinless Obedience to become theirs by his own Act of Imputation. We need indeed both the Merit of Christ's sinless Obedience and Satisfaction too to obtain for us that Act of Grace, by which we are pardon'd and entitl'd to Life upon our Compliance with the gracious, and indeed necessary Terms of it. But if his sinless Obedience be made by a*

---

[81] Joseph Boyse was a well known defender of orthodox Presbyterian doctrine against attacks from the Church of England on one side and those of the Unitarians on the other. He also played a major role in convincing the Synod of the Presbyterians in Ireland to allow their ministers to disagree with the Westminster Confession.

strict Imputation, our Personal Obedience, we need no Satisfaction to attone for the past Disobedience of our natural Persons.[82]

---

[82] We can see here from Boyse's argument that Franklin was objecting to the idea that Christians are justified by the imputation of Christ's righteousness even before they believe. There were many Calvinists of that time who taught that the Elect were born into the world already justified and already possessing the righteousness of Christ. The direct implication of this doctrine was that there was no need for the Elect to seek forgiveness of their sins since they already possessed the imputed righteousness of Christ. There was much debate over this doctrine throughout the course of the 17th and 18th centuries, and Franklin and Boyse were by no means the only ones to condemn it.

Richard Baxter, for example, once famously wrote:

"There is a particular personal Righteousness, consisting in Faith and Repentance, which by way of Condition and Evidence of our title to Christ and his Gift of Pardon and Life, is of absolute necessity in our Justification. Therefore, Imputed Righteousness is not the sole Righteousness which must justifie us." (R. Baxter, *Treatise*, 32)

Samuel Wells also opposed this doctrine when he wrote:

"It is observable, that the foresaid Expression do's very ill agree with that known Expression of Scripture, wherein Faith is said to be counted for Righteousness unto one, as Rom. 4.3,5, &c. For this last Phrase can be taken in no other Sense than this, that God do's count our Faith (viz. working by Love, as St Paul explains himself, Gal. 5.6.) for our Righteousness, and esteems it worthy to be rewarded. So that not Christ's Righteousness, but our Faith is imputed to us for Righteousness, on the alone Account of Christ's meritorious Satisfaction, whereby he obtain'd of God, that under this Condition we should become Partakers both of Righteousness and Salvation. So that according to Scripture Christ's Righteousness, properly speaking, is not That which is imputed, but That for which our Faith is imputed to us for Righteousness." (Wells, 138)

And John Sharp, the Archbishop of York, sounded very much like Franklin when he wrote:

"There is a vast Difference (if any Body will mind) between these two Propositions or Expressions; To a true Believer his Faith is reckoned or imputed for Righteousness; and this, To a true Believer the Righteousness of Christ is reckoned and imputed for his Righteousness. I say there is a vast Difference

142

"*2dly.* This Scheme of theirs is subversive of the Gospel Doctrine of Forgiveness.

"For, he that is accounted and accepted as a sinless Observer of the Law, by one that by God's Allowance and Estimation was the same Person with himself, stands in no need of Forgiveness for what he may have done in his natural Person, and is only dealt with according to the sinless Obedience of his legal Proxy, whose Obedience was perfect and sinless from his Birth to his Death, and whose Performance of it is suppos'd by God's Act of Imputation, to be made theirs, whose strict Representative he was. And therefore as far as I can see the Antinomian Writers very justly infer from this rigid Notion of Imputation that *God sees no Sin in Believers, that there never was any Guilt upon them in God's Judgment, that they have no Occasion or Need to pray for the Pardon of it.* And how this can be reconcil'd with that perfect Pattern of Prayer which our Lord has taught, that directs us as much to pray for the daily *Forgiveness of our Trespasses,* as, for *our daily Bread,* the Favourers of this

---

between these two Propositions: The Meaning of the former is, that under the Covenant of Grace (which was procured by our Lord Jesus Christ) God is pleased to accept of a true sincere Faith instead of a perfect Obedience to the Law. Whosoever truly believes in Jesus Christ, and shews forth the Fruits of his Faith, by a sincere, though not perfect, Obedience to God's Commandments, as Abraham did, (and without this his Faith is not a true Faith) such a Man is justified, is accounted righteous before God, as much as if he had performed all the Righteousness of the Law of Works: His Faith is accounted to him for Righteousness ... the latter Proposition, of Christ's Righteousness being imputed to us, hath no Foundation in Scripture." (Sharp, 289-290)

From these and several dozen additional quotes that could have been cited, it is abundantly evident that Franklin's comments on imputed righteousness are not a repudiation of Christianity or of orthodox Christian doctrine. Franklin is simply choosing a side in a debate that lies within Christianity and not a debate against Christianity.

And notice how Sharp includes the requirement that Christians must engage in "a sincere, though not perfect, Obedience to God's Commandments." Sharp is making the exact same argument regarding faith and works that Franklin made throughout his defense of Hemphill. Faith is the necessary requirement for salvation, but a faith without works "is not a true Faith."

unscriptural Scheme, wou'd do well to consider. And how this can be consistent with the constant Practice of all christian Churches, as well as private Christians, who are wont in their publick Assemblies, their Families, and their secret Devotions to implore divine Forgiveness, needs to be resolv'd by the Patrons of this Scheme. For sure the Meaning of those Prayers, is not barely that God wou'd manifest our Pardon to our own Consciences. For Desert of Punishment inseparably attends all Sin. For Sins of Ignorance, meer inadvertency, &c. God's Act of Grace provides for their Pardon, upon a general Repentance. For Sins that are wilful, a particular Pardon, upon a particular Repentance; and as to both we need to sue for Pardon, and this is God's appointed Means of our obtaining it.

"3*dly.* This Scheme weakens the Force of those powerful Motives which the Gospel sets before us to persuade us to Holiness of Heart and Life.

"The Gospel manifestly supposes us to be reasonable and free Agents plac'd in a State of Trial, and Probation for the Rewards and Punishments of a future State. And accordingly makes Use of a great Variety of Arguments to disswade us from *all ungodliness and worldly lusts,* and to perswade us to *live righteously, and soberly, and godly in this present world.* And those Arguments are suited to those various Passions of human Nature, that are the usual Springs of our moral Actions. Sometimes it uses Arguments to work upon our Fears; and such are all Threatnings of eternal Punishment it denounces against all unbelieving, impenitent and finally disobedient Sinners, against all that refuse to believe this Gospel, or to obey it when publish'd to them. Sometimes it makes Use of Arguments proper to work upon our Hopes; and such all those *exceeding great, and precious Promises* furnish us with, which assure us of God's gracious Acceptance, and liberal Reward of our sincere and persevering Obedience. Sometimes it makes use of Arguments proper to work upon our Ingenuity and Gratitude; and such are those that are drawn from the manifold Blessings of common Providence, but especially from the Consideration of the unexampled and astonishing Love of our heavenly Father, and of our Redemption and Salvation.

"Now whatever persuasive Force the Defenders of this Scheme may suppose to be in the Arguments proper to work upon our Ingenuity and Gratitude, yet their Scheme enervates the Force of all those that are proper to work upon our *Fears* and *Hopes,* those two powerful Springs of our moral Actions. For he that has already satisfy'd divine Justice, by One consider'd and allow'd to be his legal Surety, is fully secure from all Danger of Punishment for Sins committed in his *natural Person,* and he that has perform'd Sinless Obedience by the same *Legal Surety,* whose Performance of it is by Imputation made and accepted as his, has an immediate Right to the Reward, and has nothing to do as any appointed Means to obtain the actual Possession of it. And therefore not only do the Antinomian Writers make these their favourite Maxims, *that Sin can do a Believer no Hurt, and that God is not displeas'd with him on Account of it. He must work from Life, and not for Life,* (i.e. must not yield sincere Obedience as an appointed Means to obtain it) *that the Holiness of his Life, is not one Jot of the Way to his Salvation:* But even other Writers that disclaim the Title of Antinomians, yet thro' this mistaken Sense of the *Imputation of Christ's Righteousness,* adopt the same false Maxims." Thus far our judicious Author. Now let any unprejudic'd Person judge of the Tendency of this Enthusiastick Doctrine; Whether it does not tend to destroy all Religion, and to introduce all Immorality and Wickedness into the World. Is it not then the Duty of every body to disapprove and discourage the Propagation of such a Notion, that not only tends to subvert the Doctrines of the Gospel, but the Happiness and Welfare of human Society? Even heathen Moralists themselves, how inferiour soever these Theological Wits may suppose 'em to be to them, wou'd blush to teach such a palpable Absurdity. It is easy then to apprehend who they are that endeavour to render *the Cross of Christ of none Effect,*[83] *to frustrate the Grace of God, and render Christ's Death in vain,*[84] how strongly soever, they may boast themselves to be *set for the Defence of the Gospel.*[85] Noble and Worthy Defenders

---

[83] I Corinthians 1:17

[84] Galatians 2:21

[85] Philippians 1:17

undoubtedly! and if this be the Way to defend it, *Know all men by these Presents,* That, according to our Rev. Authors, the Way to defend the Gospel, is to promote Immorality and Wickedness among Mankind.

But they next proceed to observe, that *He (Hemphill) tells us, that allowing freely, that he deliver'd such a Description of Christianity as this, he nevertheless denies the Assertion of these Gentlemen, that it is inconsistent with their Confession of Faith, and more especially he denies, that it is subversive of the Gospel of Christ.*

Whether Hemphill's Notions of Christianity be or be not inconsistent with the darling Confession of Faith, he is not at all concern'd to enquire; whatever Notions he might have formerly entertain'd of this Idol Confession, he now declares it to be no more *his* Confession, &c. That his Description of Christianity is not inconsistent with, or subversive of the Gospel of Christ, is already prov'd. But our Authors attempt to prove the contrary; and indeed in such a manner as every Man of Common Sense laughs at. Hemphill has said in his *Observations,*[86] "That what he means in his Account of Christianity, is, that our Saviour's Design in coming into the World, was to restore Mankind to that State of Perfection, in which Adam was at first created; and that all those Laws that he has given us, are agreeable to that original Law, as having such a natural Tendency to our own Ease and Quiet, that they carry their own Reward, &c." That is, that our Saviour's Design in Coming into the World, was to publish such a System of Laws, as have a natural Tendency to restore Mankind to that State of Perfection, in which Adam was at first created, &c. Hemphill's Meaning being thus in a few Words explain'd, it is altogether needless to say any thing about the Observations of these incomprehensible Writers upon this part of Hemphill's Doctrine. The Scriptures they have adduc'd to prove it false, and every thing they say about it are altogether impertinent and foreign to the Purpose, as every common Reader (our Authors

---

[86] All of Franklin's pamphlets in defense of Hemphill were published anonymously, and the Synod assumed that they had been written by Hemphill. Franklin apparently thought it a good idea to allow them to continue thinking this.

excepted) will easily apprehend. And indeed if they (our Authors) had purposely endeavour'd to give the World an Idea of their impenetrable Stupidity they cou'd hardly have fallen upon more effectual Methods to do it, than they have (I'll not say in this Part of their Performance only, but) thro' the whole of it.

But before we proceed to the Consideration of the next Article, let us observe *(en passant)* how grosly these orthodox Writers, page 20, mistake the Question between them and Hemphill. The true State of the Question is, *Whether Christianity [as to its most essential and necessary Parts] be not a second Revelation of God's Will founded upon the first Revelation (the Law of Nature)? Or, Whether Christianity, [as to its most essential and necessary Parts] be not a Reinforcement of the Religion of Nature? And, Whether our Redemption by the Blood of Christ, and all the Peculiarities of the Christian Revelation, were not ultimately intended to promote the Practice of Piety, Virtue and universal Righteousness among Mankind?* Nothing need be further said upon the Question thus fairly stated, than what has been already said, 'till these Men please to put Pen to Paper again, and let us know their Sentiments about it; and the World may undoubtedly expect a wise Scheme from this quadruple Alliance. Let us then proceed to the Consideration of their Remarks upon

Article II.

Which is, That Mr. Hemphill denies the Necessity of Conversion to those born in the Church, and not degenerated into wicked Practices. This our Reverend Authors think is sufficiently justified by the Extracts mentioned in their Performance. Let us then see how sufficiently they have made their Charge good. Hemphill in his Discourse upon these Words, *For in Christ Jesus, neither Circumcision availeth any thing, nor Uncircumcision, but a new Creature,*[87] attempted among other Things to explain this Phrase, *a new Creature;* and observ'd that this metaphorical Expression is

---

[87] Galatians 6:15

sometimes made use of in Scripture, to denote that Change or Alteration made by the Grace of God in a Man, when he passes from the State or Character of a Heathen or a Jew to the happy State of Condition of a true and sincere Christian; and that it is sometimes made use of to denote in general the Change and Alteration made by the same Grace of God in wicked and immoral Persons, tho' profess'd Christians, when they sincerely endeavour to practise the Laws of the Gospel: And Hemphill in his Enlargement took Notice, that *this Change is most visible in the Conversion of Heathens to Christianity; and of wicked Professors of Christianity to a Conversation becoming the Gospel of Christ, and that it may be truly affirm'd of such, that they are new Creatures, different from what they were, and scarce to be known for the same Persons;* and that, tho' this be so, yet (as in the Extract) *the Effect of Christianity truly believ'd and duly practis'd, is the same upon those who were neither Heathens, nor wicked Christians, but were born of christian Parents, and brought up in a christian Country, and had the happiness of a virtuous Education, and were never engag'd in vicious Courses. Such as these,* he says, *tho' they can't properly be call'd new Creatures,* (that is, in the same Sense and so properly as Heathens or Jews converted to Christianity, or wicked, immoral Persons, tho' profess'd Christians, brought to a Sense of their Crimes, and a virtuous Course of Action, may be said to be New Creatures) *when compar'd with themselves, because they were always what they are,* (i.e. Christians) *except the Progress which they daily make in Virtue.*

How the Charge of Hemphill's denying the Necessity of Conversion, i.e. in one Sense of every Man's believing the Truth of Christianity, that has a fair Opportunity of being convinced of it, and of practising every Thing that Christianity recommends, or the Necessity of Conversion with Respect to wicked, immoral Christians, i.e. the Necessity of forsaking their evil Courses, and sincerely endeavouring to practise all Holiness, and Virtue;[88] how, I

---

[88] Here Franklin presents the concept of two separate and distinct kinds of conversion. The first is the quiet conversion of those who, being raised in a Christian home, eventually come to accept the truth of Christianity and continue to do the same things that they did before. The second is the dramatic

say, this Charge is founded upon this Extract, and the others mention'd in the Vindication, I confess, I am utterly at a Loss to see; and I believe, every Man of common Sense will be as much at a Loss.

Hemphill indeed supposes that Persons, who have all along had the Happiness of a christian and virtuous Education, and who have sincerely endeavour'd to practise the Laws of the Gospel, cannot so properly in the Scripture Sense be stil'd *new Creatures;* therefore say his wise Adversaries, he denies the Necessity of a Sinner's Conversion to God: Admirable Reasoning!——To which I answer, that

Asses are grave and dull Animals,
Our Authors are grave and dull Animals; therefore
Our Authors are grave, dull, or if you will, *Rev. Asses.*

---

conversion of those who have lived wickedly and who completely change the course of their lives after accepting the Gospel. In both cases, the product of the conversion is the same; only the visibility of the change is different.

Most historians completely misconstrue Franklin's argument in this section. Morgan, for example, rephrases Franklin's argument in this manner:

"People who were brought up to do right had no need of the 'spiritual Pangs and Convulsions' accompanying the conversions that were supposed to end in faith. The heathen might be converted to Christianity, but people brought up in Christian morality had no need of any kind of conversion. Nor could they expect to be saved by the righteousness of Christ. They had to earn their own salvation by their own righteousness." (Morgan, 21)

But Morgan completely misses the fact that Franklin identifies two distinct types of conversion. One that is accompanied by spiritual pangs and convulsions as a heathen turns from his former life to become a Christian and another without spiritual pangs as one who was raised in a Christian home gradually comes to accept the truth of the Gospel. Franklin does not deny the necessity of conversion for the latter. He simply denies that their conversion must be accompanied by spiritual pangs and convulsions.

This Reasoning is every Whit as conclusive, and as infallibly just as theirs.[89]

It wou'd be a needless spending of Time to make any farther Remarks upon what they say under this Article, or to take Notice of what little Use the Texts of Scripture, they mention, are to prove the

---

[89] Walter Isaacson says of this comment from Franklin that, "In a subsequent poem, he labeled Hemphill's critics 'Rev. Asses.'" (Isaacson, 109) But that is not what Franklin is saying here. What he is actually pointing out to his readers is that the Synod was using flawed logic in their condemnation of Hemphill, but instead of trying to explain that the Synod had used flawed distribution in their logic, Franklin simply presented his own, somewhat caustic, example of that flaw.

Given the explanation that preceded this example, Franklin likely thought that the Synod had committed a distribution error along the lines of:

1. All who live wickedly need to be converted.
2. No children raised in godly homes live wickedly.
3. Therefore, no children raised in godly homes need to be converted.

This particular syllogism consists of two statements made by Hemphill and the conclusion drawn from those statements by the Synod, but the Synod's conclusion is flawed in that it commits the fallacy known as the illicit major fallacy. A quick example of this fallacy can be given to simplify our own understanding of the Synod's error:

1. All fish live in water.
2. No dolphins are fish.
3. Therefore no dolphins live in water.

This example gives us a better understanding of the flaw that Franklin found in the reasoning of the Synod. It is true that fish live in water, and it is true that dolphins are not fish, but that does not necessarily mean that no dolphins live in water. There could be other things that live in water besides just fish. Similarly, Franklin claims that it is true that those who live wickedly need to be converted, and it is true that children raised in godly homes do not live wickedly, but that does not necessarily mean that children raised in godly homes do not need to be converted. There could be other people who need conversion besides just those who live wickedly, and this is precisely the point that Franklin made in the two paragraphs preceding his comments about authors and asses.

Necessity of inward Pangs and Convulsions to all truly sincere Christians; they are only different Expressions signifying the same Thing; viz. pointing to us the Necessity of Holiness and Virtue, in order to be entitl'd to the glorious Denomination of Christ's real Disciples, or true Christians.

But lest they shou'd imagine that one of their strongest Objections hinted at here, and elsewhere, is designedly overlook'd, as being unanswerable, viz. *our lost and undone State by Nature,* as it is commonly call'd, proceeding undoubtedly from the Imputation of old Father Adam's first Guilt. To this I answer once for all, that I look upon this Opinion every whit as ridiculous as that of Imputed Righteousness. 'Tis a Notion invented, a Bugbear set up by Priests (whether *Popish* or *Presbyterian* I know not) to fright and scare an unthinking Populace out of their Senses, and inspire them with Terror, to answer the little selfish Ends of the Inventors and Propagators. 'Tis absurd in it self, and therefore cannot be father'd upon the Christian Religion as deliver'd in the Gospel. Moral Guilt is so personal a Thing, that it cannot possibly in the Nature of Things be transferr'd from one Man to Myriads of others, that were no way accessary to it. And to suppose a Man liable to Punishment upon account of the Guilt of another, is unreasonable; and actually to punish him for it, is unjust and cruel.[90]

---

[90] As I mentioned previously, Franklin's comments on imputed righteousness and imputed guilt are the most misunderstood statements that he ever made. Paul Leicester Ford misquoted Franklin as saying here that "original sin was as ridiculous as imputed righteousness" (Ford, 144), and most other historians have followed suit. Lemay, for example, says that here Franklin "denounced the doctrine of original sin" (Lemay, 2: 256). However, a more careful examination of Franklin's comments reveals that he was not condemning the doctrine of original sin but rather that of imputed guilt. In the minds of the Presbyterian Synod, these two doctrines were inseparable, but when we recall that Franklin's mother was the daughter of a Baptist missionary, another possibility presents itself to us.

The Baptists have traditionally maintained a distinction between the doctrines of original sin and imputed guilt, accepting the former and denying the latter. This distinction was recently highlighted as Article Two of the "Statement of the Traditional Southern Baptist Understanding of God's Plan of Salvation." This

Statement was written for the specific purpose of combating the rise of Calvinist doctrine within the Southern Baptist Churches, and Article Two of the Statement makes the following claims:

"We affirm that, because of the fall of Adam, every person inherits a nature and environment inclined toward sin and that every person who is capable of moral action will sin. Each person's sin alone brings the wrath of a holy God, broken fellowship with Him, ever-worsening selfishness and destructiveness, death, and condemnation to an eternity in hell.

"We deny that Adam's sin resulted in the incapacitation of any person's free will or rendered any person guilty before he has personally sinned. While no sinner is remotely capable of achieving salvation through his own effort, we deny that any sinner is saved apart from a free response to the Holy Spirit's drawing through the Gospel.

"Genesis 3:15-24; 6:5; Deuteronomy 1:39; Isaiah 6:5, 7:15-16;53:6; Jeremiah 17:5,9, 31:29-30; Ezekiel 18:19-20; Romans 1:18-32; 3:9-18, 5:12, 6:23; 7:9; Matthew 7:21-23; 1 Corinthians 1:18-25; 6:9-10;15:22; 2 Corinthians 5:10; Hebrews 9:27-28; Revelation 20:11-15" (Hankins, 16)

The first paragraph affirms the doctrine of original sin while the second paragraph denies that of imputed guilt, and Adam Harwood made this distinction very clear when he wrote:

"Southern Baptists who affirm the TS explicitly reject inherited guilt. The Bible teaches that Adam's sin had devastating consequences for humanity and no one escapes sinfulness. But we are held accountable by God for our own sin and guilt, not the sin and guilt of Adam." (Harwood, 32)

According to Harwood, the dispute over the doctrine of imputed guilt began at least as early as the fourth century when it was used in support of the practice of infant baptism. The doctrine was opposed by several of the church leaders of that time including John Chrysostom, Gregory of Nazianzus and Gregory of Nyssa. Chrysostom was actually in favor of infant baptism, but he objected to the doctrine of imputed guilt when he wrote, "We do baptize infants, although they are not guilty of any sins." (Harwood, 37-38)

Lemay concluded his surmising on this section with "Franklin's opinions are neither Presbyterian nor Christian" (Lemay, 2: 257), but unless Lemay and other historians are willing to argue that the Baptists are not Christian, then such a statement is remarkably inaccurate. Franklin's view of imputed guilt certainly

152

Our Adversaries will perhaps alledge some Passages of the sacred Scriptures to prove this their Opinion; What! will they pretend to prove from Scripture a Notion that is absurd in itself, and has no Foundation in Nature? And if there was such a Text of Scripture, for my own Part, I should not in the least hesitate to say, that it could not be genuine, being so evidently contrary to Reason and the Nature of Things. But is it alledg'd, that there are some Passages in Scripture, which do, at least, insinuate the Notion here contradicted? In answer to this, I observe, that these Passages are intricate and obscure. And granting that I could not explain them after a manner more agreeable to the Nature of God and Reason, than the Maintainers of this monstrous System do yet I could not help thinking that they must be understood in a Sense consistent with them, tho' I could not find it out; and I would ingeniously confess I did not understand them, sooner than admit of a Sense contrary to Reason and to the Nature and Perfections of the Almighty God, and which Sense has no other Tendency than to represent the great Father of Mercy, the beneficent Creator and Preserver of universal Nature, as arbitrary, unjust and cruel; which is contrary to a thousand other Declarations of the same holy Scriptures. If the teaching of this Notion, pursued in its natural Consequences, be not teaching of Demonism, I know not what is.[91]

---

was not Presbyterian, but it is just as certain that his view was a Christian view nonetheless.

[91] Lemay wrote of this paragraph that:

"Though Franklin had drawn support from biblical texts several times in the controversy, he now rejected its authority. If passages supporting the doctrine of original sin exist in the Bible, they 'could not be genuine, being so evidently contrary to Reason and the Nature of Things.' Thus, reason is supposedly superior to the Bible." (Lemay, 2: 257)

Frazer made a similar claim when he identified Franklin as a theistic rationalist and wrote that:

"Theistic rationalists thought that revelation was designed to complement reason (not vice versa). Reason was the ultimate standard for learning and

All that Hemphill has to say about the Mistake of citing Words for Scripture Expressions, which he owns are not, is, that such a Mistake is not so bad, nor of so dangerous Consequence, as perverting the holy Scriptures, which these Authors are most miserably guilty of; and he thinks his Opinions still just, and

---

evaluating truth and for determining legitimate revelation from God." (Frazer, *Religious Beliefs*, 20)

For both of these men, the use of reason to determine whether any portion of the Bible is a genuine revelation from God is a sign of heresy. In fact, Frazer listed the authority of the Bible over reason as one of the ten doctrines "designed to identify who was *not* a Christian" (emphasis his), and he claimed that:

"Christians believed that the whole Bible was divinely inspired, was God's special revelation of Himself, and was the only infallible authority in all matters that it treated." (Frazer, *Religious Beliefs*, 18)

What these two men fail to realize (and what Franklin correctly realized) is the simple fact that all Scripture is dependent on human reason. The Bible itself tells us that there are false prophets, false teachers, false gospels and even false Christs; and it commands us to use reason to discern the true from the false (Matthew 7:15-20, Romans 12:2, I Thessalonians 5:21, I John 4:1). Augustine tells us that there was a dispute among the Christians of his day over whether the Hebrew manuscripts or the Greek manuscripts gave the correct ages for the patriarchs in Genesis (Augustine, 70-73); and in our day, Christians are divided over the validity of the ending of Mark (Mark 16:9-20), the Johannine Comma (I John 5:7) and the story of the woman caught in adultery (John 7:53-8:11). Frazer himself uses a Bible that denies the validity of these three passages, and yet he says of men like Franklin that:

"These guys had the audacity to decide which parts of the Bible were revelation from God and which weren't on the basis of their own reason." (Frazer, Seminar)

The simple fact of the matter is that Christians have always used human reasoning to determine which books and passages claiming to be Scripture actually are revelation from God. There is no reason to assume that Franklin was any more unorthodox on this account than Augustine was in his day or than any of our modern Bible translators are today.

agreeable to the sacred Scriptures, for any thing they have said to the contrary. Now for

Article III.

Which is, that Hemphill has declaim'd against the Doctrine of Christ's Merit and Satisfaction. A heavy Charge indeed; and to support it they produce several Extracts from his Sermons. Now, if what is advanc'd in these Extracts be false and heterodox, the contrary Propositions must be true and orthodox. Let us then compare Hemphill's Sentiments and the opposite together in the subsequent Manner. After Hemphill had observ'd that to preach Christ is universally allow'd to be the Duty of every Gospel Minister; he asks, What does this mean? and observes that "It is not to use his Name as a Charm, to work up the Hearers to a warm Pitch of Enthusiasm, without any Foundation of Reason to support it. 'Tis not to make his Person and Offices incomprehensible. 'Tis not to exalt his Glory, as a kind condescending Saviour, to the dishonouring of the supreme and unlimited Goodness of the Creator and Father of the Universe, who is represented as stern and inexorable, as expressing no Indulgence to his guilty Creatures, but demanding full and rigorous Satisfaction for their Offences."

The opposite and orthodox Principles of the Presbyterian Ministers of Pensylvania are, that *to preach Christ is to use his Name as a Charm, to work up the Hearers to a warm Pitch of Enthusiasm, without any Foundation of Reason to support it. 'Tis to make his Person and Offices incomprehensible. 'Tis to exalt his Glory as a kind, condescending Saviour, to the dishonouring of the supreme and unlimited Goodness of the Creator and Father of the Universe, who is really a stern and inexorable Being, expressing no Indulgence to his guilty Creatures but demanding full and rigorous Satisfaction for their Offences.* Well, these are glorious Principles, and a most excellent Method of preaching Christ.

These gloomy Writers after a Story of a Cock and a Bull, observe that Hemphill can't pretend to instance in any Preachers of Christ, that ever directly or in terms applied these Epithets, *stern, rigorous,*

&c. to the glorious God. Suppose this granted; yet it is easy to mention some who pretend to preach Christ, that maintain Doctrines, which, if pursued thro' their just and natural Consequences, would lead any unprejudic'd Mind to entertain such unworthy Conceptions of our glorious, good and beneficent God.

But Hemphill is charg'd with denying the Merits and Satisfaction of Christ, and that too for preaching the Laws of Christ. Let us then consider what the Scripture Doctrine of this Affair is, and in a Word it is this: Christ by his Death and Sufferings has purchas'd for us those easy Terms and Conditions of our Acceptance with God, propos'd in the Gospel, to wit, Faith and Repentance:[92] By his Death and Sufferings, he has assur'd us of God's being ready and willing to accept of our sincere, tho' imperfect Obedience to his reveal'd Will; By his Death and Sufferings he has atton'd for all Sins forsaken and amended, but surely not for such as are wilfully and obstinately persisted in. This is Hemphill's Notion of this Affair, and this he has always preach'd; and he believes, 'tis what no wise Man will contradict.

That the ultimate End and Design of Christ's Death, of our Redemption by his Blood, &c. was to lead us to the Practice of all Holiness, Piety and Virtue, and by these Means to deliver us from future Pain an Punishment, and lead us to the Happiness of Heaven, may, (besides what has been already suggested) be prov'd from innumerable Passages of the holy Scriptures. If St. Paul's Authority be of any Weight with these Rev. and Ghostly Fathers, he distinctly tells us that the Design of Christ's giving himself for us, was, *that he*

---

[92] As far as I have been able to determine, this very important statement from Franklin had never been referenced by any historian prior to my bringing it to light in 2012. A Google search for this phrase conducted at the time that this book was being written in December of 2014 returned only 76 results, and all of them were references to my work. Nearly every historian who has written about Franklin's religion has referenced his defense of Samuel Hemphill, yet I have not found a single one who has addressed the fact that Franklin believed that man's acceptance with God was purchased by the death of Jesus Christ and is available only through faith and repentance.

might redeem us from all Iniquity, and purify unto himself a peculiar People, zealous of good Works.[93] And he elsewhere tells us, that *Christ dyed for all, that they which live, should not henceforth live unto themselves, but unto him,* (i.e. in Obedience to his Laws) *which died for them, and rose again.*[94] And St. Peter expresly tells us the same thing, when he says, that *Jesus Christ bore our Sins in his own Body on the Tree, that we being dead unto Sin should live unto Righteousness.*[95] Our Saviour himself, as was before observ'd, tells us, that he *came to call Sinners to Repentance.*[96] But what need I trouble the Reader with quoting any more Passages to this Purpose? To proceed then,

It is most astonishing to find those who pretend to be christian Ministers finding Fault with Hemphill, p. 40, for teaching, that *to preach Christ is not to encourage undue and presumptuous Reliances on his Merits and Satisfaction, to the Contempt of Virtue and good Works? This,* say they, *is a most dangerous Doctrine.*

And wou'd they really have Hemphill preach the contrary Doctrine? Wou'd they have him encourage impenitent Sinners with the Hopes of Salvation, by teaching them an undue and presumptuous Reliance on Christ's Merits and Satisfaction? And was it for this that God sent his Son into the World? If then Christ has shed his Blood to save such as wilfully continue in their Sins, and obstinately persist in a vicious Course of Action, then in Order to evidence our Trust and Reliance upon the Merits and Satisfaction of our Lord Jesus Christ, we must continue quietly in a State of Impenitence and

---

[93] Titus 2:14

[94] II Corinthians 5:15

[95] I Peter 2:24

[96] Matthew 9:13

Wickedness, and promise ourselves Favour and Acceptance with God, notwithstanding all our Sins.[97]

If this be not Antinomianism, if it be not to preach the Doctrine of Devils, instead of the Gospel of Jesus, I know not what is. How great and valuable soever the Merits and Satisfaction of Christ may be (as undoubtedly they are great and valuable beyond Conception) yet, they are no more with Respect to us, than what God in his Word has declar'd them to be. They will be of no Use to us, without sincerely endeavouring to conform to his Will. And when Christians sincerely endeavor to obey God's Commands, and perform their Duty really and affectionately, tho' very imperfectly; to rely then and depend upon the Merits and Satisfaction of Christ for our final Acceptance with God, is undoubtedly not only the Duty, but the Comfort of all Christians. This is a Trust and Reliance founded upon the Gospel. But when Men continue in a vicious Course of Action, and imagine that God, notwithstanding their impenitence, will save them at last, and that because of the Merits and Satisfaction of our Lord and Redeemer Jesus Christ, provided they at particular Times, when they happen to fall into a Paroxysm of Devotion, confidently declare their Trust and Dependence thereupon, and apply them to themselves, as our unmeaning Authors sometimes talk; when Sinners, I say, trust and rely upon this; it is a foolish, presumptuous and extravagantly unreasonable Reliance, and it is obvious to the meanest Capacity (our Authors still excepted) that such a Dependance is no way founded upon the Gospel.[98] Besides, such a

---

[97] This is an identical argument to that made by the Apostle Paul in Romans 6 where he asked, "What shall we say then? Shall we continue in sin, that grace may abound?" And the answer is found in the next verse: "God forbid. How shall we, that are dead to sin, live any longer therein?" Franklin is correctly contrasting true salvation through a living faith that produces good works against the false gospel of antinomianism which teaches that salvation is possible for those whose faith produces no fruit and even for those with no faith at all.

[98] Here Franklin is referring to those who occasionally make public professions of faith in Christ, but who have never repented of their sins. This is evident by his use of the phrase "notwithstanding their impenitence." Christ Himself made a similar statement when He said, "Except ye repent, ye shall all likewise perish." (Luke 13:3) Franklin is just agreeing with Christ when he claims that they are not

Trust and Reliance as this, is to injure and affront the great Redeemer of Mankind in the most extravagant manner imaginable; as if he came from Heaven, as if he suffer'd so much, not *to lead Sinners to Repentance,* but to encourage them in their Impenitence. But enough of this; every unbias'd Reader will easily see how ill-grounded the Charge of Hemphill's denying the Merits and Satisfaction of Christ is, and also the ridiculous Impertinence of the Whole of what our Reverend Authors have said upon the Affair; and they will easily apprehend too, the Truth of this Position of Hemphill's, found so much Fault with by our Authors, viz. *That God hath no Regard to any thing but Men's inward Merits and Deserts;* that is, no Regard to any thing *in Men* but their inward Merits; What else can the Almighty regard in them?

'Twould be a needless Trouble (and the Reader would hardly forgive the doing it) to follow these dark Authors Step by Step, thro' all their incoherent Starts and Hints. I shall therefore only take Notice of one Thing more under this Article. Hemphill is condemn'd for advancing this Piece of Heresy, viz. *They who have no other Knowledge of God and their Duty, but what the Light of Nature teaches them; no Law for the Government of their Actions, but the Law of Reason and Conscience; will be accepted, if they live up to the Light which they have, and govern their Actions accordingly.* To this our stern Authors answer, *Will the Heathen be accepted of God, by living up to the Light which they have, and governing their Actions accordingly?* then, say they, *there is no need of Christ's Merits and Satisfaction, in order to our Acceptance with God.* Well concluded! Pray, how came these Rev. Gentlemen to know that the Heathen, living up to the Light of Nature, may not have an Interest in the Merits and Satisfaction of Christ, or that they may not be accepted of God upon account thereof. The Merits of Christ's Death and Sufferings may be so great as to extend to the Heathen World, they may reap the Advantages of it, tho' they never had an Opportunity of hearing of him, provided they make a good Use of their Reason, and other Principles of Action within them. And to say

---

really Christians who make a public profession of faith while never repenting of their sins.

otherwise is actually to lessen and diminish the Merits of the Redeemer of Mankind: The Holy Scriptures represent his Mission as a general Benefit, a Benefit which Regards all Men, and in Fact, tell us that *Christ dyed for all.*[99] And can any imagine that our good God, as is here suppos'd, will eternally damn the Heathen World for not obeying a Law they never heard of; that is, damn them for not doing an Impossibility. Surely none can imagine such a thing; except such as form their Ideas of the great Governor of the Universe, by reflecting upon their own cruel, unjust and barbarous Tempers, as our Authors seem to do. If God requir'd Obedience to an unknown Law, Obedience to the Gospel from those that never heard of it, or who never were in a Capacity or Circumstances of being reasonably convinc'd of it, it would be in the first Place manifest Injustice; for surely, Promulgation or Publishing of a Law must be allow'd necessary, before Disobedience to it can be accounted criminal. It is utterly impossible to reconcile the contrary Notion with the Idea of a good and just God; and is a most dreadful and shocking Reflection upon the Almighty. In the next Place, we should find the Mission of our Saviour so far from being a general Benefit, as the Scripture teaches, that on the contrary it would be but a particular one, distributed only to the smallest Part of Mankind: But, which is more, this Mission of our Saviour wou'd be a very great Misfortune and Unhappiness to the greatest Part (three Fourths) of Mankind. For it is probable, that without this Necessity of Obedience to an unknown Law, many would be able to save themselves by a good Use of their Reason and the Light of Nature; whereas by the Mission of our Redeemer, and the Imposition of an unknown Law, a Law which they could not observe (I mean what is peculiar to Christianity) they are reduc'd to an utter Impossibility of being sav'd. I do not think that these Observations can be contradicted without saying Things very injurious to the Deity, and therefore erroneous. Agreable to the general Notion here advanc'd are the Sentiments of St. Paul in Rom. 4:15 where he says, *For*

---

[99] II Corinthians 5:15

where no Law is there is no Transgression. And Rom. 5:13 *Sin is not imputed when there is no Law.* See also Rom. 2:14, 15.[100]

I know that some Passages of Scripture are adduc'd by the Maintainers of this Notion to prove the Truth of it. But some of the Observations made in page 32, are applicable here, which I need not repeat. And give me leave to remark here by the by, that if after all

---

[100] Franklin's belief in the possibility of salvation extending to those who have never heard the Gospel is a commonly held view among non-Calvinist Christians, and it is very similar to the view expressed by the great hymn writer and theologian, Isaac Watts. Watts wrote that Christ's offer of salvation might extend to:

"a Heathen Deist according to the general Revelations of Grace made to Adam or Noah, if any such Person should be found diligent and sincere in the Search of Truth by the Light of Nature, and constant in the daily Worship of one true God, and zealous to practise the common Rules of Virtue among Men, who is humbly penitent where he falls short and trusts in the general Mercy of God, while he has never yet heard of the Gospel of Christ, nor ever enjoy'd any Opportunity of Acquaintance with Jesus and his Salvation." (Watts, *The Redeemer*, 116)

And in his *Caveat against Infidelity*, Watts devotes nearly twenty pages to a discussion of the salvation of those who have never heard the Gospel. He concludes his discussion with this explanation:

"Where there is an intire and invincible Ignorance of all God's appointed Methods of Grace, both Patriarchal, Jewish and Christian, if there should be any Person humbly asking Forgiveness of God, and diligent in following every Dictate of his own Conscience, and longing after some further Discoveries of divine Grace and his own Duty, I will not deny but that God may condescend to save him, thro' the extensive Merits of the Mediator, by sovereign and unpromised Mercy; tho' he cannot claim the Pardon of his Sins or Acceptance with God, because he has no Revelation of Grace made to him.

"Or if God see it necessary to acquaint him with any explicit Methods of his Grace, in order to his Salvation, I am persuaded wheresoever he finds such a sincere Soul, he will inwardly illuminate him by his own Spirit of Revelation, or will send an Angel or an Apostle to him, as he did to Cornelius to speak Words to him whereby he shall be saved." (Watts, *Caveat*, 118-120)

requisite Care and Pains, Reason clearly teaches the Truth of such or such a Proposition, and that we find in the holy Scriptures some Passage that seems to contradict the clear Decisions of Reason, we ought not, for we really cannot, admit that Sense of the Passage that does so, altho' it shou'd be receiv'd by all the Divines, that call themselves *orthodox,* upon Earth; So that any Man must be altogether in the right to look out for another Sense of the Passage in Question, which will not contradict the clear Decisions of Reason.

This Principle is to be extended only to Propositions, which evidently contradict the clear and manifestly well-founded Decisions of Reason in general (as in the Case before us;) and I say that such Propositions, such Doctrines cannot be contain'd in divine Revelation; so that we must look for another Sense of the Passages, by which they wou'd pretend to establish these Propositions or Doctrines; we must, I say, look for a Sense agreeable to Reason and the known Perfections of God; and it is absolutely impossible to reconcile the Opinion here contradicted to either; and if this Notion be not to represent the Almighty, as stern, arbitrary, inexorable, &c. pray what is?

As for those Passages of Scripture, which are often adduc'd to prove the absolute Necessity of all Men's believing in Jesus Christ without Distinction, in order to Salvation; Reason, common Sense, Equity and Goodness oblige us to understand and apply them only to those to whom infinite Wisdom has thought proper to send the Gospel.

These Gentlemen can hardly take it amiss to be advis'd to take the utmost Care of saying any thing, or interpreting Scripture after a Manner injurious to the infinite Justice, Goodness and Mercy of God, and contradictory to Reason. If the christian Scheme of Religion be not a reasonable one, they wou'd make but a dull Piece of Work on't in attempting to vindicate the Truth of it.

But they ask, What are the Benefits and Advantages of the christian Revelation, if the Heathen World living up to the Light of Nature and Reason may be sav'd? For Answer to this, I refer them to that excellent Defence of Christianity by Mr. Foster, Chap. 1.[101] But not to insist any more upon this Point, their remaining Objections against Hemphill, under this Article are easily obviated from what has been already said.

Article IV.

---

[101] Here Franklin reveals yet another evidence of the influence of the Baptists on his theology, for the Mr. Foster that he is referring to is Dr. James Foster, a Baptist theologian in England. The book here referenced is *The Usefulness, Truth, and Excellency of the Christian Revelation* which was written to defend the Bible against attacks by the Christian Deist, Matthew Tindal. If Franklin were a Deist as many historians assert, he would be far more likely to quote Tindal than Foster. In any case, here is an excerpt from Foster's book which summarizes the argument that Franklin references:

"If we suppose ... that the reason of mankind is capable of discovering all the important principles, and precepts of natural religion, all those duties they owe to God and their fellow creatures, or which relate to the right government of their affections and appetites ... all that can be infer'd from hence is, that it may, but not that it certainly will produce that desirable effect. On the contrary, 'tis as plain that it may not, but that notwithstanding their rational faculties, men may be ignorant of some great and essential branches of morality. For reason can only be serviceable to us in directing our moral conduct, if it be cultivated and improv'd; and even self-evident truths may be unknown, if they are not consider'd and attended to; and ... may be so perverted by vitious and irregular prejudices, that the very men who are thus dignified by their reason, and capable by a right use of it of forming a true judgment of what is fit and becoming in every circumstance, may grow rude and wild, having very little sense of the eternal difference of good and evil, and being almost intirely govern'd by animal instincts and passions.

"...And in such a state of corruption as this ... the advantage of a revelation will be altogether as great, as if men were unavoidably ignorant of the great truths of morality. For how they come to be out of the way is not the question, whether it proceeds from a defect in their natural powers, or from want of attention, and not using those powers as they ought. In both cases 'tis certain that they need to be set right, and recover'd to a just sense of their duty, and happiness; and that an external revelation which rectifies their errors in points of morality ... must whatever we determine concerning the sufficiency of reason, if rightly exercis'd, to have taught them better, be eminently useful, and an instance of great goodness in the supreme governour of the world." (Foster, 10-12)

The next Article of Accusation exhibited against Hemphill, is that *he describ'd saving Faith, but an Assent to, or Perswasion of the Gospel upon rational Grounds;* as they word it. Which Article, say they, is supported by this Extract; viz. *That by saving Faith is always intended such a firm Perswasion of Mind of the Truths of the Gospel, as is founded on reasonable and good Grounds, and produces suitable Effects.* "The Commission," say the Vindicators, "complain that this Description is too general, as not explicitly mentioning our receiving of Christ upon the Terms of the Gospel."

Pray, what do the Commission or their learn'd Advocates mean by this Enthusiastick Cant, more than what is included in Hemphill's Definition? What is it to receive Christ upon the Terms of the Gospel? I should be apt to suspect some Charm in this, and the Authors of Sorcery and Witchcraft, had they not given so many Instances of a contemptible Stupidity; and among the rest is the following, viz. their concluding that Hemphill's Description of Saving Faith *may be apt dangerously to mislead Persons, and encourage them to trust to a naked Assent to the Gospel Revelation,* when the very contrary is included in the Definition itself. Saving Faith, in Hemphill's Sense, is always attended with suitable Effects; that is, with Piety and Virtue, or Love to God and Mankind; this in the Opinion of our worthy Authors and Rev. Commission, is apt dangerously to mislead People, &c. This is New-Light indeed! But *How,* as Hemphill has already said in his Observations, *can such a Faith, in the Description of which Good Works are mention'd, be a Means to lead Men from Good Works,* or mislead them?

One would imagine these Men were jesting about this Affair, or that they really wrote with a Design to burlesque Christianity, did not a dull, phlegmatic Air of Seriousness run thro' their whole Performance; when they in the very next Page condemn him for saying, *the only End of Faith is Obedience.* Pray what is the End of it, if Obedience be not? Is Disobedience the End of it? He, surely, must deserve to be as heartily laught at, as our Authors themselves, that would undertake a formal Refutation of what so sufficiently refutes it self. Let's try if we can find any better Sense in the Accusation contain'd in

Article V.

And here we are told, that Hemphill has *open'd the Door of the Church wide enough to admit all honest Heathens as such into it.* Well, these Men have the rarest Knack of Writing unintelligibly of any I ever met with! What do these Words of theirs mean? Would they be for shutting the Doors of their Churches against honest Heathens that had a mind to come in, and so deprive them of any Opportunity of being convinc'd of the Truth of the Christian Religion? Wonderful Charity indeed! of a Piece with their damning them to all Eternity for an Impossibility. What Connexion there is between the Accusation, and the Extracts upon which they say it is founded, I own I am not able to see. And till they please to explain themselves, if they know what they would be at, I have nothing further to say, but *Darapti Felapton Disamis Datisi Ferison Bocardo Bamarip Cameres Dimatis Festapo Fresison,*[102]

Article VI.

The next and last Article of Accusation is, *that Hemphill has subverted the Doctrine of Justification by Faith.* The Observations of these unlucky Writers, and their pretended Proofs of this, are every whit as impertinent and senseless as the rest.

In the Discourse from whence the Extracts are taken, upon which this ridiculous Censure is foolishly suppos'd to be grounded, Hemphill, among other Things considered how, or in what Senses, Christians might be said to be sav'd by Faith. One Sense in which he alledg'd they might be said to be sav'd by their Faith in Jesus Christ was, that this their *Faith saves them from the Guilt of their Sins committed before their Faith;* that is, when, for Instance, a Jew or a Gentile commenc'd Christian, or profess'd his Faith in Jesus Christ, all Sins committed while a Jew or a Gentile, were forgiven him upon Account of this his first sincerely professing to believe, &c. and this

---

[102] This is a partial listing of the terms used by classical logicians to help them identify the various moods of syllogisms. Franklin recites part of the list here as if he is a teacher chiding a class of forgetful students. This is obviously a sarcastic criticism of the logic used by the Synod in arriving at their conclusions.

Notion seems still to be agreeable to the christian Scheme of Religion: And he farther observ'd this to be a *Priviledge peculiarly belonging to the first Christians, converted at Years of Discretion from a Life of Sin and Impurity; and therefore, this first Justification,* or Forgiveness of past Sins, *is often inculcated by St. Paul in his Epistles, and attributed to Faith; but this doth not concern those who have been educated and instructed in the Knowledge of the Christian Religion.* And it is very true indeed, that Justification, or Forgiveness of past Sins, in the Sense here mention'd, is not, nor can it be applicable to such as were always Christians, or *were educated and instructed in the Knowledge of the Christian Religion;* except you'll suppose, that those that were always Christians, were notwithstanding Jews or Gentiles, before they were Christians, tho' they were always Christians. An Absurdity which our Rev. Authors alone are capable of.

Tho' Hemphill, upon farther Reflection, will own that Justification, in the Sense above, is not a Privilege so peculiarly belonging to the first Christians, but that it may be applicable now-a-days; yet this will not at all answer their foolish Design, because the Case is exactly the same with that of the first Christians, or those converted from Judaism or Gentilism to Christianity, at the first Propagation of it. What Hemphill means, is this; Suppose an Indian, for Instance, now converted to Christianity, Justification in the Sense above might as well be apply'd to him, as to the first Christians: If the Reason of Things continue the same, God Almighty, according to the Christian Scheme of Religion, would forgive our suppos'd Indian, upon his Conversion, all his past Sins, as he did the Sins of the first Christians upon their Conversion, or upon Account of their believing in Jesus Christ. Now the Question with respect to our new Convert, or new Christian, is, What are the Terms or Conditions of *his* final Acceptance with God? In Hemphill's Opinion, and according to his Notions of Christianity, a sincere Endeavour to conform to all the Laws of true Goodness, Piety, Virtue, and universal Righteousness, or the Laws of Morality both with respect to God and Man, are the Terms of his final Acceptance with God; and when he fails in any Instances, a sincere Repentance and a renew'd Endeavour, begging divine Assistance, to practise the contrary Virtues; and when our Convert, and all other Christians, have thus endeavour'd sincerely to conform to the Laws of Piety and Virtue, tho' their Obedience be attended with many Imperfections, they will, as Christians, or as Believers in Christ Jesus, be accepted of by God, according to the christian Scheme of Religion, the Imperfections of their Virtue will be forgiven upon account of the Merits and Satisfaction of Christ, as was before observ'd. So that what Hemphill farther says (as in the Extract) is still true, if rightly understood, viz. *that all Hopes of Happiness but what are built upon Purity of Heart and a virtuous Life, are, according to the Christian Scheme, vain and delusory.* That is, *all Hopes of Happiness* to Christians, as such, consider'd separately and distinctly from the Practice of the Moral Virtues, *are vain and delusory.* If these Gentlemen assert the contrary, they must infallibly run into Antinomianism, how angry soever, they may appear to be at the Charge. Now, how justly the Accusation of Hemphill's denying our Justification by Faith is founded upon the Extracts before us, is obvious to every body. The first Extract has nothing to do with us at all, who were all along educated and instructed in the Christian Religion; the second has been shewn to contain in it the Terms or Conditions of our Acceptance with God, as Christians, for Christ's Sake, or upon Account of his Merits and Satisfaction. How ridiculously silly and impertinent then are all their Observations upon these Extracts!

These Authors in very angry Terms condemn a Remark of Hemphill's in his Observations, which yet appears to be a very just one. *He* (Hemphill) *supposes, that all Christians (Antimonians excepted) will allow, that Faith will not be imputed for Righteousness to those Men who have been educated in the Christian Religion, and yet have never endeavour'd to practise its Precepts; that such Men,* says he, *have no reason to expect that they shall be justify'd by a bare Faith, as the primitive Christians were, who embrac'd Christianity as soon as they heard it preached;* that is, have no reason to expect the Forgiveness of their Sins upon account of a bare Faith, as the primitive Christians were forgiven their past Sins upon their first Conversion, or their Believing in Jesus Christ.

To this our very reverend Authors, with a pious and orthodox Sneer, answer, *It is scarce possible for a Man to bind together a greater Bundle of Error, Ignorance and Impertinence in so few Words, than this Gentleman has done.* Hah! a home Thrust! a bold Stroke! next Turn's mine. Here they suppose this Position of Hemphill's to be erroneous, &c. And yet in the next Paragraph tell us, with a sanctify'd Leer, that *the whole Protestant World, the Antinomians only excepted, have constantly taught, that those Men who have been educated in the Christian Religion, are justifyed by a Faith, that from the very Nature of it is necessarily accompanied with Good Works, by a Faith that can no more exist without good Works, than the Body can live without the Spirit,* &c. So then we are now justify'd by a Faith, the very Life and Soul of which consists in good Works, as certainly as the Life of the Body consists in the Spirit. Such Inconsistency! Such Self-contradiction! Surely these Men's Spirits must be strangely muffled up with Phlegm, and their Brains, if they have any, *encompass'd with a Fence of a most impenetrable Thickness.*[103]

---

[103] I have explained Franklin's view of the correlation between faith and works in a previous note, so I will only add here that Franklin's view is very similar to the Lordship Salvation view that is held by John MacArthur. MacArthur is a prominent Christian leader of our day. He is the host of the *Grace to You* radio program, the pastor of Grace Community Church, the president of both The Master's College and The Master's Seminary, and ironically, the pastor of historian Gregg Frazer whom I have referenced several times in this book. Frazer claims that Franklin held to a works based salvation, and he wrote in his book that:

"According to Franklin, morality was the means of 'salvation' for the individual ... His views in this regard were made clear in his defense of a young heterodox preacher named Samuel Hemphill." (Frazer, *Religious Beliefs*, 143)

But compare what Franklin says in regards to faith and works with MacArthur's statements in his book *The Gospel According to Jesus*:

"We have seen that Jesus' lordship includes the ideas of dominion, authority, sovereignty, and the right to govern. If those ideas are implicit in the phrase "confess ... Jesus as Lord" (Rom. 10:9), then it is clear that people who come to

168

Thus, I think, I have examin'd the principal Things in this Vindication of the Rev. Commission; and upon the whole, it appears even from a plain Narration of Matter of Fact, that they (the leading Men among them at least) came to Philadelphia with Malice, Rancour and Prejudice in their Hearts, resolv'd at all Hazards to condemn the Man and his Doctrines; and their Aversion to both carry'd them those shameful Lengths which we have here shewn in their true Light. For if to justify a known Perjury, to lye openly and frequently in the Face of the World; if to condemn Doctrines agreeable to the main End and Design of the Gospel, and calculated for the common Welfare of Men; if to stamp an Appearance of Sanctity upon Animosity, false Zeal, Injustice, Fraud, Oppression, by their own open Example as well as Precept; and to behave as bitter Adversaries instead of impartial Judges; if to do all this be

---

Christ for salvation must do so in obedience to Him - that is, with a willingness to surrender to Him as Lord...

"The signature of saving faith is surrender to the lordship of Jesus Christ. The definitive test of whether a person belongs to Christ is a willingness to bow to His divine authority...

"It includes acknowledging Him as Lord by obeying Him, by surrendering one's will to His lordship, by affirming Him with one's deeds as well as one's words...

"Any message that omits this truth cannot be called the gospel. It is a defective message that presents a savior who is not Lord, a redeemer who does not demonstrate authority over sin, a weakened, sickly messiah who cannot command those he rescues...

"Those who refuse Him as Lord cannot use Him as Savior. Everyone who receives Him must surrender to His authority, for to say we receive Christ when in fact we reject His right to reign over us is utter absurdity. It is a futile attempt to hold on to sin with one hand and take Jesus with the other. What kind of salvation is it if we are left in bondage to sin?" (MacArthur, *The Gospel According to* Jesus, 230-232)

The similarity between Franklin's view and MacArthur's Lordship Salvation is blindingly obvious, and yet, Frazer claims one of these men as his pastor and spiritual leader and rejects the other as a heretic specifically because he held to this opinion.

truly *christian Candour, Charity and Truth,* then will I venture to say, these Rev. Gentlemen have given the most lively Instances of theirs. For all these Things have been so strongly charg'd and fairly prov'd upon 'em, that they must of Necessity confess their Guilt in Silence, or by endeavouring a Refutation of the plain Truth, plunge themselves deeper into the Dirt and Filth of Hypocrisy, Falsehood and Impiety, 'till at length they carry their quibbling Absurdities far enough to open the Eyes of the weakest and most unthinking Part of the Laity, from whom alone they can expect Support and Proselytes.

I have one Thing to desire of the Vindicators, before I come to a Conclusion, viz. that they wou'd, for Shame, take in the Motto they have hung out in the Title Page of their Performance, from II Tim. 3, since 'tis plainly applicable to none but themselves, and can by no means touch Hemphill; for, he contended for the *Power of Godliness,* denying the *Form;* and 'tis well known, that none but the Men of Sense were on his Side, and that all the *silly Women* of the Congregation were inveterately bent against him, being zealous Abettors of Mr. Andrews, who *crept into their Houses, and led them away captive* to the Commission to say and swear whatever he had prepar'd for them. This Motto therefore was the most improper one they cou'd possibly have pick'd out of the whole Bible.

The Rev. Mr. David Evans, one of the Commission, in his Sermon at the Ordination of Mr. Treat, says, Page 49, *That it is a* Wonder *to see* any *truly gracious, considerate wise Man in the Gospel Ministry.* And confirms it at the End of the Paragraph, by saying, *It is no* Wonder *to see thousands of Ignorant, inconsiderate, carnal Ministers, but a* Wonder *to see* any *truly understanding, considerate, gracious ones.* I am really inclin'd to be of his Opinion; especially, if he confines his Observations to the Presbyterian Ministers of this Part of the World. I am sure, however, that their Proceedings against Hemphill has convinc'd Multitudes, that this Wonder was not to be seen in the late Commission.

I might therefore divide the Gentlemen that were concern'd in this Affair (and I trust, I should do them no Injustice), into these three Classes; first, the Men of Honesty who wanted Sense; secondly the

Men of Sense, who wanted Honesty; and lastly, those who had neither Sense, nor Honesty. And I believe this Division may comprehend the whole Commission.

Poor Richard – 1737

God offer'd to the Jews Salvation
And 'twas refus'd by half the Nation:[104]
Thus, (tho' 'tis Life's great Preservation)
Many oppose *Inoculation.*
We're told by one of the black Robe
The Devil inoculated Job:
Suppose 'tis true, what he does tell;
Pray, Neighbours, *Did not Job do well?*

Poor Richard – 1738

If he then be a Fool whose Thought denies
There is a God, how desp'rately unwise,
How much more Fool is he whose Language shall
Proclaim in publick, *There's no God at all:*
What then are they, nay Fools in what degree
Whose Actions shall maintain 't? *Such Fools are we.*

...

In Christendom we all are *Christians* now,
And thus I answer, if you ask me how;
Where with *Christ's Rule* our Lives will not comply,
We bend it like a Rule of Lead, say I;
Making it thus comply with what we be,
And only thus our Lives with th' Rule agree.
But from our Fathers we've the Name (perchance)

---

[104] This short poem was written in defense of the smallpox vaccine, but in it, we can see that Franklin recognized that God had offered salvation to the Jews and that they had refused it. Franklin correlated this salvation with "Life's great Preservation" in reference to the vaccine.

Ay, so our King is call'd *the King of France.*[105]

Autobiography

I had been religiously educated as a Presbyterian; and tho' some of the Dogmas of that Persuasion, such as the Eternal Decrees of God, Election, Reprobation, &c. appear'd to me unintelligible,[106] others doubtful, and I early absented myself from the Public Assemblies of the Sect, Sunday being my Studying-Day, I never was without some religious Principles; I never doubted, for instance, the Existance of the Deity, that he made the World, and govern'd it by his Providence; that the most acceptable Service of God was the doing Good to Man; that our Souls are immortal; and that all Crime will be punished and Virtue rewarded eithcr here or hereafter; these I esteem'd the Essentials of every Religion, and being to be found in all the Religions we had in our Country I respected them all, tho' with different degrees of Respect as I found them more or less mix'd with other Articles which without any Tendency to inspire, promote or confirm Morality, serv'd principally to divide us and make us unfriendly to one another. This Respect to all, with an Opinion that the worst had some good Effects, induc'd me to avoid all Discourse that might tend to lessen the good Opinion another might have of his own Religion; and as our Province increas'd in People and new Places of worship were continually wanted, and generally erected by

---

[105] George II was the king of England at this time and his official title was:

"George the Second, by the Grace of God, King of Great Britain, France and Ireland, Defender of the Faith, Duke of Brunswick-Lüneburg, Archtreasurer and Prince-Elector of the Holy Roman Empire"

The actual king of France, however, was Louis XV. Franklin was criticizing the idea that Christianity could be inherited by saying that it was just as foolish as the claim that George II was the king of France even though none of the English kings had actually ruled over France since the end of the Hundred Years' War in 1453.

[106] Here, Franklin states very plainly that his dispute with his parents in the area of religion was focused primarily on the doctrines of Calvinism.

voluntary Contribution, my Mite for such purpose, whatever might be the Sect, was never refused.[107]

Tho' I seldom attended any Public Worship, I had still an Opinion of its Propriety, and of its Utility when rightly conducted, and I regularly paid my annual Subscription for the Support of the only Presbyterian Minister or Meeting we had in Philadelphia. He us'd to visit me sometimes as a Friend, and admonish me to attend his Administrations, and I was now and then prevail'd on to do so, once for five Sundays successively. Had he been, *in my Opinion,* a good Preacher perhaps I might have continued, notwithstanding the occasion I had for the Sunday's Leisure in my Course of Study: But his Discourses were chiefly either polemic Arguments, or Explications of the peculiar Doctrines of our Sect, and were all to me very dry, uninteresting and unedifying, since not a single moral Principle was inculcated or enforc'd, their Aim seeming to be rather to make us Presbyterians than good Citizens. At length he took for his Text that Verse of the 4th Chapter of Philippians, *Finally, Brethren, Whatsoever Things are true, honest, just, pure, lovely, or of good report, if there be any virtue, or any praise, think on these Things*; and I imagin'd in a Sermon on such a Text, we could not miss of having some Morality: But he confin'd himself to five Points only as meant by the Apostle, viz. 1. Keeping holy the Sabbath Day. 2. Being diligent in Reading the Holy Scriptures. 3. Attending duly the Publick Worship. 4. Partaking of the Sacrament.

---

[107] Sidney Mead wrote of this paragraph that:

"Men whose primary interest was in good citizens, and who could see that even the worst sects 'had some good effects' in producing them, were prepared to note that all sects were good enough." (Mead, 64)

But this could not have been the case with Franklin. He was very vocal in his disagreements with the Catholic Church and certainly would not have considered Catholicism to be "good enough." In fact, even in this paragraph, Franklin writes that his respect for all the religions in America was not the kind of respect which viewed all religions as equal. He simply recognized that each of those religions had at least some measure of benefit. This did not cause Franklin to view all religions as equal, but rather encouraged him to be more considerate of others in his remarks.

5. Paying a due Respect to God's Ministers. These might be all good Things, but as they were not the kind of good Things that I expected from that Text, I despaired of ever meeting with them from any other, was disgusted, and attended his Preaching no more. I had some Years before compos'd a little Liturgy or Form of Prayer for my own private Use, viz, in 1728. entitled, *Articles of Belief and Acts of Religion.* I return'd to the Use of this, and went no more to the public Assemblies. My Conduct might be blameable, but I leave it without attempting farther to excuse it, my present purpose being to relate Facts, and not to make Apologies for them.

To Josiah and Abiah Franklin – April 13, 1738

I have your Favour of the 21st of March in which you both seem concern'd lest I have imbib'd some erroneous Opinions. Doubtless I have my Share, and when the natural Weakness and Imperfection of Human Understanding is considered, with the unavoidable Influences of Education, Custom, Books and Company, upon our Ways of thinking, I imagine a Man must have a good deal of Vanity who believes, and a good deal of Boldness who affirms, that all the Doctrines he holds, are true; and all he rejects, are false. And perhaps the same may be justly said of every Sect, Church and Society of men when they assume to themselves that Infallibility which they deny to the Popes and Councils. I think Opinions should be judg'd of by their Influences and Effects; and if a Man holds none that tend to make him less Virtuous or more vicious, it may be concluded he holds none that are dangerous; which I hope is the Case with me. I am sorry you should have any Uneasiness on my Account, and if it were a thing possible for one to alter his Opinions in order to please others, I know none whom I ought more willingly to oblige in that respect than your selves: But since it is no more in a Man's Power to think than to look like another, methinks all that should be expected from me is to keep my Mind open to Conviction, to hear patiently and examine attentively whatever is offered me for that end; and if after all I continue in the same Errors, I believe your usual Charity will induce you rather to pity and excuse than blame me. In the mean time your Care and Concern for me is what I am very thankful for.

As to the Freemasons, unless she will believe me when I assure her that they are in general a very harmless sort of People; and have no principles or Practices that are inconsistent with Religion or good Manners, I know no Way of giving my Mother a better Opinion of them than she seems to have at present, (since it is not allow'd that Women should be admitted into that secret Society). She has, I must confess, on that Account, some reason to be displeas'd with it; but for any thing else, I must entreat her to suspend her Judgment till she is better inform'd, and in the mean time exercise her Charity.

My Mother grieves that one of her Sons is an Arian, another an Arminian.[108] What an Arminian or an Arian is, I cannot say that I

---

[108] Frazer wrote of this letter that Franklin here "confessed that his mother 'grieves' over his denial of the Trinity," (Frazer, *Religious Beliefs*, 149) but Frazer ignored two very important facts. First, up to this point in time, there is no record of Franklin ever saying or writing anything that could be construed as an indicator that he was an Arian. An Arian is someone who follows the teachings of Arius, a Christian minister in Egypt during the third and fourth centuries. Arius once explained his beliefs in a letter expressing that:

"We say and believe, and have taught, and do teach, that the Son is not unbegotten, nor in any way part of the unbegotten; and that He does not derive His subsistence from any matter; but that by His own will and counsel He has subsisted before time, and before ages, as perfect God, only begotten and unchangeable, and that before He was begotten, or created, or purposed, or established, He was not. For He was not unbegotten. We are persecuted, because we say that the Son has a beginning, but that God is without beginning. This is the cause of our persecution, and likewise, because that we say that He is of the non-existent. And this we say, because He is neither part of God, nor of any essential being. For this we are persecuted." (Schaff, 41)

The idea that Christ is not God but rather a separate being who was created by God before they created everything else is the distinguishing feature of Arianism, but Franklin never even mentions Christ in any of his writings before his defense of Hemphill, and none of his references to Christ at that time give any indication that Franklin was an Arian.

This, of course, leads us to the second fact that Frazer ignored: by this point in his life, Franklin had already written many things which could easily have been viewed as consistent with Arminianism. Arminianism is one of the most well

very well know; the Truth is, I make such Distinctions very little my Study; I think vital Religion has always suffer'd, when Orthodoxy is more regarded than Virtue. And the Scripture assures me, that at the last Day, we shall not be examin'd what we thought, but what we did; and our Recommendation will not be that we said Lord, Lord, but that we did Good to our Fellow Creatures. See Matth. 26.[109]

Autobiography

I proceeded the next Day, and got in the Evening to an Inn within 8 or 10 Miles of Burlington, kept by one Dr. Brown. He entered into Conversation with me while I took some Refreshment, and finding I had read a little, became very sociable and friendly. Our Acquaintance continu'd as long as he liv'd. He had been, I imagine, an itinerant Doctor, for there was no Town in England, or Country in Europe, of which he could not give a very particular Account. He had some Letters, and was ingenious, but much of an Unbeliever, and wickedly undertook some Years after to travesty the Bible in doggrel Verse as Cotton had done Virgil. By this means he set many of the Facts in a very ridiculous Light, and might have hurt weak minds if his Work had been publish'd: but it never was.[110]

---

known systems opposed to Calvinism, and we have already seen several examples of Franklin's frequent condemnations of Calvinism.

Given these two facts, that Franklin had given no indication of Arianism and several of Arminianism, it is far more likely that his mother thought he had become one of the latter rather than one of the former.

[109] Franklin should have written Matthew 25 instead of 26. Here Franklin writes to his father that God judges men by their actions and not by their thoughts. This has led several historians to conclude that Franklin viewed good works as the path to salvation, but Franklin dispels this idea in a letter to his sister in 1743.

[110] It is interesting to note here that Franklin thought it was both wicked and dangerous for an unbeliever to corrupt the text of the Bible.

Autobiography

In 1739 arriv'd among us from England the Rev. Mr. Whitefiel, who had made himself remarkable there as an itinerant Preacher. He was at first permitted to preach in some of our Churches; but the Clergy taking a Dislike to him, soon refus'd him their Pulpits and he was oblig'd to preach in the Fields. The Multitudes of all Sects and Denominations that attended his Sermons were enormous, and it was matter of Speculation to me who was one of the Number, to observe the extraordinary Influence of his Oratory on his Hearers, and how much they admir'd and respected him, notwithstanding his common Abuse of them, by assuring them they were naturally *half Beasts and half Devils.* It was wonderful to see the Change soon made in the Manners of our Inhabitants; from being thoughtless or indifferent about Religion, it seem'd as if all the World were growing Religious; so that one could not walk thro' the Town in an Evening without Hearing Psalms sung in different Families of every Street. And it being found inconvenient to assemble in the open Air, subject to its Inclemencies, the Building of a House to meet in was no sooner propos'd and Persons appointed to receive Contributions, but sufficient Sums were soon receiv'd to procure the Ground and erect the Building which was 100 feet long and 70 broad, about the Size of Westminster-hall; and the Work was carried on with such Spirit as to be finished in a much shorter time than could have been expected. Both House and Ground were vested in Trustees, expressly for the Use of any Preacher of any religious Persuasion who might desire to say something to the People of Philadelphia, the Design in building not being to accommodate any particular Sect, but the Inhabitants in general, so that even if the Mufti of Constantinople were to send a Missionary to preach Mahometanism to us, he would find a Pulpit at his Service. (The Contributions being made by People of different Sects promiscuously, Care was taken in the Nomination of Trustees to avoid giving a Predominancy to any Sect, so that one of each was appointed, viz. one Church of England-man, one Presbyterian, one Baptist, one Moravian, &c.).

Mr. Whitfield, in leaving us, went preaching all the Way thro' the Colonies to Georgia. The Settlement of that Province had lately been begun; but instead of being made with hardy industrious Husbandmen accustomed to Labour, the only People fit for such an Enterprise, it was with Families of broken Shopkeepers and other insolvent Debtors, many of indolent and idle habits, taken out of the Goals, who being set down in the Woods, unqualified for clearing Land, and unable to endure the Hardships of a new Settlement, perished in Numbers, leaving many helpless Children unprovided for. The Sight of their miserable Situation inspired the benevolent Heart of Mr. Whitefield with the Idea of building an Orphan House there, in which they might be supported and educated. Returning northward he preach'd up this Charity, and made large Collections; for his Eloquence had a wonderful Power over the Hearts and Purses of his Hearers, of which I myself was an Instance. I did not disapprove of the Design, but as Georgia was then destitute of Materials and Workmen, and it was propos'd to send them from Philadelphia at a great Expence, I thought it would have been better to have built the House here and brought the Children to it. This I advis'd, but he was resolute in his first Project, and rejected my Counsel, and I thereupon refus'd to contribute. I happened soon after to attend one of his Sermons, in the Course of which I perceived he intended to finish with a Collection, and I silently resolved he should get nothing from me. I had in my Pocket a Handful of Copper Money, three or four silver Dollars, and five Pistoles in Gold. As he proceeded I began to soften, and concluded to give the Coppers. Another Stroke of his Oratory made me asham'd of that, and determin'd me to give the Silver; and he finish'd so admirably, that I empty'd my Pocket wholly into the Collector's Dish, Gold and all. At this Sermon there was also one of our Club, who being of my Sentiments respecting the Building in Georgia, and suspecting a Collection might be intended, had by Precaution emptied his Pockets before he came from home; towards the Conclusion of the Discourse however, he felt a strong Desire to give, and apply'd to a Neighbour who stood near him to borrow some Money for the Purpose. The Application was unfortunately to perhaps the only Man in the Company who had the firmness not to be affected by the Preacher. His Answer was, *At any other time, Friend Hopkinson, I would lend to thee freely; but not now; for thee seems to be out of thy right Senses.*

Some of Mr. Whitfield's Enemies affected to suppose that he would apply these Collections to his own private Emolument; but I, who was intimately acquainted with him, (being employ'd in printing his Sermons and Journals, &c..) never had the least Suspicion of his Integrity, but am to this day decidedly of Opinion that he was in all his Conduct, a perfectly *honest Man.* And methinks my Testimony in his Favour ought to have the more Weight, as we had no religious Connection. He us'd indeed sometimes to pray for my Conversion, but never had the Satisfaction of believing that his Prayers were heard. Ours was a mere civil Friendship, sincere on both Sides, and lasted to his Death.[111]

---

[111] Many historians have taken this statement from Franklin to mean that he refused to become a Christian, but the conversion that Whitefield preached is not necessarily the same as becoming a Christian. Whitefield taught that the only true Christians are those who have experienced a great, all encompassing change as a result of the gospel. In a sermon entitled "Repentance and Conversion," he once said:

"They that are truly converted to Jesus, and are justified by faith in the Son of God, will take care to evidence their conversion, not only by the having grace implanted in their hearts, but by that grace diffusing itself through every faculty of the soul, and making a universal change in the whole man ... Any thing short of this is but the shadow instead of the substance ... There will be new principles, new ways, new company, new works; there will be a thorough change in the heart and life; this is conversion." (Whitefield, 435)

And in a 1755 letter to Franklin, Whitefield advised him to "get a feeling possession of Christ." (Epitaph, 1728) This type of experiential conversion was often referred to as "spiritual pangs," and Whitefield was not alone in thinking that it was necessary for salvation. Thomas Watson once wrote:

"There are pangs before the birth; so before Christ be born in the heart, there are spiritual pangs ... all have not the same pangs of sorrow and humiliation, yet all have pangs. If Christ be born in thy heart, thou hast been deeply afflicted for sin. Christ is never born in the heart without pangs. Many thank God they never had any trouble of spirit, they were always quiet: a sign Christ is not yet formed in them." (Watson, 184)

That Franklin rejected this view of conversion can be seen in his "Observations of the Proceedings against Mr. Hemphill" where he wrote:

The following Instance will show something of the Terms on which we stood. Upon one of his Arrivals from England at Boston, he wrote to me that he should come soon to Philadelphia, but knew not where he could lodge when there, as he understood his old kind Host Mr. Benezet was remov'd to Germantown. My Answer was; You know my House, if you can make shift with its scanty Accommodations you will be most heartily welcome. He reply'd, that if I made that kind Offer for Christ's sake, I should not miss of a Reward. And I return'd, *Don't let me be mistaken; it was not for Christ's sake, but for your sake.* One of our common Acquaintance jocosely remark'd that knowing it to be the Custom of the Saints, when they receiv'd any favour, to shift the Burthen of the Obligation from off their own Shoulders, and place it in Heaven, I had contriv'd to fix it on Earth.

Poor Richard – 1742

A sober Diet makes a Man die without Pain; it maintains the Senses in Vigour; it mitigates the Violence of Passions and Affections. It preserves the Memory, it helps the Understanding, it allays the Heat of Lust; it brings a Man to a Consideration of his latter End; it makes the Body a fit Tabernacle for the Lord to dwell in; which

---

"I may add, that whoever preaches up the absolute necessity of spiritual Pangs and Convulsions in those whose Education has been in the Ways of Piety and Vertue, and who therefore are not to pass from a State of Sin to a State of Holiness, but to go on and improve in the State wherein they already are, represent Christianity to be unworthy of its divine Author."

As can be seen in his Hemphill pamphlets, Franklin believed that there were two different paths to faith in Christ. The first was a glorious redemption from a life of sin, and the second was the slow and steady acceptance of truths of the gospel by those who were raised in Christian homes. The conversion of the former would evidence the kind of spectacular change that Whitefield wrote of while the conversion of the latter would seem to be just the next step in the progression of their lives. Franklin's conversion to Christianity, though taking place in his adult years rather than in his childhood, would likely have been similar to this second type, and thus, would not have been accepted by Whitefield as a true conversion.

makes us happy in this World, and eternally happy in the World to come, through Jesus Christ our Lord and Saviour.[112]

Poor Richard – 1743

How many observe Christ's Birth-day! How few, his Precepts![113]

To Jane Mecom – July 28, 1743

I took your Admonition very kindly, and was far from being offended at you for it. If I say any thing about it to you, 'tis only to rectify some wrong Opinions you seem to have entertain'd of me,

---

[112] Here, Franklin not only identifies himself as a Christian by referring to Christ as his Lord and Savior but as a Trinitarian Christian as well. Franklin's claim that the Lord wants to dwell within us is a recognition that Jesus is alive even though He died, that He indwells those who accept Him as Savior, and that He is the same being as the Holy Ghost mentioned in I Corinthians 6:19:

"What? know ye not that your body is the temple of the Holy Ghost which is in you, which ye have of God, and ye are not your own?"

Thus Franklin here recognizes Christ's resurrection and His inclusion in the Godhead.

[113] Once again, we find Franklin referring to Jesus as "Christ." Frazer claims in his lectures on the founders that:

"They didn't talk about Jesus Christ. They didn't talk about Christ. It was just Jesus or Jesus of Nazareth to emphasize His humanity." (Frazer, "One Nation," 34:00)

And yet of the fourteen times that Franklin refers to Jesus outside of his defense of Hemphill and of the many references to Jesus in the Hemphill pamphlets, there are only two occasions in which Franklin did not identify Jesus as either the Christ, the Messiah, or the Savior, and in one of those, he was quoting a statement made by Ezra Styles. I've confronted Frazer on this point, and I've received several responses from him, but he still maintains that Franklin's "normal/routine/general usage" was to refer to Jesus as "just Jesus or Jesus of Nazareth." (Fortenberry, "Frazer, Fortenberry and Franklin")

and that I do only because they give you some Uneasiness, which I am unwilling to be the Occasion of. You express yourself as if you thought I was against Worshipping of God, and believed Good Works would merit Heaven; which are both Fancies of your own, I think, without Foundation. I am so far from thinking that God is not to be worshipped, that I have compos'd and wrote a whole Book of Devotions for my own Use: And I imagine there are few, if any, in the World, so weake as to imagine, that the little Good we can do here, can *merit* so vast a Reward hereafter. There are some Things in your New England Doctrines and Worship, which I do not agree with, but I do not therefore condemn them, or desire to shake your Belief or Practice of them. We may dislike things that are nevertheless right in themselves. I would only have you make me the same Allowances, and have a better Opinion both of Morality and your Brother. Read the Pages of Mr. Edward's late Book entitled Some Thoughts concerning the present Revival of Religion in NE. from 367 to 375; and when you judge of others, if you can perceive the Fruit to be good, don't terrify your self that the Tree may be evil, but be assur'd it is not so; for you know who has said, *Men do not gather Grapes of Thorns or Figs of Thistles.*[114] I have not time to add but that I shall always be Your affectionate Brother.[115]

---

[114] Matthew 7:16

[115] Franklin is often accused of abandoning Christianity in favor of a deistic religion of morality. Fea wrote of him that:

"Franklin's religious beliefs were less about Christian doctrine and more about virtue - moral behavior that serves the public good." (Fea, 221)

Isaacson claimed that Franklin opposed the evangelism of the Great Awakening and instead:

"sought to bring [America] into an Enlightenment era that exalted tolerance, individual merit, civic virtue, good deeds, and rationality." (Isaacson, 109)

And Lubert said of Franklin that:

To John Franklin – May, 1745

Our people are extremely impatient to hear of your success at Cape Breton. My shop is filled with thirty inquiries at the coming in of every post. Some wonder the place is not yet taken. I tell them I

"Franklin invoked religious language and ritual in order to promote socially beneficial behavior, arguing that the most acceptable form of worship is to do good works and going so far as to suggest that good works, not piety, are the path to salvation." (Lubert, 157)

However, when Franklin's own sister accused him of holding to the position attributed to him by the historians, Franklin assured her that she was mistaken. In an attempt to explain his view of morality to his sister, Franklin directed her to read a section from Jonathan Edwards' defense of the Great Awakening. And in that section, Edwards made the following observations:

"But another Thing I would mention, which it is of much greater Importance, that we should attend to; and that is the Duty, that is incumbent upon God's People at this Day ... such as Acts of Righteousness, Truth, Meekness, Forgiveness & Love towards our Neighbour; which are of much greater Importance in the Sight of God, than all the Externals of his Worship." (Edwards, 367)

And:

"Of this inward Religion, there are two Sorts of external Manifestations or Expressions. The one Sort, are outward Acts of Worship, such as meeting in religious Assemblies, attending Sacraments, & other outward Institutions, & honouring God with Gestures, such as bowing, or kneeling before him, or with Words, in speaking honourably of him, in Prayer, Praise, or religious Conference. And the other Sort, are the Expressions of our Love to God, by obeying his moral Commands, of Self-denial, Righteousness, Meekness, and Christian Love, in our Behaviour among Men. And the latter are of vastly the greatest Importance in the Christian Life. God makes little Account of the former, in Comparison of them." (Edwards, 367-368)

Edwards proceeded to defend his claims by giving example after example from Scripture to demonstrate that God desires virtue and good deeds far more than He desires public expressions of prayer, praise and worship. And yet, Edwards, much like Franklin, maintained that, as important as good works may be, they are still incapable of guaranteeing our entrance into Heaven. Both men taught that the only way to heaven was through faith in the sacrifice of Jesus Christ.

shall be glad to hear that news three months hence. Fortified towns are hard nuts to crack; and your teeth have not been accustomed to it. Taking strong places is a particular trade, which you have taken up without serving an apprenticeship to it. Armies and veterans need skilful engineers to direct them in their attack. Have you any? But some seem to think forts are as easy taken as snuff. Father Moody's prayers look tolerably modest.[116] You have a fast and prayer day for

---

[116] This is a reference to Samuel Moody, the pastor of the First Parish Congregational Church in York, Maine and also the chaplain of the troops stationed in that town. Moody was renowned throughout the colonies for his bold and effective prayers, (Moody, 58-61) and Franklin mentions him here in order to stress how fervently the people of New England were praying for the success of the attack against Cape Breton. The prayers of the colonists were so fervent that Moody's prayers seemed modest in comparison.

That Franklin expected these prayers to be successful is obvious from the hopeful tone of the letter. Although he speaks of the difficulty of the task, he does so light heartedly joking about how foolish it was for the people to expect news of victory so soon. He speaks of reassuring the people that he expects to hear the good news eventually, but he does not ridicule them for expecting good news instead of bad. Even in the second paragraph, Franklin makes no mention of the very serious effect that a loss would have had on the colonies but instead jokes with his brother that a loss would cause him to become indifferent to the efficacy of Presbyterian prayers.

For some reason, historians have taken a much different view of this letter. Most of them link these statements to Franklin's earlier Deism and view Franklin's jocularity as ridicule and contempt for the foolish faith of the colonists. Marsden, for example, said of this letter that "Benjamin Franklin mocked New England's piety" (Marsden, 312), and Isaacson introduced this letter by saying that Franklin:

"did not, however, stray too far from deism; he placed little faith in the use of prayers for specific personal requests or miracles. In an irreverent letter he later wrote to his brother John, he calculated that 45 million prayers were offered in all of New England seeking victory over a fortified French garrison in Canada." (Isaacson, 87)

How these men have arrived at the idea that Franklin is ridiculing the colonist's prayers is beyond me. The brother to whom this letter is addressed was actually one of the men engaged in the battle against Cape Breton. How heartless do

that purpose; in which I compute five hundred thousand petitions were offered up to the same effect in New England, which added to the petitions of every family morning and evening, multiplied by the number of days since January 25th, make forty-five millions of prayers; which, set against the prayers of a few priests in the garrison, to the Virgin Mary, give a vast balance in your favor.

If you do not succeed. I fear I shall have but an indifferent opinion of Presbyterian prayers in such cases, as long as I live. Indeed, in attacking strong towns I should have more dependence on *works,* than on *faith;* for, like the kingdom of heaven, they are to be taken by force and violence; and in a French garrison I suppose there are devils of that kind, that they are not to be cast out by prayers and fasting, unless it be by their own fasting for want of provisions. I believe there is Scripture in what I have wrote, but I cannot adorn the margin with quotations, having a bad memory, and no Concordance at hand; besides no more time than to subscribe myself, &c.

To Thomas Hopkinson – Oct. 16, 1746

---

they imagine Franklin to be to assume that he would write to a brother in battle for no other reason than to mock the people who were praying for his brother's safety and success?

But as preposterous as such an opinion may be, at least these two were not as openly deceitful in their recounting as Lemay turned out to be in his book. In order to make Franklin's comments appear even more critical toward prayer, Lemay split the letter in two and presented it as if the second paragraph had been written after Franklin learned of the victory at Cape Breton. He claimed that:

"Franklin ridiculed the 'forty five millions of prayers' offered by the New Englanders for the taking of Cape Breton in 1745. The Americans succeeded, but Franklin hardly credited the victory to prayer. He later wrote: 'Indeed, in attacking strong towns I should have more dependence on works, than on faith...'" (Lemay, 1: 351)

In reality, this letter does not contain a single word of ridicule, and Franklin's jocularity shows he fully expected the prayers of the colonists to be answered.

I imagine I may venture to conclude my Observations on this Piece, almost in the Words of the Author, "That if the Doctrines of the Immateriality of the Soul, and the Existence of God, and of Divine Providence are demonstrable from *no plainer* Principles, the *Deist* hath a desperate Cause in Hand." I oppose my *Theist* to his *Atheist,* because I think they are diametrically opposite and not near of kin, as Mr. Whitefield seems to suppose where (in his Journal) he tells us, *Mr. B. was a Deist, I had Almost said an Atheist.* That is, *Chalk,* I had almost said *Charcoal.*[117]

Shall I hazard a Thought to you [that?] for aught I know is new, viz, If God was before all Things, and fill'd all Space; then, when he form'd what we call Matter, he must have done it out of his own Thinking immaterial Substance. The same, tho' he had not fill'd all Space; if it be true that *ex nihilo nihil fit.* From hence may we not draw this Conclusion, That if any Part of Matter does not at present act and think, 'tis not from an Incapacity in its Nature [but from] a

---

[117] James Parton once wrote of this paragraph that:

"In conversation with familiar friends, he called himself a Deist, or a Theist, and he resented a sentence in Mr. Whitefield's Journal, which seemed to imply that between a Deist and an Atheist, there was little difference." (Parton, 319-320)

But Parton has completely missed the point of Franklin's statement. Franklin was not identifying himself as a Deist in this statement. He was explaining why he inserted the word "Deist" in the quote that he had just presented. That quote was taken from the book *An Inquiry into the Nature of the Human Soul* by Andrew Baxter. Thomas Hopkinson had asked Franklin to review the book, and Franklin concluded his review with a slightly modified form of this statement from Baxter's book:

"If the immateriality of the soul, the existence of God, and the necessity of a most particular, incessant providence in the world, are demonstrable from such plain and easy principles, the Atheist hath a desperate cause in hand." (A. Baxter, 8)

Franklin thought that Baxter's argument would be better used against Deists than Atheists, and he explained to Hopkins that he viewed the two as being very different from each other and not similar as Whitfield did. There is no indication in this letter or in any other that Franklin considered himself a Deist.

positive Restraint. I know not yet [what other] Consequences may follow the admitting of [this position] and therefore I will not be oblig'd to defend [it. *Torn*] 'tis with some Reluctance that I either [*torn*] in the metaphysical Way. The great Uncertainty I have found in that Science; the wide Contradictions and endless Disputes it affords; and the horrible Errors I led my self into when a young Man, by drawing a Chain of plain Consequences as I thought them, from true Principles, have given me a Disgust to what I was once extreamly fond of.[118]

Plain Truth – Nov. 17, 1747

It is said the wise Italians make this proverbial Remark on our Nation, viz. *The English* feel, *but they do not* see. That is, they are sensible of Inconveniencies when they are present, but do not take sufficient Care to prevent them: Their natural Courage makes them too little apprehensive of Danger, so that they are often surpriz'd by it, unprovided of the proper Means of Security. When 'tis too late they are sensible of their Imprudence: After great Fires, they provide Buckets and Engines: After a Pestilence they think of keeping clean their Streets and common Shores: and when a Town has been sack'd by their Enemies, they provide for its Defence, &c. This Kind of After-Wisdom is indeed so common with us, as to occasion the vulgar, tho' very significant Saying, *When the Steed is stolen, you shut the Stable Door.*

But the more insensible we generally are of publick Danger, and indifferent when warn'd of it, so much the more freely, openly, and earnestly, ought such as apprehend it, to speak their Sentiments; that if possible, those who seem to sleep, may be awaken'd, to think of some Means of Avoiding or Preventing the Mischief before it be too late.

---

[118] In the margin of this letter, Franklin wrote that he was referring to "my Pamphlet call'd a Dissertation on Liberty and Necessity, Pleasure and Pain, printed in London in 1725." (Labaree, 89) Stewart wrote that Franklin "never gave reason to think that he ever departed from the convictions acquired as a youthful bibliophile," (Stewart, 471) but here we find Franklin doing that very thing.

Believing therefore that 'tis my Duty, I shall honestly speak my Mind in the following Paper.

War, at this Time, rages over a great Part of the known World; our News-Papers are Weekly filled with fresh Accounts of the Destruction it every where occasions. Pennsylvania, indeed, situate in the Center of the Colonies, has hitherto enjoy'd profound Repose; and tho' our Nation is engag'd in a bloody War, with two great and powerful Kingdoms, yet, defended, in a great Degree, from the French on the one Hand by the Northern Provinces, and from the Spaniards on the other by the Southern, at no small Expence to each, our People have, till lately, slept securely in their Habitations.

There is no British Colony excepting this, but has made some Kind of Provision for its Defence; many of them have therefore never been attempted by an Enemy; and others that were attack'd, have generally defended themselves with Success. The Length and Difficulty of our Bay and River has been thought so effectual a Security to us, that hitherto no Means have been entered into that might discourage an Attempt upon us, or prevent its succeeding.

But whatever Security this might have been while both Country and City were poor, and the Advantage to be expected scarce worth the Hazard of an Attempt, it is now doubted whether we can any longer safely depend upon it. Our Wealth, of late Years much encreas'd, is one strong Temptation, our defenceless State another, to induce an Enemy to attack us; while the Acquaintance they have lately gained with our Bay and River, by Means of the Prisoners and Flags of Truce they have had among us; by Spies which they almost every where maintain, and perhaps from Traitors among ourselves; with the Facility of getting Pilots to conduct them; and the known Absence of Ships of War, during the greatest Part of the Year, from both Virginia and New-York, ever since the War began, render the Appearance of Success to the Enemy far more promising, and therefore highly encrease our Danger.

That our Enemies may have Spies abroad, and some even in these Colonies, will not be made much doubt of, when 'tis considered,

188

that such has been the Practice of all Nations in all Ages, whenever they were engaged, or intended to engage in War. Of this we have an early Example in the Book of Judges (too too pertinent to our Case, and therefore I must beg leave a little to enlarge upon it) where we are told, Chap. xviii, v. 2, That *the Children of Dan sent of their Family five Men from their Coasts to spie out the Land, and search it, saying, Go, search the* Land. These Danites it seems were at this Time not very orthodox in their Religion, and their Spies met with a certain idolatrous Priest of their own Persuasion, v. 3, and they said to him, *Who brought thee hither! what makest thou in this Place? and what hast thou here?* [would to God no such Priests were to be found, among us.] And they said unto him, verse 5, *Ask Counsel of God, that we may know whether our Way which we go shall be prosperous? And the Priest said unto them, Go in Peace; before the Lord is your Way wherein you go.* [Are there no Priests among us, think you, that might, in the like Case, give an Enemy as good Encouragement? 'Tis well known, that we have Numbers of the same Religion with those who of late encouraged the French to invade our Mother-Country.] [119] *And they came,* Verse 7, *to Laish, and saw the People that were therein, how they dwelt* careless, *after the Manner of the Zidonians,* quiet *and* secure. They *thought* themselves secure, no doubt; and as they *never had been* disturbed, vainly imagined they *never should.* 'Tis not unlikely that some might see the Danger they were exposed to by living in that *careless* Manner, but that if these publickly expressed their Apprehensions, the rest reproached them as timorous Persons, wanting Courage or Confidence in their Gods, who (they might say) had hitherto protected them. But the Spies, Verse 8, returned, and said to their Countrymen, Verse 9, *Arise that we may go up against them; for we have seen the Land, and behold it is very good! And are ye still? Be not slothful to go.* Verse 10, *When ye go, ye shall come unto a People* secure; [that is, a People that apprehend no Danger, and therefore have made no Provision against it; great Encouragement this!] *and to a large Land, and a Place where there is no Want of any Thing.* What could they desire more? Accordingly we find, in the following Verses, that *Six hundred Men* only, *appointed with*

---

[119] Here again we see that Franklin was very anti-Catholic.

Weapons of War, undertook the Conquest of this *large Land;* knowing that 600 Men, armed and disciplined, would be an Overmatch perhaps for 60,000, unarmed, undisciplined, and off their Guard. And when they went against it, the idolatrous Priest, Verse 17, *with his graven Image, and his Ephod, and his Teraphim, and his molten Image,* [Plenty of superstitious Trinkets] joined with them, and, no doubt, gave them all the Intelligence and Assistance in his Power; his Heart, as the Text assures us, *being glad,* perhaps for Reasons more than one. And now, what was the Fate of poor Laish! The 600 Men being arrived, found, as the Spies had reported, a People quiet and secure, Verse 20, 21. *And they smote them with the Edge of the Sword, and burnt the City with* Fire; *and there was no* Deliverer, *because it was far from Zidon.* Not so far from Zidon, however, as Pennsylvania is from Britain; and yet we are, if possible, more *careless* than the People of Laish! As the Scriptures are given for our Reproof, Instruction and Warning,[120] may we make a due Use of this Example, before it be too late!

And is our *Country,* any more than our City, altogether free from Danger? Perhaps not. We have, 'tis true, had a long Peace with the Indians: But it is a long Peace indeed, as well as a long Lane, that has no Ending. The French know the Power and Importance of the Six Nations, and spare no Artifice, Pains or Expence, to gain them to their Interest. By their Priests they have converted many to their Religion, and these have openly espoused their Cause. The rest appear irresolute which Part to take; no Persuasions, tho' enforced with costly Presents, having yet been able to engage them generally on our Side, tho' we had numerous Forces on their Borders, ready to second and support them. What then may be expected, now those Forces are, by Orders from the Crown, to be disbanded; when our boasted Expedition is laid aside, thro' want (as it may appear to them) either of Strength or Courage; when they see that the French, and their Indians, boldly, and with Impunity, ravage the Frontiers of NewYork, and scalp the Inhabitants; when those few Indians that engaged with us against the French, are left exposed to their

---

[120] This is a reference to II Timothy 3:16, and it reveals to us once again that Franklin viewed the Bible with great reverence.

Resentment: When they consider these Things, is there no Danger that, thro' Disgust at our Usage, joined with Fear of the French Power, and greater Confidence in their Promises and Protection than in ours, they may be wholly gained over by our Enemies, and join in the War against us? If such should be the Case, which God forbid, how soon may the Mischief spread to our Frontier Counties? And what may we expect to be the Consequence, but deserting of Plantations, Ruin, Bloodshed and Confusion!

Perhaps some in the City, Towns and Plantations near the River, may say to themselves, *An Indian War on the Frontiers will not affect us; the Enemy will never come near our Habitations; let those concern'd take Care of themselves.* And others who live in the Country, when they are told of the Danger the City is in from Attempts by Sea, may say, *What is that to us? The Enemy will be satisfied with the Plunder of the Town, and never think it worth his while to visit our Plantations: Let the Town take care of itself.* These are not mere Suppositions, for I have heard some talk in this strange Manner. But are these the Sentiments of true Pennsylvanians, of Fellow-Countrymen, or even of Men that have common Sense or Goodness? Is not the whole Province one Body, united by living under the same Laws, and enjoying the same Priviledges? Are not the People of City and Country connected as Relations both by Blood and Marriage, and in Friendships equally dear? Are they not likewise united in Interest, and mutually useful and necessary to each other? When the Feet are wounded, shall the Head say, *It is not me; I will not trouble myself to contrive Relief?* Or if the Head is in Danger, shall the Hands say, *We are not affected, and therefore will lend no Assistance!* No. For so would the Body be easily destroyed: But when all Parts join their Endeavours for its Security, it is often preserved. And such should be the Union between the Country and the Town; and such their mutual Endeavours for the Safety of the Whole. When New-England, a distant Colony, involv'd itself in a grievous Debt to reduce Cape-Breton, we freely gave *Four Thousand Pounds* for *their* Relief. And at another Time, remembering that Great Britain, still more distant, groan'd under heavy Taxes in Supporting the War, we threw in our Mite to their Assistance, by a free Gift of *Three Thousand Pounds:* And shall

Country and Town join in helping Strangers (as those comparatively are) and yet refuse to assist each other?

But whatever different Opinions we have of our Security in other Respects, our Trade, all seem to agree, is in Danger of being ruin'd in another Year. The great Success of our Enemies, in two different Cruizes this last Summer in our Bay, must give them he greatest Encouragement to repeat more frequently their Visits, the Profit being almost certain, and the Risque next to nothing. Will not the first Effect of this be, an Enhauncing of the Price of all foreign Goods to the Tradesman and Farmer, who use or consume them? For the Rate of Insurance will increase in Proportion to the Hazard of Importing them; and in the same Proportion will the Price of those Goods increase. If the Price of the Tradesman's Work and the Farmer's Produce would encrease equally with the Price of foreign Commodities, the Damage would not be so great: But the direct contrary must happen. For the same Hazard, or Rate of Insurance, that raises the Price of what is imported, must be deducted out of, and lower the Price of what is exported. Without this Addition and Deduction, as long as the Enemy cruize at our Capes, and take those Vessels that attempt to *go out,* as well as those that endeavour to *come in,* none can afford to trade, and Business must be soon at a Stand. And will not the Consequences be, A discouraging of many of the Vessels that us'd to come from other Places to purchase our Produce, and thereby a Turning of the Trade to Ports that can be entered with less Danger, and capable of furnishing them with the same Commodities, as New-York, &c? A Lessening of Business to every Shopkeeper, together with Multitudes of bad Debts; the high Rate of Goods discouraging the Buyers, and the low Rates of their Labour and Produce rendering them unable to pay for what they had bought: Loss of Employment to the Tradesman, and bad Pay for what little he does: And lastly, Loss of many Inhabitants, who will retire to other Provinces not subject to the like Inconveniencies; whence a Lowering of the Value of Lands, Lots, and Houses.

The Enemy, no doubt, have been told, That the People of Pennsylvania are Quakers, and against all Defence, from a Principle of Conscience; this, tho' true of a Part, and that a small Part only of the Inhabitants, is commonly said of the Whole; and what may make it look probable to Strangers, is, that in Fact, nothing is done by any Part of the People towards their Defence. But to refuse Defending one's self or one's Country, is so unusual a Thing among Mankind, that possibly they may not believe it, till by Experience they find, they can come higher and higher up our River, seize our Vessels, land and plunder our Plantations and Villages, and retire with their Booty unmolested. Will not this confirm the Report, and give them the greatest Encouragement to strike one bold Stroke for the City, and for the whole Plunder of the River?

It is said by some, that the Expence of a Vessel to guard our Trade, would be very heavy, greater than perhaps all the Enemy can be supposed to take from us at Sea would amount to; and that it would be cheaper for the Government to open an Insurance-Office, and pay all Losses. But is this right Reasoning? I think not: For what the Enemy takes is clear Loss to us, and Gain to him; encreasing his Riches and Strength as much as it diminishes ours, so making the Difference double; whereas the Money paid our own Tradesmen for Building and Fitting out a Vessel of Defence, remains in the Country, and circulates among us; what is paid to the Officers and Seamen that navigate her, is also spent ashore, and soon gets into other Hands; the Farmer receives the Money for her Provisions; and on the whole, nothing is clearly lost to the Country but her Wear and Tear, or so much as she sells for at the End of the War less than her first Cost. This Loss, and a trifling one it is, is all the Inconvenience: But how many and how great are the Conveniencies and Advantages! And should the Enemy, thro' our Supineness and Neglect to provide for the Defence both of our Trade and Country, be encouraged to attempt this City, and after plundering us of our Goods, either *burn it,* or put it to Ransom; how great would that Loss be! Besides the Confusion, Terror, and Distress, so many Hundreds of Families would be involv'd in!

The Thought of this latter Circumstance so much affects me, that I cannot forbear expatiating somewhat more upon it. You have, my dear Countrymen, and Fellow Citizens, Riches to tempt a considerable Force to unite and attack you, but are under no Ties or

Engagements to unite for your Defence. Hence, on the first Alarm, *Terror* will spread over All; and as no Man can with Certainty depend that another will stand by him, beyong Doubt very many will seek Safety by a speedy Flight. Those that are reputed rich, will flee, thro' Fear of Torture, to make them produce more than they are able. The Man that has a Wife and Children, will find them hanging on his Neck, beseeching him with Tears to quit the City, and save his Life, to guide and protect them in that Time of general Desolation and Ruin. All will run into Confusion, amidst Cries and Lamentations, and the Hurry and Disorder of Departers, carrying away their Effects. The Few that remain will be unable to resist. *Sacking* the City will be the first, and *Burning* it, in all Probability, the last Act of the Enemy. This, I believe, will be the Case, if you have timely Notice. But what must be your Condition, if suddenly surprized, without previous Alarm, perhaps in the Night! Confined to your Houses, you will have nothing to trust to but the Enemy's Mercy. Your best Fortune will be, to fall under the Power of Commanders of King's Ships, able to controul the Mariners; and not into the Hands of *licentious Privateers.* Who can, without the utmost Horror, conceive the Miseries of the Latter! when your Persons, Fortunes, Wives and Daughters, shall be subject to the wanton and unbridled Rage, Rapine and Lust, of *Negroes, Molattoes,* and others, the vilest and most abandoned of Mankind. A dreadful Scene! which some may represent as exaggerated. I think it my Duty to warn you: Judge for yourselves.

'Tis true, with very litte Notice, the Rich may shift for themselves. The Means of speedy Flight are ready in their Hands; and with some previous Care to lodge Money and Effects in distant and secure Places, tho' they should lose much, yet enough may be left them, and to spare. But most unhappily circumstanced indeed are we, the middling People, the Tradesmen, Shopkeepers, and Farmers of this Province and City! We cannot all fly with our Families; and if we could, how shall we subsist? No; we and they, and what little we have gained by hard Labour and Industry, must bear the Brunt: The Weight of Contributions, extorted by the Enemy (as it is of Taxes among ourselves) must be surely borne by us. Nor can it be avoided as we stand at present; for tho' we are numerous, we are quite defenceless, having neither Forts, Arms, Union, nor Discipline. And tho' it were true, that our Trade might be protected at no great Expence, and our Country and our City easily defended, if proper Measures were but taken; yet who shall take these Measures? Who shall pay that Expence? On whom may we fix our Eyes with the least Expectation that they will do any one Thing for our Security? Should we address that wealthy and powerful Body of People, who have ever since the War governed our Elections, and filled almost every Seat in our Assembly; should we intreat them to consider, if not as Friends, at least as Legislators, that *Protection* is as truly due from the Government to the People, as *Obedience* from the People to the Government; and that if on account of their religious Scruples, they themselves could do no Act for our Defence, yet they might retire, relinquish their Power for a Season, quit the Helm to freer Hands during the present Tempest, to Hands chosen by their own Interest too, whose Prudence and Moderation, with regard to them, they might safely confide in; secure, from their own native Strength, of resuming again their present Stations, whenever it shall please them: Should we remind them, that the Publick Money, raised *from All,* belongs *to All;* that since they have, for their own Ease, and to secure themselves in the quiet Enjoyment of their Religious Principles (and may they long enjoy them) expended such large Sums to oppose Petitions, and engage favourable Representations of their Conduct, if they themselves could by no Means be free to appropriate any Part of the Publick Money for our Defence; yet it would be no more than Justice to spare us a reasonable Sum for that Purpose, which they might easily give to the King's Use as heretofore, leaving all the Appropriation to others, who would faithfully apply it as we desired: Should we tell them, that tho' the Treasury be at present empty, it may soon be filled by the outstanding Publick Debts collected; or at least Credit might be had for such a Sum, on a single Vote of the Assembly: That tho' *they* themselves may be resigned and easy under this naked, defenceless State of the Country, it is far otherwise with a very great Part of the People; with *us,* who can have no Confidence that God will protect those that neglect the Use of rational Means for their Security; nor have any Reason to hope, that our Losses, if we should suffer any, may be made up by Collections in our Favour at Home? Should we conjure them by all the Ties of Neighbourhood, Friendship, Justice and Humanity, to consider these Things; and what Distraction, Misery and Confusion, what Desolation and Distress, may possibly be the Effect of their *unseasonable* Predominancy and Perseverance; yet all would be in vain: For they have already been by great Numbers of the People petitioned in vain. Our late Governor did for Years sollicit, request, and even threaten them in vain. The Council have since twice remonstrated to them in vain. Their religious Prepossessions are unchangeable, their Obstinacy invincible. Is there then the least Hope remaining, that from that Quarter any Thing should arise for our Security?

And is our Prospect better, if we turn our Eyes to the Strength of the *opposite Party,* those Great and rich Men, Merchants and others, who are ever railing at Quakers for doing what their Principles seem to require, and what in Charity we ought to believe they think their Duty, but take no one Step themselves for the Publick Safety? They have so much Wealth and Influence, if they would use it, that they might easily, by their Endeavours and Example, raise a military Spirit among us, make us fond, studious of, and expert in Martial Discipline, and effect every Thing that is necessary, under God, for our Protection. But Envy seems to have taken Possession of their Hearts, and to have eaten out and destroyed every generous, noble, Publick-spirited Sentiment. *Rage* at the Disappointment of their little Schemes for Power, gnaws their Souls, and fills them with such cordial Hatred to their Opponents, that every Proposal, by the Execution of which *those* may receive Benefit as well as themselves, is rejected with Indignation. *What,* say they, *shall we lay out our Money to protect the Trade of Quakers? Shall we fight to defend Quakers? No; Let the Trade perish, and the City burn; let what will happen, we shall never lift a Finger to prevent it.* Yet the Quakers have *conscience* to plead for their Resolution not to fight, which these Gentlemen have not: *Conscience* with you, Gentlemen, is on the other Side of the Question: *Conscience* enjoins it as a Duty on you (and indeed I think it such on every Man) to defend your Country, your Friends, your Aged Parents, your Wives, and helpless Children: And yet you resolve not to perform this Duty, but act *contrary* to *your own* Consciences, because the Quakers act *according* to *theirs.* 'Till of late I could scarce believe the Story of him who refused to pump in a sinking Ship, because one on board, whom he hated, would be saved by it as well as himself. But such, it seems, is the Unhappiness of human Nature, that our Passions, when violent, often are too hard for the united Force of *Reason, Duty* and *Religion.*

Thus unfortunately are we circumstanc'd at this Time, my dear Countrymen and Fellow-Citizens; we, I mean, the middling People, the Farmers, Shopkeepers and Tradesmen of this City and Country. Thro' the Dissensions of our Leaders, thro' *Mistaken Principles* of *religion,* join'd with a Love of Worldly Power, on the one Hand; thro' *Pride, Envy* and *implacable Resentment* on the other; our Lives, our Families and little Fortunes, dear to us as any Great Man's can be to him, are to remain continually expos'd to Destruction, from an enterprizing, cruel, now well-inform'd, and by Success encourag'd Enemy. It seems as if Heaven, justly displead'd at our growing Wickedness, and determin'd to punish this once favour'd Land, had suffered our Chiefs to engage in these foolish and mischievous Contentions, for *little Posts* and *paltry Distinctions,* that our Hands might be bound up, our Understandings darkned and misled, and every Means of our Security neglected. It seems as if our greatest Men, our *Cives nobilissimi* of both Parties, had *sworn the Ruin of the Country, and invited the French, our most inveterate Enemy, to destroy it.* Where then shall we seek for Succour and Protection? The Government we are immediately under denies it to us; and if the Enemy comes, we are *far from* Zidon, *and there is no Deliverer near.* Our Case indeed is dangerously bad; but perhaps there is yet a Remedy, if we have but the Prudence and the Spirit to apply it.

If this now flourishing City, and greatly improving Colony, is destroy'd and ruin'd, it will not be for want of Numbers of Inhabitants able to bear Arms in its Defence. 'Tis computed that we have at least (exclusive of the Quakers) 60,000 Fighting Men, acquainted with Fire-Arms, many of them Hunters and Marksmen, hardy and bold. All we want is Order, Discipline, and a few Cannon. At present we are like the separate Filaments of Flax before the

Thread is form'd, without Strength because without Connection; but Union would make us strong and even formidable: Tho' the *Great* should neither help nor join us; tho' they should even oppose our Uniting from some mean Views of their own, yet, if we resolve upon it, and it please God to inspire us with the necessary Prudence and Vigour, it *may* be effected. Great Numbers of our People are of British Race, and tho' the fierce fighting Animals of those happy Islands, are said to abate their native Fire and Intrepidity, when removed to a Foreign Clime, yet with the People 'tis not so; Our Neighbours of New-England afford the World a convincing Proof, that Britons, tho' a Hundred Years transplanted, and to the remotest Part of the Earth, may yet retain, even to the third and fourth Descent, that *Zeal* for the *Publick Good,* that *military Prowess,* and that *undaunted Spirit,* which has in every Age distinguished their Nation. What Numbers have we likewise of *those brave People,* whose Fathers in the last Age made so glorious a Stand for our Religion and Liberties, when invaded by a powerful French Army, join'd by Irish Catholicks, under a bigotted Popish King! Let the Memorable Siege of Londonderry, and the signal Actions of the Iniskillingers, by which the Heart of that Prince's Schemes was broken, be perpetual Testimonies of the *Courage* and *Conduct* of those *noble Warriors!* Nor are there wanting amongst us, Thousands of *that Warlike Nation,* whose Sons have ever since the Time of Caesar maintained the Character he gave their Fathers, of joining the most *obstinate Courage* to all the other military Virtues. I mean the *Brave* and *steady* Germans. Numbers of whom have actually borne Arms in the Service of their respective Princes; and if they fought well for their Tyrants and Oppressors, would they refuse to unite with us in Defence of their *newly acquired* and most precious *Liberty* and *Property?* Were this Union form'd, were we once united, thoroughly arm'd and disciplin'd, was every Thing in our Power done for our Security, as far as human Means and Foresight could provide, we might then, *with more Propriety,* humbly ask the Assistance of Heaven, and a Blessing on our lawful Endeavours.[121]

---

[121] In this statement Franklin reveals the relationship which he saw between self-sufficiency and prayers for God's assistance. He did not view the preparations of men for their own safety as more important than the aid of Heaven. Rather, he

The very Fame of our Strength and Readiness would be a Means of Discouraging our Enemies; for 'tis a wise and true Saying, that *One Sword often keeps another in the Scabbard.* The Way to secure Peace is to be prepared for War. They that are on their Guard, and appear ready to receive their Adversaries, are in much less Danger of being attack'd, than the supine, secure and negligent. We have yet a Winter before us, which may afford a good and almost sufficient Opportunity for this, if we seize and improve it with a becoming Vigour. And if the Hints contained in this Paper are so happy as t meet with a suitable Disposition of Mind in his Countrymen and Fellow Citizens, the Writer of it will, in a few Days, lay before them a Form of an Association for the Purposes herein mentioned, together with a practicable Scheme for raising the Money necessary for the Defence of our Trade, City, and Country, without laying a Burthen on any Man.

May the God *of* Wisdom, Strength *and* Power, *the Lord of the Armies of Israel, inspire us with Prudence in this Time of* Danger; *take away from us all the Seeds of Contention and Division, and unite the Hearts and Counsels of all of us, of whatever* Sect *or* Nation, *in one Bond of Peace, Brotherly Love, and generous Publick spirit; May he give us Strength and Resolution to amend our Lives, and remove from among us every Thing that is displeasing to him; afford us his most Gracious Protection, confound the Designs of our Enemies, and give* Peace *in all our Borders, is the sincere Prayer of*

A Tradesman of Philadelphia.[122]

---

viewed human effort as a necessary precursor to prayer, and he had an excellent example of this in the very book of the Bible that he quoted earlier in this essay.

In chapter seven of the book of Judges, God refused to deliver Israel by aiding Gideon's army until all of those who lacked proper military discipline were sent home. Franklin's proposal that Pennsylvania form a disciplined militia before relying on God's deliverance is perfectly consistent with this example.

[122] This prayer reveals several things about Franklin's view of God. First, it shows us that Franklin recognized the God of Israel as the true God. Second, it demonstrates that he knew that God was displeased with certain actions among

Autobiography

My Activity in these Operations was agreable to the Governor and Council; they took me into Confidence, and I was consulted by them in every Measure wherein their Concurrence was thought useful to the Association. Calling in the Aid of Religion, I propos'd to them the Proclaiming a Fast, to promote Reformation, and implore the Blessing of Heaven on our Undertaking. They embrac'd the Motion, but as it was the first Fast ever thought of in the Province, the Secretary had no Precedent from which to draw the Proclamation. My Education in New England, where a Fast is proclaim'd every Year, was here of some Advantage. I drew it in the accustomed Stile, it was translated into German, printed in both Languages and divulg'd thro' the Province. This gave the Clergy of the different Sects an Opportunity of Influencing their Congregations to join in the Association; and it would probably have been general among all but Quakers if the Peace had not soon interven'd.[123]

---

men and that the remedy for this situation required God's assistance. And third, that God was a personal God who could be relied upon to intervene in the affairs of men in order to protect those who sought His aid. This is a far cry from the distant and impersonal God of Deism.

[123] It is very important to note that it was Franklin who first proposed the idea of proclaiming a day of public prayer and fasting in Pennsylvania, and it was Franklin who personally wrote the proclamation for that day of fasting. Isaacson wrote of Franklin's view of prayer that:

"Franklin was a believer, even more so as he grew older, in a rather general and at times nebulous divine providence, the principle that God had a benevolent interest in the affairs of men. But he never showed much faith in the more specific notion of special providence, which held that God would intervene directly based on personal prayer." (Isaacson, 451)

And yet, we find here another example of Franklin stating just the opposite. The same Franklin that Isaacson accuses of placing no faith in the efficacy of prayer was the one who introduced the concept of the efficacy of public prayer and fasting to the Province of Pennsylvania.

Proclamation for a General Fast – Dec. 9, 1747

By the Honourable the President and Council of the Province of Pennsylvania, A Proclamation For a General Fast.

Forasmuch as it is the Duty of Mankind, on all suitable Occasions, to acknowledge their Dependance on the Divine Being, to give Thanks for the Mercies received, and no less to deprecate his Judgments, and humbly pray for his Protection: And as the Calamities of a bloody War, in which our Nation is now engaged, seem every Year more nearly to approach us, and the Expedition form'd for the Security of these Plantations, hath been laid aside: As the Inhabitants of this Province and City have been sorely visited with mortal Sickness in the Summer past, and there is just Reason to fear, that unless we humble ourselves before the Lord, and amend our Ways, we may be chastised with yet heavier Judgments: We have therefore thought fit, on due Consideration thereof, to appoint Thursday, the seventh Day of January next, to be observed throughout this Province as a Day of Fasting and Prayer; exhorting all, both Ministers and People, to observe the same with becoming Seriousness and Attention, and to join with one Accord in the most humble and fervent Supplications, That Almighty God would mercifully interpose, and still the Rage of War among the Nations, and put a Stop to the Effusion of Christian Blood: That he would preserve and bless our Gracious King, guide his Councils, and give him Victory over his Enemies, to the Establishing a speedy and lasting Peace: That he would bless, prosper and preserve all the British Colonies, and particularly, that he would take this Province under his Protection, confound the Designs and defeat the Attempts of its Enemies, and unite our Hearts, and strengthen our Hands in every Undertaking that may be for the Publick Good, and for our Defence and Security in this Time of Danger: That he would graciously please to bless the succeeding Year with Health, Peace and Plenty, and enable us to make a right Use of his late afflicting Hand, in a sincere and thorough Reformation of our Lives and Manners, to which the Ministers of all religious Societies are desired earnestly to exhort their People. And it is recommended to all Persons to abstain from servile Labour on the said Day.

Given at Philadelphia, under the Great Seal of the said Province, the Ninth Day of December, in the Twenty-first Year of the Reign of our Sovereign Lord George II. by the Grace of God, of Great-Britain, France and Ireland, King, Defender of the Faith, &c. Annoq; Domini, 1747.

Poor Richard – Feb. 1748

To lead virtuous Life, my Friends, and get to Heaven in Season, You've just so much more Need of Faith, as you have less of Reason.[124]

Poor Richard Improved – Feb. 1749

Wak'd by the Call of Morn, on early Knee,
Ere the World thrust between thy God and thee,
Let thy pure Oraisons, ascending, gain
His Ear, and Succour of his Grace obtain,
In Wants, in Toils, in Perils of the Day,
And strong Temptations that beset thy Way.
Thy best Resolves then in his Strength renew
To walk in Virtue's Paths, and Vice eschew.[125]

---

[124] In this short witticism, Franklin advocates the idea that faith and reason are equally necessary for entrance into heaven. The important role of reason in the process of salvation is evident throughout the Scriptures in passages such as Isaiah 1:18 where we read:

"Come now, and let us reason together, saith the LORD: though your sins be as scarlet, they shall be as white as snow; though they be red like crimson, they shall be as wool."

[125] Here again we find Franklin exhorting his readers to pray. If Franklin really was as opposed to prayer as the historians often claim, why would we find so many unnecessary exhortations such as these?

Proposals Relating to the Education of Youth in Pennsylvania – 1749

History will also afford frequent Opportunities of showing the Necessity of a Publick Religion, from its Usefulness to the Publick; the Advantage of a Religious Character among private Persons; the Mischiefs of Superstition, &c . and the Excellency of the CHRISTIAN RELIGION above all others antient or modern. (19)

Footnote 19: See Turnbull on this Head, from p. 386 to 390. very much to the Purpose, but too long to be transcribed here.[126]

---

[126]According to Lemay, Franklin here "gave four reasons, none of which had to do with truth, God, or theology." He also said that "In an undercurrent, Franklin may have been questioning the validity of any religion." (Lemay, 3:185) The problem with Lemay's conclusion is that it completely ignores Franklin's own footnote to this section. When we turn to the source that Franklin cited, we can see that his four reasons had a great deal to do with truth, God and theology. For example, Franklin's source included the statement that:

"The Lord's supper being nothing else but a serious grateful commemoration of all the blessed doctrines, i. e. all the blessed and glorious hopes set before us by Christianity thro' Jesus Christ, who came to call us to virtue and glory, that we being made partakers of the divine nature, through holiness, might be qualified to dwell with God for ever." (Trumbull, 387-388)

And Trumbull further wrote:

"He who is persuaded of the intrinsic excellence of the Christian institution, will not hesitate long about giving his assent to the external evidence it offers of its divine authority. For the works Jesus Christ wrought and gave his apostles power to work, bear the same relation to his doctrines that experiments have in natural philosophy to the doctrines or conclusions inferred from them, or which they are brought to prove, i. e. they were specimens or samples analogous in kind, and commensurate in quantity or moment to the knowledge and power he pretended to as a superior teacher, authorised by God to instruct mankind in several important truths relating to God, providence, virtue, vice, and a future state." (Trumbull, 388)

I doubt that Lemay would say of these statements that they have nothing to do with truth, God, or theology.

Poor Richard Improved – May, 1751

Vice luring, in the Way of Virtue lies,
God suffers This; but tempts not; tho' He tries.
Go wrong, go right, 'tis your own Action still;
He leaves you to your Choice, of Good, or Ill.
Then chuse the Good! the Ill submisly bear!
The Man of Virtue is above Despair.
Safe on this Maxim with the Writer rest,
That all that happens, happens for the best.[127]

Oath as Trustee of University of Pennsylvania – June 10, 1755

And all these Things I do plainly and sincerely acknowledge and Swear, according to these express Words by me spoken, and according to the plain, and common Sense and Understanding of the same Words, without any Equivocation, Mental Evasion, or secret Reservation whatsoever. And I do make this Recognition, Acknowledgment, Abjuration, Renunciation and Promise, heartily, willingly and truly, upon the true Faith of a Christian: So help me God ... I do believe that there is not any Transubstantiation in the Sacrament of the Lords Supper, or in the Elements of Bread and Wine, at or after the Consecration thereof by any Person whatsoever.[128]

---

[127] In this poem, Franklin references both James 1:13 and Romans 8:28 and also presents yet another evidence of his rejection of Calvinism.

[128] I have yet to find a single historian who has made reference to the oath taken by Franklin as a member of the board of Trustees of the University of Pennsylvania. Lemay devotes a significant portion of his third volume to Franklin's efforts to start the university, but I did not notice any comment from him in regards to Franklin swearing fealty upon his "true Faith of a Christian."
204

Last Will and Testament – June 22, 1750

And now humbly returning sincere Thanks to God for producing me into Being, and conducting me hitherto thro' Life so happily, so free from Sickness, Pain and Trouble, and with such a Competency of this World's Goods as might make a reasonable Mind easy: That he was pleased to give me such a Mind, with moderate Passions, or so much of his gracious Assistance in governing them; and to free it early from Ambition, Avarice and Superstition, common Causes of much Uneasiness to Men. That he gave me to live so long in a Land of Liberty, with a People that I love, and rais'd me, tho' a Stranger, so many Friends among them; bestowing on me moreover a loving and prudent Wife, and dutiful Children. For these and all his other innumerable Mercies and Favours, I bless that Being of Beings who does not disdain to care for the meanest of his Creatures. And I reflect on those Benefits received with the greater Satisfaction, as they give me such a Confidence in his Goodness, as will, I hope, enable me always in all things to submit freely to his Will, and to resign my Spirit chearfully into his Hands whenever he shall please to call for it; reposing myself securely in the Lap of God and Nature as a Child in the Arms of an affectionate Parent.

To Samuel Johnson – Aug. 23, 1750

Your tenderness of the church's peace is truly laudable; but, methinks, to build a new church in a growing place is not properly *dividing* but *multiplying;* and will really be a means of increasing the number of those who worship God in that way. Many who cannot now be accommodated in the church, go to other places, or stay at home; and if we had another church, many who go to other places, or stay at home, would go to church. I suppose the interest of the church has been far from suffering in Boston by the building of two churches there in my memory. I had for several years nailed against the wall of my house a pigeon box that would hold six pair; and though they bred as fast as my neighbours' pigeons, I never had more than six pair, the old and strong driving out the young and weak, and obliging them to seek new habitations. At length I put up an additional box with apartments for entertaining twelve pair more;

and it was soon filled with inhabitants, by the overflowing of my first box, and of others in the neighbourhood. This I take to be a parallel case with the building a new church here.

Appeal for the Hospital – August 8, 1751

The great Author of our Faith, whose Life should be the constant Object of our Imitation, as far as it is not inimitable, always shew'd the greatest Compassion and Regard for the Sick; he disdain'd not to visit and minister Comfort and Health to the meanest of the People; and he frequently inculcated the same Disposition in his Doctrine and Precepts to his Disciples. For this one Thing, (in that beautiful Parable of the Traveller wounded by Thieves) the Samaritan (who was esteemed no better than a *Heretick,* or an *Infidel* by the *Orthodox* of those Times) is preferred to the Priest and the Levite; because he did not, like them, pass by, regardless of the Distress of his Brother Mortal; but when he came to the Place where the half-dead Traveller lay, *he had Compassion on him, and went to him, and bound up his Wounds, pouring in Oil and Wine, and set him on his own Beast, and brought him to an Inn, and took Care of him.*[129] Dives, also, the rich Man, is represented as being excluded from the Happiness of Heaven, because he fared sumptuously every Day, and had Plenty of all Things, and yet neglected to comfort and assist his poor Neighbour, who was helpless and *full of Sores,* and might perhaps have been revived and restored with small care, *by the Crumbs that fell from his Table,*[130] or, as we say, *with his loose Corns.—I was Sick, and ye Visited me,*[131] is one of the Terms of Admission into Bliss, and the Contrary, a Cause of Exclusion: That is, as our Saviour himself explains it,[132] *Ye have visited, or ye have*

---

[129] Luke 10:30-37

[130] Luke 16:19-21

[131] Matthew 25:36

[132] Here Franklin refers to Jesus Christ as "our Saviour," and earlier in this article he referred to Christ as "The great Author of our Faith." Statements such as these demonstrate that Franklin publicly proclaimed himself to be a Christian.

not visited, assisted and comforted those who stood in need of it, even tho' they were the least, or meanest of Mankind. This Branch of *Charity* seems essential to the true Spirit of Christianity; and should be extended to all in general, whether Deserving or Undeserving, as far as our Power reaches. Of the ten Lepers who were cleansed, *nine* seem to have been much more unworthy than the *tenth,* yet in respect to the Cure of their Disease, they equally shared the Goodness of God.[133] And the great Physician in sending forth his Disciples, always gave them a particular Charge, *that into whatsoever City they entered, they should heal* All *the Sick,*[134] without Distinction.

When the good Samaritan left his Patient at the Inn, *he gave Money to the Host, and said,* Take Care of Him, *and what thou spendest more, I will repay thee.* We are in this World mutual Hosts to each ohther; the Circumstances and Fortunes of Men and Families are continually changing; in the Course of a few Years we have seen the Rich become Poor, and the Poor Rich; the Children of the Wealthy languishing in Want and Misery, and those of their Servants lifted into Estates, and abounding in the good Things of this Life. Since then, our present State, how prosperous soever, hath no Stability, but what depends on the good Providence of God, how careful should we be not to *harden our Hearts* against the Distresses of our Fellow Creatures, lest He who owns and governs all, should punish our Inhumanity, deprive us of a Stewardship in which we have so unworthily behaved, *laugh at our Calamity, and mock when our Fear cometh.*[135] Methinks when Objects of Charity, and Opportunities of relieving them, present themselves, we should hear the Voice of this Samaritan, as if it were the Voice of God sounding in our Ears, Take Care of Them, *and whatsoever thou spendest, I will repay thee.*

---

[133] Luke 17:11-19

[134] Luke 10:8-9

[135] Proverbs 1:26

Second Appeal for the Hospital – 1751

This Motto, taken from a Pagan Author, expresses the general Sense of Mankind, even in the earliest Ages, concerning that great Duty and extensive Charity, the *administring Comfort and Relief to the Sick.* If Men without any other Assistance than the Dictates of natural Reason, had so high an Opinion of it, what may be expected from Christians, to whom it has been so warmly recommended by the best Example of human Conduct. To visit the Sick, to feed the Hungry, to clothe the Naked, and comfort the Afflicted, are the inseparable Duties of a christian Life.[136]

Accordingly 'tis observable, that the Christian Doctrine hath had a real Effect on the Conduct of Mankind, which the mere Knowledge of Duty without the Sanctions Revelation affords, never produc'd among the Heathens: For History shows, that from the earliest Times of Christianity, in all well-regulated States where Christians obtain'd sufficient Influence, publick Funds and private Charities have been appropriated to the building of Hospitals, for receiving, supporting and curing those unhappy Creatures, whose Poverty is aggravated by the additional Load of bodily Pain. But of these Kind of Institutions among the Pagans, there is no Trace in the History of their Times.

Poor Richard Improved – Dec. 1751

Ere the Foundations of the World were laid,
Ere kindling Light th'Almighty Word obey'd,
Thou wert; and when the subterraneous Flame,
Shall burst its Prison, and devour this Frame,
From angry Heav'n when the keen Lightning flies,
When fervent Heat dissolves the melting Skies,
Thou still shalt be; still as thou wert before,
And know no Change when *Time* shall be no more.[137]

---

[136] Matthew 25:34-46

[137] This poem is likely a reference to the wisdom of God which is personified in Proverbs 8.

To Joseph Huey – June 6, 1753

For my own Part, when I am employed in serving others, I do not look upon my self as conferring Favours, but as paying Debts. In my Travels and since my Settlement I have received much Kindness from Men, to whom I shall never have any Opportunity of making the least direct Return. And numberless Mercies from God, who is infinitely above being benefited by our Services. These Kindnesses from Men I can therefore only return on their Fellow-Men; and I can only show my Gratitude for those Mercies from God, by a Readiness to help his other Children and my Brethren. For I do not think that Thanks, and Compliments, tho' repeated Weekly, can discharge our real Obligations to each other, and much less those to our Creator.

You will see in this my Notion of Good Works, that I am far from expecting (as you suppose) that I shall merit Heaven by them.[138] By

---

[138] One would think that such a plain and direct statement from Franklin himself would be sufficient to establish that Franklin did not believe he could earn salvation by doing good works, but consider the logical contortions that Lemay utilizes in order to avoid that conclusion. Here is what he wrote in regards to this letter:

"Though he did not believe that good works would earn him admittance to heaven, he nevertheless suggested that God was good to those who were not evil and implied that perhaps there was no hell – which may have implied that he was denying an afterlife." (Lemay, 3:312)

Where Lemay discovers these suggestions and implications in Franklin's letter is beyond me. There is nothing in this letter about God doing good to those who are not evil nor even a hint of an implication that Franklin did not believe in hell or an afterlife. All Franklin is asserting here is that he does not believe that good works give us any spiritual merit. He viewed good works to be his duty because of the debt that he owed to his Creator and Savior.

Franklin's conclusion, by the way, is exactly what is taught in Scripture in passages such as II Corinthians 5:15 and Luke 17:10. Both of these passages teach that we should offer Christ our service and our good works because of the great debt that we owe to Him as a result of His great goodness to us.

Heaven we understand, a State of Happiness, infinite in Degree, and eternal in Duration: I can do nothing to deserve such Reward: He that for giving a Draught of Water to a thirsty Person should expect to be paid with a good Plantation, would be modest in his Demands, compar'd with those who think they deserve Heaven for the little Good they do on Earth. Even the mix'd imperfect Pleasures we enjoy in this World are rather from God's Goodness than our Merit; how much more such Happiness of Heaven. For my own part, I have not the Vanity to think I deserve it, the Folly to expect it, nor the Ambition to desire it; but content myself in submitting to the Will and Disposal of that God who made me, who has hitherto preserv'd and bless'd me, and in whose fatherly Goodness I may well confide, that he will never make me miserable, and that even the Afflictions I may at any time suffer shall tend to my Benefit.

The Faith you mention has doubtless its use in the World; I do not desire to see it diminished, nor would I endeavour to lessen it in any Man. But I wish it were more productive of Good Works than I have generally seen it: I mean real good Works, Works of Kindness, Charity, Mercy, and Publick Spirit; not Holiday-keeping, Sermon-Reading or Hearing, performing Church Ceremonies, or making long Prayers, fill'd with Flatteries and Compliments, despis'd even by wise Men, and much less capable of pleasing the Deity. The Worship of God is a Duty, the hearing and reading of Sermons may be useful; but if Men rest in Hearing and Praying, as too many do, it is as if a Tree should value itself on being water'd and putting forth Leaves, tho' it never produc'd any Fruit.[139]

---

[139] This paragraph is often misconstrued as a rejection of faith in favor of good works. Frazer, for example, writes of this paragraph that:

"Franklin could hardly have made clearer his reliance upon works or his rejection of a 'faith' based on the claim that there is salvation only by that name and that Jesus is the only way to salvation." (Frazer, *Religious Beliefs*, 145)

But that is not what Franklin is saying. The argument presented here is the same as that presented in Franklin's defenses of Hemphill and as that presented in his letter to his sister in which he referenced the writings of Jonathan Edwards.

Your great Master tho't much less of these outward Appearances and Professions than many of his modern Disciples. He prefer'd the Doers of the Word to the meer Hearers;[140] the Son that seemingly refus'd to obey his Father and yet perform'd his Commands, to him that profess'd his Readiness but neglected the Works;[141] the heretical but charitable Samaritan, to the uncharitable tho' orthodox Priest and sanctified Levite:[142] and those who gave Food to the hungry, Drink to the Thirsty, Raiment to the Naked, Entertainment to the Stranger, and Relief to the Sick, &c. tho' they never heard of his Name, he declares shall in the last Day be accepted, when those who cry Lord, Lord; who value themselves on their Faith tho' great enough to perform Miracles but have neglected good Works shall be rejected.[143] He profess'd that he came not to call the Righteous but Sinners to Repentance;[144] which imply'd his modest Opinion that there were some in his Time who thought themselves so good that they need not hear even him for Improvement; but now a days we have scarce a little Parson, that does not think it the Duty of every Man within his Reach to sit under his petty Ministrations, and that whoever omits them offends God. I wish to such more Humility, and to you Health and Happiness, being Your Friend and Servant.[145]

Franklin claims that he does not desire to see faith diminished or lessened but only that it should be accompanied by good works.

[140] James 1:22-25

[141] Matthew 21:28-32

[142] Luke 10:30-36

[143] Matthew 25:35-46

[144] Matthew 9:13

[145] In commenting on this paragraph, Lemay makes yet another feeble attempt to distract his readers from the importance of Franklin's statements. Lemay introduces this paragraph by saying that:

"In the letter's last paragraph, Franklin referred to several biblical passages, thereby making it seem as if he were primarily reflecting Christian doctrine." (Lemay, 3:313)

To Elizabeth Hubbart – Feb. 22, 1756

I condole with you, we have lost a most dear and valuable relation, but it is the will of God and Nature that these mortal bodies be laid aside, when the soul is to enter into real life; 'tis rather an embrio state, a preparation for living; a man in not completely born until he be dead: Why then should we grieve that a new child is born among the immortals? A new member added to their happy society? We are spirits. That bodies should be lent us, while they can afford us pleasure, assist us in acquiring knowledge, or doing good to our fellow creatures, is a kind and benevolent act of God— when they become unfit for these purposes and afford us pain instead of pleasure—instead of an aid, become an incumbrance and answer none of the intentions for which they were given, it is equally kind and benevolent that a way is provided by which we may get rid of them. Death is that way. We ourselves prudently choose a partial death. In some cases a mangled painful limb, which cannot be restored, we willingly cut off. He who plucks out a tooth, parts with it freely since the pain goes with it, and he that quits the whole body, parts at once with all pains and possibilities of pains and diseases it was liable to, or capable of making him suffer.

Then, after quoting the paragraph, Lemay repeated his introductory comment with a perplexing difference:

"Perhaps few persons other than ministers who read the letter would have recognized all the allusions, but almost all its readers would have recognized that the letter frequently used biblical teaching. Thus, as with his advocacy of the Golden Rule near the letter's beginning, Franklin made it seem as if he believed in the Christian virtues – as he generally did." (Lemay, 3:314)

If Franklin generally did believe in the Christian virtues, then why would he have to refer to passages from Scripture in a special effort to make it seem as if he agreed with the Christian virtues? If he really did believe in those virtues, then he would not need to make it seem as if he did. Lemay's view of this letter simply does not make sense.

Our friend and we are invited abroad on a party of pleasure— that is to last for ever. His chair was first ready and he is gone before us. We could not all conveniently start together, and why should you and I be grieved at this, since we are soon to follow, and we know where to find him.[146]

To George Whitefield – July 2, 1756

You mention your frequent Wish that you were a Chaplain to an American Army. I sometimes wish, that you and I were jointly employ'd by the Crown to settle a Colony on the Ohio. I imagine we could do it effectually, and without putting the Nation to much Expence. But I fear we shall never be call'd upon for such a Service. What a glorious Thing it would be, to settle in that fine Country a large Strong Body of Religious and Industrious People! What a Security to the other Colonies; and Advantage to Britain, by Increasing her People, Territory, Strength and Commerce. Might it not greatly facilitate the Introduction of pure Religion among the Heathen, if we could, by such a Colony, show them a better Sample of Christians than they commonly see in our Indian Traders, the most vicious and abandoned Wretches of our Nation?[147] Life, like a

---

[146] This letter soundly refutes Lemay's claim that Franklin's letter to Joseph Huey "may have implied that he was denying an afterlife."

[147] Here is another comment by Franklin that has been largely ignored by the historians. Lemay barely mentions it in passing with the comment that Franklin "appealed to Whitefield – and also to his own sense of what religion should be." (Lemay, 3:396) Few others even mention it at all. Yet, this statement contains a significant admission from Franklin in regards to his view of Christianity. By asking Whitefield to accompany him on a mission to found a society based on the "pure Religion," Franklin was admitting that Whitefield's evangelistic messages were proclamations of the same pure Religion that Franklin sought to inculcate into society.

Williams addressed this letter with the statement that "it might be inferred that Franklin was attracted, however briefly, to orthodox Christianity," (Williams, 411) but he dismissed that possibility on the grounds that Franklin resisted Whitefield's attempts to convert him. Unfortunately, Williams failed to account

dramatic Piece, should not only be conducted with Regularity, but methinks it should finish handsomely. Being now in the last Act, I begin to cast about for something fit to end with. Or if mine be more properly compar'd to an Epigram, as some of its few Lines are but barely tolerable, I am very desirous of concluding with a bright Point. In such an Enterprize I could spend the Remainder of Life with Pleasure; and I firmly believe God would bless us with Success, if we undertook it with a sincere Regard to his Honour, the Service of our gracious King, and (which is the same thing) the Publick Good.

Poor Richard Improved – July, 1756

It is observable that God has often called Men to Places of Dignity and Honour, when they have been busy in the honest Employment of their Vocation. Saul was seeking his Father's Asses, and David keeping his Father's Sheep when called to the Kingdom. The Shepherds were feeding their Flocks, when they had their glorious Revelation. God called the four Apostles from their Fishery, and Matthew from the Receipt of Custom;[148] Amos from among the Herdsmen of Tekoah, Moses from keeping Jethro's Sheep, and Gideon from the Threshing Floor, &c. God never encourages Idleness, and despises not Persons in the meanest Employments.

Poor Richard Improved – Dec. 1756

Mysterious Impulse! that more clear to know,
Exceeds the finite Reach of Art below.
 Forbear, bold Mortal! 'tis an impious Aim;
Own God immediate acting thro' the Frame.
'Tis HE, unsearchable, in all resides;
He the First Cause their Operations guides,

---

for the fact that Whitefield and Franklin disagreed over the definition of the term "conversion" as I have pointed out in several other places.

[148] This may be a reference to the Deity of Christ, for it was Jesus who called Matthew and the other Apostles. At the very least, it is a recognition that Jesus was doing the work of God.

Fear on his awful Privacy to press,
But, honouring Him, thy Ignorance confess.

Poor Richard Improved – Feb, 1757

Is there any Duty in Religion more generally agreed on, or more justly required by God, than a perfect Submission to his Will in all Things? Can any Disposition of Mind, either please him more, or become us better, than that of being satisfied with all he gives, and content with all he takes away? None, certainly, can be of more Honour to God, nor of more Ease to ourselves; for if we consider him as our Maker, we dare not contend with him; if as our Father, we ought not to mistrust him; so that we may be confident whatever he does is for our Good, and whatever happens that we interpret otherwise, yet we can get nothing by Repining, nor save anything by Resisting.

To Deborah Franklin – July 17, 1757

The bell ringing for church, we went thither immediately, and with hearts full of gratitude, returned sincere thanks to God for the mercies we had received: were I a Roman Catholic, perhaps I should on this occasion vow to build a chapel to some saint; but as I am not, if I were to vow at all, it should be to build a *lighthouse.*[149]

Poor Richard Improved – Dec. 1757

Learning is a valuable Thing in the Affairs of this Life, but of infinitely more Importance is *Godliness,* as it tends not only to make us happy here but hereafter. At the Day of Judgment, we shall not be asked, what Proficiency we have made in Languages or Philosophy; but whether we have liv'd virtuously and piously as Men endued with Reason, guided by the Dictates of Religion. In that Hour it will

---

[149] This paragraph is the original source of the quote "Lighthouses are better than churches" which is frequently cited by uneducated atheists like Richard Dawkins. (Dawkins, 64) What Franklin is actually saying here is that building a lighthouse would be a better way to express his gratitude toward God than building a shrine to a Catholic saint.

more avail us, that we have thrown a Handful of Flour or Chaff in Charity to a Nest of contemptible Pismires, than that we could muster all the Hosts of Heaven, and call every Star by its proper Name. For then the Constellations themselves shall disappear, the Sun and Moon shall give no more Light, and all the Frame of Nature shall vanish. But our good or bad Works shall remain forever, recorded in the Archives of Eternity.[150]

Unmov'd alone the *Virtuous* now appear,[151]
And in their Looks a calm Assurance wear.[152]
From East, from West, from North and South they come,[153]
To take from the most righteous Judge their Doom;[154]
Who thus, to them, with a serene Regard;
(The Books of Life before him laid,
And all the secret Records wide display'd)[155]
"According to your Works be your Reward:[156]
Possess immortal Kingdoms as your Due,[157]
Prepar'd from an eternal Date for you."[158]

---

[150] Franklin is often viewed as a skeptic and as a champion of the enlightenment, but here he says himself that Godliness is infinitely more important than learning and that men of reason should be guided by the dictates of religion. Such statements are incompatible with the generally accepted view of Franklin.

[151] II Corinthians 11:2, Ephesians 5:26-27

[152] Hebrews 4:16, Hebrews 10:19-22, Ephesians 3:12

[153] Luke 13:29

[154] II Corinthians 5:10

[155] Revelation 20:12

[156] I Corinthians 3:11-15

[157] Revelation 3:5, Revelation 21:27

[158] John 14:2-3, Hebrews 11:16

A Letter from Father Abraham to his Beloved Son – Aug. 1758

Dear Isaac,

You frequently desire me to give you some *Advice,* in Writing. There is, perhaps, no other valuable Thing in the World, of which so great a Quantity is *given,* and so little *taken.* Men do not generally err in their Conduct so much through Ignorance of their Duty, as through Inattention to their own Faults, or through strong Passions and bad Habits; and, therefore, till that Inattention is cured, or those Passions reduced under the Government of Reason, *Advice* is rather resented as a Reproach, than gratefully acknowledged and followed.

Supposing then, that from the many good Sermons you have heard, good Books read, and good Admonitions received from your Parents and others, your Conscience is by this Time pretty well informed, and capable of advising you, if you attentively listen to it, I shall not fill this Letter with Lessons or Precepts of Morality and Religion; but rather recommend to you, that in order to obtain a *clear* Sight and *constant* Sense of your Errors, you would set apart a Portion of every Day for the Purpose of *Self-Examination,* and trying your daily Actions by that Rule of Rectitude implanted by God in your Breast. The properest Time for this, is when you are retiring to Rest; then carefully review the Transactions of the past Day; and consider how far they have agreed with *what you know* of your Duty to God and to Man, in the several Relations you stand in of a Subject to the Government, Servant to your Master, a Son, a Neighbour, a Friend, &c. When, by this Means, you have discovered the Faults of the Day, acknowledge them to God, and humbly beg of him not only Pardon for what is past, but Strength to fulfil your solemn Resolutions of guarding against them for the Future. Observing this Course steadily for some Time, you will find (through God's Grace assisting) that your Faults are continually diminishing, and your Stock of Virtue encreasing; in Consequence of which you will grow in Favour both with God and Man.

I repeat it, that for the Acquirement of solid, uniform, steady Virtue, nothing contributes more, than a daily strict Self-Examination, by the Lights of Reason, Conscience, and the Word of God; joined with firm Resolutions of amending what you find amiss, and fervent Prayer for Grace and Strength to execute those Resolutions. This Method is very antient. 'Twas recommended by Pythagoras, in his truly *Golden Verses,* and practised since in every Age, with Success, by Men of all Religions. Those golden Verses, as translated by Rowe, are well worth your Reading, and even getting by Heart. The Part relating to this Matter I have transcribed, to give you a Taste of them, *viz.*

Let not the stealing God of Sleep surprize,
Nor creep in Slumbers on thy weary Eyes,
Ere ev'ry Action of the former Day,
Strictly thou dost, and *righteously* survey.
With Rev'rence at thy own Tribunal stand,
And answer justly to thy own Demand.
Where have I been? In what have I transgrest?
What Good or Ill has this Day's Life exprest?
Where have I fail'd in what I ought to do?
In what to God, to Man, or to myself I owe?
Inquire severe whate'er from first to last,
From Morning's Dawn till Ev'nings Gloom has past.
If Evil were thy Deeds, repenting mourn,
And let thy Soul with strong Remorse be torn:
If Good, the Good with Peace of Mind repay,
And to thy secret Self with Pleasure say,
Rejoice, my Heart, for all went well to Day.

And that no Passage to your Improvement in Virtue may be kept secret, it is not sufficient that you make Use of *Self-Examination* alone; therefore I have also added a *golden Extract* from a *favourite* Old Book, to instruct you in the prudent and deliberate Choice of some disinterested Friend, to remind you of such Misconduct as must necessarily escape your severest Inquiry: Which is as follows;

Every prudent Man ought to be jealous and fearful of himself, lest he run away too hastily with a Likelihood instead of Truth; and abound too much in his own Understanding. All Conditions are

218

equal, that is, Men may be contented in every Condition: For Security is equal to Splendor; Health to Pleasure, &c. Every Condition of Life has its Enemies, for *Deus posuit duo et duo, unum contra unum.*[159] A rich Man hath Enemies sometimes for no other Reason than because he is rich; the poor Man hath as poor Neighbours, or rich Ones that gape after that small Profit which he enjoys. The Poor very often subsist merely by Knavery and Rapine among each other. Beware, therefore, how you offend any Man, for he that is displeased at your Words or Actions, commonly joins against you, without putting the *best* Construction on (or endeavouring to find out a reasonable Excuse for) them. And be sure you *hate* no Man, though you think him a worthless or unjust Person. Never *envy* any one above you: You have Enemies enough by the common Course of Human Nature; be cautious not to encrease the Number; and rather procure as many Friends as you can, to countenance and strengthen you. Every Man has also an Enemy within himself. Every Man is choleric and covetous, or gentle and generous by Nature. Man is naturally a beneficent Creature: But there are many external Objects and Accidents, met with as we go through Life, which *seem* to make great Alterations in our natural Dispositions and Desires. A Man naturally passionate and greedy, may, to all Appearance, become complaisant and hospitable, merely by Force of Instruction and Discipline; and so the Contrary. 'Tis in vain for a passionate Man to say, *I am pardonable* because *it is natural to me,* when we can perhaps point out to him an Example in his next Neighbour, who was *once* affected in the very same Manner, and could say as much to defend himself, who is now exceedingly *different* in his Behaviour, and quite free from those unhappy Affections which disturbed his Repose so often, not long ago, and became a chearful, facetious, and profitable Companion to his Friends, and a Pattern of Humility to all around him.

Nothing was ever well done or said *in a Passion.* One Man's Infirmities and bad Inclinations may be harder to conquer than another Man's, according to the various and *secret* Circumstances

---

[159] Translation: God placed two and two, and one against another.

that attend them; but they are all capable of being conquered, or very much improved for the better, except they have been suffered to *take Root in* Old *Age*; in this Case it is most convenient to let them have their own Way, as the Phrase is.

The strongest of our natural Passions are seldom perceived by us; a choleric Man does not always discover when he is angry, nor an envious Man when he is invidious; at most they think they commit no great Faults.

Therefore it is necessary that you should have a Monitor. Most Men are very indifferent Judges of themselves, and often think they do well when they sin; and, imagine they commit only small Errors, when they are guilty of Crimes. It is in Human Life as in the Arts and Sciences; their Plainest Doctrines are easily comprehended, but the finest Points cannot be discovered without the closest Attention; of these Parts only the wise and skilful in the Art or Science, can be deemed competent Judges. Many Vices and Follies resemble their opposite Virtues and Prudence; they border upon, and seem to mix with each other; and therefore the exact Line of Division betwixt them is hard to ascertain. Pride resembles a generous Spirit; Superstition and Enthusiasm frequently resemble true Religion; a laudable worthy Ambition resembles an unworthy Self-Sufficiency; Government resembles Tyranny; Liberty resembles Licentiousness; Subjection resembles Slavery; Covetousness resembles Frugality; Prodigality resembles Generosity; and so of the Rest. Prudence chiefly consists in that Excellence of Judgement, which is capable of discerning the Medium; or of acting so as not to intermingle the one with the other; and in being able to assign to every Cause its *proper* Actions and Effects. It is therefore necessary for every Person who desires to be a wise Man, to *take particular Notice of* his own *Actions,* and of his own *Thoughts and Intentions* which are the Original of his actions; with great Care and Circumspection; otherwise he can never arrive to that Degree of Perfection which constitutes the amiable Character he aspires after. And, lest all this Diligence should be insufficient, as Partiality to himself will certainly render it, it is very requisite for him to *chuse a* Friend, or Monitor, who must be allowed the greatest Freedom to advertise and remind him of his Failings, and to point out Remedies. Such a One, I mean, as is a discreet and virtuous Person; but especially One that does not creep after the Acquaintance of, or play the Spaniel to, *great* Men; One who does not covet Employments which are known to be scandalous for Opportunities of Injustice: One who can bridle his Tongue and curb his Wit; One that can converse with himself, and industriously attends upon his own Affairs whatever they be. Find out such a *Man*; insinuate yourself into a Confidence with him; and desire him to observe your Conversation and Behaviour; intreat him to admonish you of what he thinks amiss, in a serious and friendly Manner; importune his Modesty till he condescends to grant your Request. Do not imagine that you live one Day without Faults, or that those Faults are undiscovered. Most Men see that in another, which they can not or will not see in themselves: And he is happiest, who through the whole Course of his Life, can attain to a reasonable Freedom from Sin and Folly, even by the Help of *Old Age,* that great Mortifier and Extinguisher of our Lusts and Passions. If such a Monitor informs you of any Misconduct, whether you know his Interpretations to be true or false, take it not only *patiently,* but *thankfully*; and be careful to reform. Thus you get and keep a Friend, break the inordinate and mischievous Affection you bore towards your Frailities, and advance yourself in Wisdom and Virtue. When you consider that you must give an Account of your Actions to your vigilant Reprover; that other Men see the same Imperfections in you as he does; and that it is impossible for a good Man to enjoy the Advantages of Friendship, except he first puts off those Qualities which render him subject to Flattery, that is, except he first cease to flatter himself. A good, a generous Christian Minister, or worthy sensible Parents, may be suitable Persons for such a difficult Office; difficult, though it should be performed by *familiar* Conversation. And how much more meritorious of Entertainment are People of such a Character, than those who come to your Table to *make Faces,* talk Nonsense, devour your Substance, censure their Neighbours, flatter and deride you? Remember that if a Friend tells you of a Fault, always imagine that he does not tell you the whole, which is commonly the Truth; for he desires your Reformation, but is loth to offend you. And *nunquam sine querela aegra tanguntur*.

I know, dear Son, *Ambition* fills your Mind,
And in Life's Voyage, is th' impelling Wind;
But, at the Helm, let sober Reason stand,
To steer the Bark with Heav'n directed Hand;
So shall you safe *Ambition's* Gales receive,
And ride securely, though the Billows heave;
So shall you shun the giddy Hero's Fate,
And by her Influence be both good and great.
  She bids you first, in Life's soft vernal Hours,
With active Industry wake Nature's Pow'rs;
With rising Years still rising Arts display,
With new-born Graces mark each new-born Day.
'Tis now the Time *young Passion* to command,
While yet the pliant Stem obeys the Hand;
Guide now the Courser with a steady Rein,
E'er yet he bounds o'er Pleasure's flowry Plain;
In Passion's Strife no Medium you can have;
You rule, a Master; or submit, a Slave.

To conclude. You are just entering into the World: Beware of the
first Acts of Dishonesty: They present themselves to the Mind under
specious Disguises, and *plausible Reasons* of Right and Equity: But
being admitted, they open the Way for admitting others, that are *but
a little* more dishonest, which are followed by others *a little* more
knavish than they, till by Degrees, however slow, a Man becomes an
habitual Sharper, and at length a *consummate Rascal* and Villain.
Then farewell all Peace of Mind, and inward Satisfaction; all
Esteem, Confidence, and Reputation among Mankind. And indeed if
outward Reputation could be preserved, what Pleasure can it afford
to a Man that must *inwardly* despise himself, whose own Baseness
will, in Spite of his Endeavours to forget it, be ever presenting itself
to his View. If you have a *Sir-Reverence* in your Breeches, what
signifies it if you *appear* to Others neat and clean and genteel, when
you *know* and *feel* yourself to be b---t. I make no Apology for the
Comparison, however coarse, since none can be too much so for a
defiled and foul Conscience. But never flatter yourself with
Concealment; 'tis impossible to last long. One Man may be too
cunning for another Man, but not for *all Men*: Some Body or other

will smell you out, or some Accident will discover you; or who can be sure that he shall never be heard to talk in his Sleep, or be delirious in a Fever, when the working Mind usually throws out Hints of what has inwardly affected it? Of this there have been many Instances; some of which are within the Compass of your own Knowledge.

Whether you chuse to act in a public or a private Station, if you would maintain the personal Character of a Man of Sincerity, Integrity and Virtue, there is a Necessity of becoming *really good,* if you would *do good*: For the thin Disguises of *pretended* private Virtue and Public Spirit, are easily seen through; the Hypocrite detected and exposed. For this Reason then, *My dear* Isaac, as well as for many others, be sincere, candid, honest, well-meaning, and upright, in all you do and say; be *really* good, if you would *appear* so: Your Life then shall give Strength to your *Counsels*; and though you should be found but an indifferent *Speaker* or *Writer,* you shall not be without Praise for the Benevolence of your Intention.

But, again, suppose it possible for a Knave to preserve a fair Character among Men, and even to approve his own Actions, what is that to the Certainty of his being discovered and detested by the all-seeing Eye of *that righteous* Being, who made and governs the World, whose just Hand never fails to do right and to punish Iniquity, and whose Approbation, Favour, and Friendship, is worth the Universe?

Heartily wishing you every Accomplishment that can make a Man amiable and valuable, to HIS Protection I commit you, being, with sincere Affection, *dear Son,* Your very loving Father,

Abraham.

To Jane Mecom – Sept. 16, 1758

We have been together over a great part of England this Summer; and among other places visited the Town our Father was born in and found some Relations in that part of the Country Still living. Our

Cousin Jane Franklin, daughter of our Unkle John, died but about a Year ago. We saw her Husband Robert Page, who gave us some old Letters to his Wife from unkle Benjamin. In one of them, dated Boston July 4. 1723 he writes "Your Unkle Josiah has a Daughter Jane about 12 years Old, a good humour'd Child" So Jenny keep up your Character, and don't be angry when you have no Letters.

In a little Book he sent her, call'd None but Christ, he wrote an Acrostick on her Name, which for Namesakes' Sake, as well as the good Advice it contains, I transcribe and send you

Illuminated from on High,
And shining brightly in your Sphere
Nere faint, but keep a steady Eye
Expecting endless Pleasures there
Flee Vice, as you'd a Serpent flee,
Raise Faith and Hope three Stories higher
And let Christ's endless Love to thee
N-ere cease to make thy Love Aspire.
Kindness of Heart by Words express
Let your Obedience be sincere,
In Prayer and Praise your God Address
Nere cease 'till he can cease to hear.

After professing truly that I have a great Esteem and Veneration for the pious Author, permit me a little to play the Commentator and Critic on these Lines. The Meaning of *Three Stories* higher seems somewhat obscure, you are to understand, then, that *Faith, Hope* and *Charity* have been called the three Steps of Jacob's Ladder, reaching from Earth to Heaven. Our Author calls them *Stories,* likening Religion to a Building, and those the three Stories of the Christian Edifice; Thus Improvement in Religion, is called *Building Up,* and *Edification. Faith* is then the Ground-floor, *Hope* is up one Pair of Stairs. My dearly beloved Jenny, don't delight so much to dwell in these lower Rooms, but get as fast as you can into the Garret; for in truth the best Room in the House is *Charity*. For my part, I wish the House was turn'd upside down; 'tis so difficult (when one is fat) to get up Stairs; and not only so, but I imagine *Hope* and *Faith* may be more firmly built on *Charity,* than *Charity* upon *Faith* and *Hope.*

To Lord Kames – May 3, 1760

I will shortly send you a Copy of the Chapter you are pleas'd to mention in so obliging a Manner; and shall be extreamly oblig'd in receiving a Copy of the Collection of Maxims for the Conduct of Life, which you are preparing for the Use of your Children. I purpose, likewise, a little Work for the Benefit of Youth, to be call'd *The Art of Virtue.* From the Title I think you will hardly conjecture what the Nature of such a Book may be. I must therefore explain it a little. Many People lead bad Lives that would gladly lead good ones, but know not *how* to make the Change. They have frequently *resolv'd* and *endeavour'd* it; but in vain, because their Endeavours have not been properly conducted. To exhort People to be good, to be just, to be temperate, &c. without *shewing* them *how* they shall *become* so, seems like the ineffectual Charity mention'd by the Apostle, which consisted in saying to the Hungry, the Cold, and the Naked, *be ye fed, be ye warmed, be ye clothed,* without shewing them how they should get Food, Fire or Clothing.[160] Most People

---

[160] James 2:14-18. Franklin's choice of reference here is significant, for it reveals that his goal in teaching the art of virtue was not to supplant faith but rather to bring it to life. As we read in verse 17, "faith, if it hath not works, is dead, being alone."

Lemay writes of this letter that:

"He deliberately did not found his virtues on religion or on an ethic of ends. Since religious beliefs differed and since he, at times, believed in none of the great religions of the world, he separated virtues from religion." (Lemay, 2:58)

But Franklin did not separate virtue from religion, nor indeed could he, for the Bible itself teaches that pure religion is nothing else but virtue. (James 1:27) Franklin established the need for virtue by quoting Scripture, and he presented a plan for meeting that need in practice. Those who simply instructed people to be good without showing them how were in violation of the principles of Scripture, and Franklin sought to avoid that error in his own life by writing a manual for behaving virtuously.

have naturally *some* Virtues, but none have naturally *all* the Virtues. To *acquire* those that are wanting, and *secure* what we acquire as well as those we have naturally, is the Subject of *an Art.* It is as properly an Art, as Painting, Navigation, or Architecture. If a Man would become a Painter, Navigator, or Architect, it is not enough that he is *advised* to be one, that he is *convinc'd* by the Arguments of his Adviser that it would be for his Advantage to be one, and that he *resolves* to be one, but he must also be taught the Principles of the Art, be shewn all the Methods of Working, and how to acquire the *Habits* of using properly all the Instruments; and thus regularly and gradually he arrives by Practice at some Perfection in the Art. If he does not proceed thus, he is apt to meet with Difficulties that discourage him, and make him drop the Pursuit. My *Art of Virtue* has also its Instruments, and teaches the Manner of Using them. Christians are directed to have *Faith in Christ,* as the effectual Means of obtaining the Change they desire. It may, when sufficiently strong, be effectual with many. A full Opinion that a Teacher is infinitely wise, good, and powerful, and that he will certainly reward and punish the Obedient and Disobedient, must give great Weight to his Precepts, and make them much more attended to by his Disciples.[161] But all Men cannot have Faith in Christ; and many have it in so weak a Degree, that it does not produce the Effect. Our *Art of Virtue* may therefore be of great Service to those who have not Faith, and come in Aid of the weak Faith of others. Such as are naturally well-disposed, and have been carefully educated, so that good Habits have been early established, and bad ones prevented, have less Need of this Art; but all may be more or less benefited by it. It is, in short, to be adapted for universal Use. I imagine what I have now been writing will seem to

---

[161] The "Faith in Christ" that Franklin mentions here is not a reference to the faith of salvation, but rather to an assurance of Christ's future judgment of our works. Franklin claimed that the assurance that Christ will judge each individual for his works should be enough to produce virtue among Christians, but it does not do so because there are many who either do not have that assurance at all or who do not have it in sufficient strength to overcome their desire for sin. As a result, "many People lead bad Lives that would gladly lead good ones." Franklin's goal was to help those who desire to lead good lives actually fulfill that desire even if they did not believe that Christ would judge them according to their works.

savour of great Presumption; I must therefore speedily finish my little Piece, and communicate the Manuscript to you, that you may judge whether it is possible to make good such Pretensions. I shall at the same time hope for the Benefit of your Corrections.

To George Whitefield – June 19, 1764

Your frequently repeated Wishes and Prayers for my Eternal as well as temporal Happiness are very obliging. I can only thank you for them, and offer you mine in return. I have my self no Doubts that I shall enjoy as much of both as is proper for me. That Being who gave me Existence, and thro' almost threescore Years has been continually showering his Favours upon me, whose very Chastisements have been Blessings to me, can I doubt that he loves me? And if he loves me, can I doubt that he will go on to take care of me not only here but hereafter? This to some may seem Presumption; to me it appears the best grounded Hope; Hope of the Future; built on Experience of the Past.[162]

---

[162] Fea has this to say about this letter:

"Whitefield would have rejected much of what Franklin said in this letter about the afterlife. As an evangelical Christian he believed that human beings were saved by faith in the death, burial, and resurrection of Jesus Christ. Franklin's 'hope' was a false one. Indeed, Franklin's view of the afterlife … departs significantly from traditional Christian views of salvation." (Fea, 220)

But Fea is very much mistaken on the beliefs of both men. Whitefield did not believe that everyone who had faith in the death, burial and resurrection of Christ would go to Heaven. As explained in a previous note, Whitefield believed that one must experience a conversion of spiritual pangs in order to be a true Christian. In regards to Franklin, Fea has overlooked his admission in the Hemphill pamphlets that he did in fact believe in the atoning death and resurrection of Christ. Had Fea considered these two facts, he may have come to a different conclusion regarding this letter.

To William Strahan – June 25, 1764

I enjoy the Pleasure with which you speak of your Children. God has been very good to you, from whence I think you may be *assured* that he loves you, and that he will take at least as good Care of your future Happiness as he has done of your present. What Assurance of the *Future* can be better founded, than that which is built on Experience of the *Past?* Thank me for giving you this Hint, by the Help of which you may die as chearfully as you live. If you had Christian Faith, quantum suff[icit].[163] This might not be necessary: But as Matters are, it may be of Use.

To Jane Mecom – July 10, 1764

We all condole with you most sincerely on the Death of your Daughter. She always appear'd to me of a sweet and amiable Temper, and to have many other good Qualities that must make the Loss of her more grievous for Brother and you to bear. Our only Comfort under such Afflictions is, that God knows what is best for us, and can bring Good out of what appears Evil. She is doubtless happy: which none of us are while in this Life.

To Sarah Franklin – Nov. 8, 1764

My dear Child, the natural Prudence and goodness of heart that God has blessed you with, make it less necessary for me to be particular in giving you Advice; I shall therefore only say, that the more attentively dutiful and tender you are towards your good Mama, the more you will recommend your self to me; But why shou'd I mention *me,* when you have so much higher a Promise in the Commandment, that such a conduct will recommend you to the favour of God.[164] You know I have many Enemies (all indeed on the Public Account, for I cannot recollect that I have in a private Capacity given just cause of offence to any one whatever) yet they

---

[163] Translation: "that much would suffice." Franklin advised his friend that Christian faith would be sufficient to enable him to die cheerfully.

[164] Ephesians 6:1-3

are Enemies and very bitter ones, and you must expect their Enmity will extend in some degree to you, so that your slightest Indiscretions will be magnified into crimes, in order the more sensibly to wound and afflict me. It is therefore the more necessary for you to be extreamly circumspect in all your Behaviour that no Advantage may be given to their Malevolence. Go constantly to Church whoever preaches. The Acts of Devotion in the common Prayer Book, are your principal Business there; and if properly attended to, will do more towards mending the Heart than Sermons generally can do. For they were composed by Men of much greater Piety and Wisdom, than our common Composers of Sermons can pretend to be. And therefore I wish you wou'd never miss the Prayer Days. Yet I do not mean that you shou'd despise Sermons even of the Preachers you dislike, for the Discourse is often much better than the Man, as sweet and clear Waters come to us thro' very dirty Earth. I am the more particular on this Head, as you seem'd to express a little before I came away some Inclination to leave our Church, which I wou'd not have you do.[165]

To Deborah Franklin – Nov. 9, 1765

[As] to that pious Presbyterian Countryman of mine [whom you] say sets the People a madding, by telling them [that I] plann'd the Stamp Act, and am endeavo[uring to] bring the Test over to America, I thank him he does not charge me (as they do their God) with having plann'd Adam's Fall, and the Damnation of Mankind. It might be affirm'd with equal Truth and Modesty. He certainly was intended for a Wise Man; for he has the wisest Look of any Man I know; and if he would only nod and wink, and could but hold his Tongue, he might deceive an Angel. Let us pity and forget him.[166]

---

[165] This is hardly the advice that a committed Deist would give to his daughter.

[166] Here Franklin again reveals his vehement opposition to the Calvinist portions of Presbyterian doctrine.

N.N. – January 1766

I have read that the whale swallowed Jonah; and as that is in Holy Writ, to be sure I ought to believe it. But if I were told, that, in fact, it was Jonah that swallowed the whale, I fancy I could myself as easily swallow the whale as the story.[167]

Homespun – January 1766

Pray, Sir, who informed you that our *"laws* are Scottish?" The same, I suppose, that told you our Indian corn is unwholesome. Indeed, Sir, your information is very imperfect. The common law of England, is, I assure you, the common law of the colonies: and if the civil law is what you mean by the Scottish law, we have none of it but what is forced upon us by England, in its courts of Admiralty, depriving us of that inestimable part of the common law, trials by juries. And do you look upon keeping the *Sabbath,* as part of the Scottish law? "The Americans, like the Scots, (you say,) observe what *they call* the Sabbath." Pray, Sir, you who are so zealous for your church (in abusing other Christians) what *do you call* it? and where the harm of their *observing* it? If you look into your prayer-book, or over your altars, you will find these words written, *Remember to keep holy the* sabbath *Day.*[168] This law, tho' it may be observed in Scotland, and has been *countenanced* by some of your statutes, is, Sir, originally one of *God's Commandments*: a body of laws still in force in America, tho' they may have become *obsolete* in *some other* countries.[169]

A New Version of the Lord's Prayer – 1768

---

[167] In this brief, parenthetical statement, Franklin points out that the story of Jonah being swallowed by the whale should be believed simply because it is written in Scripture.

[168] Exodus 20:8

[169] It is interesting to note that Franklin actually defended the use of laws forbidding work on Sunday and that he did so on the grounds that such laws are consistent with the commandments of God.

Heavenly Father, may all revere thee, and become thy dutiful Children and faithful Subjects; may thy Laws be obeyed on Earth as perfectly as they are in Heaven: Provide for us this Day as thou hast hitherto daily done: Forgive us our Trespasses, and enable us likewise to forgive those that offend us. Keep us out of Temptation, and deliver us from Evil.[170]

Old Version. *Our Father which art in Heaven* New V. *Heavenly Father,* is more concise, equally expressive, and better modern English. Old. *Hallowed be thy Name.* This seems to relate to an Observance among the Jews not to pronounce the proper or peculiar Name of God, they deeming it a Profanation so to do. We have in our Language no *proper Name* for God; the Word *God* being a common or general Name, expressing all chief Objects of Worship, true or false. The Word *hallowed* is almost obsolete: People now have but an imperfect Conception of the Meaning of the Petition. It is therefore proposed to change the Expression into New. *May all revere thee.* Old V. *Thy Kingdom come.* This Petition seems suited to the then Condition of the Jewish Nation. Originally their State was a Theocracy: God was their King. Dissatisfied with that kind of

---

[170] During the seventeenth and eighteenth centuries, there was a great deal of debate among Presbyterians as to whether the Lord's prayer should be quoted verbatim or whether it was given as a pattern for Churches to follow in composing their own prayers. Franklin apparently held to the second opinion, and his rendition of the Lord 's Prayer seems to fit well with the view expressed by William Carstares in a letter to Sir Hugh Campbell.

"We all heartily acknowledge, that it is an excellent and incomparable Pattern, and we bless our Redeemer, the great Apostle and High Priest of our Profession, that he hath left it on record in his Scriptures, for our Instruction and conduct, in the great duty of Prayer. And we hope, we desire and endeavour, to improve it for these ends, and we have not the least doubt, but that it may be Lawfully used, in the very terms, in which it is expressed. But that we are obliged, by a Divine Command, in all publick Prayers, to use the very words and Syllables, of that Holy Pattern, and that successively too, without the intermixing such Pious Paraphrases upon the several parts of it, as, Sir, your self gives in your Book, is that, which I confess, I have not yet seen a cogent reason, to perswade my belief of it." (Campbell, 7)

Government, they desired a visible earthly King in the manner of the Nations round them. They had such King's accordingly; but their Happiness was not increas'd by the Change, and they had reason to wish and pray for a Return of the Theocracy, or Government of God. Christians in these Times have other Ideas when they speak of the Kingdom of God, such as are perhaps more adequately express'd by New V. *And become thy dutiful Children and faithful Subjects.* Old V. *Thy Will be done on Earth as it is in Heaven.* More explicitly, New V. *May thy Laws be obeyed on Earth as perfectly as they are in Heaven.* Old V. *Give us this Day* our *daily Bread.* Give us what is *ours,* seems to put in a Claim of Right, and to contain too little of the grateful Acknowledgment and Sense of Dependance that becomes Creatures who live on the daily Bounty of their Creator. Therefore it is changed to New V. *Provide for us this Day, as thou hast hitherto daily done.* Old V. *Forgive us our Debts as we forgive our Debtors.* Matthew. *Forgive us our Sins, for we also forgive every one that is indebted to us.* Luke. Offerings were *due* to God on many Occasions by the Jewish Law, which when People could not pay, or had forgotten as Debtors are apt to do, it was proper to pray that those Debts might be forgiven. Our Liturgy uses neither the *Debtors* of Matthew, nor the *indebted* of Luke, but instead of them speaks of *those that trespass against us.* Perhaps the Considering it as a Christian Duty to forgive Debtors, was by the Compilers thought an inconvenient Idea in a trading Nation. There seems however something presumptious in this Mode of Expression, which has the Air of proposing ourselves as an Example of Goodness fit for God to imitate. *We hope you will at least be as good as we are;* you see we forgive one another, and therefore we pray that you would forgive us. Some have considered it in another Sense, *Forgive us* as *we forgive others;* i.e. If we do not forgive others we pray that thou wouldst not forgive us. But this being a kind of conditional *Imprecation* against ourselves, seems improper in such a Prayer; and therefore it may be better to say humbly and modestly New V. *Forgive us our Trespasses, and enable us likewise to forgive those that offend us.* This instead of assuming that we have already in and of ourselves the Grace of Forgiveness, acknowledges our Dependance on God, the Fountain of Mercy, for any Share we may have of it, praying that he would communicate of it to us. Old V.

And lead us not into Temptation. The Jews had a Notion, that God sometimes tempted, or directed or permitted the Tempting of People. Thus it was said he tempted Pharaoh; directed Satan to tempt Job; and a false Prophet to tempt Ahab, &c. Under this Persuasion it was natural for them to pray that he would not put them to such severe Trials. We now suppose that Temptation, so far as it is supernatural, comes from the Devil only; and this Petition continued, conveys a Suspicion which in our present Conceptions seems unworthy of God, Therefore might be altered to New V. Keep *us* out of *Temptation.*

To Mary Stevenson – Oct. 28, 1768

In fine, nothing can contribute to true Happiness that is inconsistent with Duty; nor can a Course of Action conformable to it, be finally without an ample Reward. For, God governs; and he is *good.* I pray him to direct you: And indeed you will never be without his Direction, if you humbly ask it, and show yourself always ready to obey it.

To George Whitefield – Between Jan. and Aug. 1769

I am under continued apprehensions that we may have bad news from America. The sending soldiers to Boston always appeared to me a dangerous step; they could do no good, they might occasion mischief. When I consider the warm resentment of a people who think themselves injured and oppressed, and the common insolence of the soldiery, who are taught to consider that people as in rebellion, I cannot but fear the consequences of bringing them together. It seems like setting up a smith's forge in a magazine of gunpowder. I see with you that our affairs are not well managed by our rulers here below; I wish I could believe with you, that they are well attended to by those above; I rather suspect, from certain circumstances, that though the general government of the universe is well administered, our particular little affairs are perhaps below notice, and left to take the chance of human prudence or imprudence, as either may happen to be uppermost. It is, however, an uncomfortable thought, and I leave it.[171]

To Jane Mecom – Dec. 30, 1770

I send you by this Opportunity the 2 Books you wrote for. They cost 3*s.* a piece. When I was first in London, about 45 Years since, I knew a person who had an Opinion something like your Author's — —Her Name was *Ilive,* a Printer's Widow. She dy'd soon after I left England, and by her Will oblig'd her son to deliver publickly in Salter's Hall a Solemn Discourse, the purport of which was to prove, that this World is the true Hell or Place of Punishment for the Spirits who had transgress'd in a better State, and were sent here to suffer for their sins in Animals of all Sorts. It is long since I saw the

---

[171] Here we find Franklin depressed by the news which he has received from America, and he writes to his friend that this news has caused him to suspect that God does not care about their plight in the least. Upon receiving this letter, Whitefield penned the following statement across the bottom of the page:

"*Uncomfortable* indeed! and, blessed be God, *unscriptural*, for we are fully assured that 'the Lord reigneth,' and are directed to cast all our own care on him, because he careth for us."

Scholars are prone to view this letter as confirmation of Franklin's Deism, but that conclusion is easily dismissed when it is considered in light of Franklin's multiple attestations to the contrary. For example, Stout writes of this letter that:

"Franklin hoped, but could never believe, in an actively involved, caring deity ... Here we see the greatest difference separating the religious worlds of Franklin and Whitefield. For Franklin, the experience of personal friendship could not be translated into an experience of personal faith. The result was profound pessimism." (Stouts, 230-231)

The error in this conclusion is painfully obvious when it is listed, as it is here, in such proximity with Franklin's 1768 letter to Mary Stevenson whom he assured, "God governs; and he is *good*." Franklin's writings are filled with similar assurances, and in light of these, his letter to Whitefield is much more likely to have been a fleeting bout with depression than an admission of Deism.

Discourse, which was printed. I think a good deal of Scripture was cited in it, and that the Supposition was, that tho' we now remember'd nothing of such pre-existent State; yet after Death we might recollect it, and remember the Punishments we had suffer'd, so as to be the better for them; and others who had not yet offended, might now behold and be warn'd by our Sufferings. In fact we see here that every lower Animal has its Enemy with proper Inclinations, Faculties and Weapons, to terrify, wound and destroy it; and that Men, who are uppermost, are Devils to one another; So that on the establish'd Doctrine of the Goodness and Justice of the great Creator, this apparent State of general and systematical Mischief, seem'd to demand some such Supposition as Mrs. Ilives, to account for it consistent with the Honour of the Diety. But our reasoning Powers when employ'd about what may have been before our Existence here, or shall be after it, cannot go far for want of History and Facts: Revelation only can give us the necessary Information, and that (in the first of these Points especially) has been very sparingly afforded us.[172]

To Jane Mecom – Dec. 30, 1770

In some former Letter I believe I mention'd the Price of the Books, which I have now forgotten: But I think it was 3s. each. To be sure there are Objections to the Doctrine of Pre-existence: But it seems to have been invented with a good Intention, to save the Honour of the Deity, which was thought to be injured by the Supposition of his bringing Creatures into the World to be miserable, without any previous misbehaviour of theirs to deserve it. This, however, is perhaps an officious Supporting of the Ark, without being call'd to such Service. Where he has thought fit to draw a Veil, our Attempting to remove it may be deem'd at least an offensive Impertinence. And we shall probably succeed little better in such an

---

[172] Here Franklin gives yet another indication that he believed the Scriptures to be a genuine revelation from God.

Adventure to gain forbidden Knowledge, than our first Parents did when they ate the Apple.[173]

I meant no more by saying Mankind were Devils to one another than that being in general superior to the Malice of the other Creatures, they were not so much tormented by them as by themselves. Upon the whole I am much disposed to like the World as I find it, and to doubt my own Judgment as to what would mend it. I see so much Wisdom in what I understand of its Creation and Government, that I suspect equal Wisdom may be in what I do not understand. And thence have perhaps as much Trust in God as the most pious Christian.

To Samuel Cooper – Jan, 1772

Your Story of the Clergyman and Proclamation is a pleasant one. I can only match it with one I had from my Father, I know not if it was ever printed. Charles I. ordered his Proclamation, authorizing Sports on a Sunday, to be read in all Churches. Many Clergymen comply'd, some refus'd and others hurry'd it through as indistinctly as possible. But one, whose Congregation expected no such thing from him, did nevertheless, to their great Surprize, read it distinctly. He follow'd it, however, with the Fourth Commandment, *Remember to keep holy the Sabbath Day,* and then said, Bretheren, I have laid before you the Command of your King and the Commandment of your God. I leave it to your selves to judge which of the two ought rather to be observed.

Toleration in Old and New England – June 3, 1772

I Understand from the public papers, that in the debates on the bill for relieving the Dissenters in the point of subscription to the Church Articles, sundry reflections were thrown out against that people, importing, "that they themselves are of a persecuting intolerant spirit, for that when they had here the superiority they persecuted the

---

[173] We previously examined Franklin's view of original sin in his defense of Samuel Hemphill, and here we see another evidence that Franklin did not reject that doctrine.

church, and still persecute it in America, where they compel its members to pay taxes for maintaining the Presbyterian or independent worship, and at the same time refuse them a toleration in the full exercise of their religion by the administrations of a bishop."

If we look back into history for the character of present sects in Christianity, we shall find few that have not in their turns been persecutors, and complainers of persecution. The primitive Christians thought persecution extremely wrong in the Pagans, but practised it on one another. The first Protestants of the Church of England, blamed persecution in the Roman church, but practised it against the Puritans: these found it wrong in the Bishops, but fell into the same practice themselves both here and in New England. To account for this we should remember, that the doctrine of *toleration* was not then known, or had not prevailed in the world. Persecution was therefore not so much the fault of the sect as of the times. It was not in those days deemed wrong *in itself.* The general opinion was only, that those *who are in error* ought not to persecute *the truth:* But the *possessors of truth* were in the right to persecute *error,* in order to destroy it. Thus every sect believing itself possessed of *all truth,* and that every tenet differing from theirs was *error,* conceived that when the power was in their hands, persecution was a duty required of them by the God whom they supposed to be offended with heresy. By degrees more moderate *and more modest* sentiments have taken place in the christian world; and among Protestants particularly all disclaim persecution, none vindicate it, and few practise it. We should then cease to reproach each other with what was done by our ancestors, but judge of the present character of sects or churches by their *present conduct* only.[174]

Now to determine on the justice of this charge against the present dissenters, particularly those in America, let us consider the following facts. They went from England to establish a new country for themselves, *at their own expence,* where they might enjoy the

---

[174] In using the terms "we," "each other" and "our," Franklin is identifying himself as a Christian.

free exercise of religion in their own way. When they had purchased the territory of the natives, they granted the lands out in townships, requiring for it neither purchase-money nor quit-rent, but this condition only to be complied with, that the freeholders should for ever support a gospel minister (meaning probably one of the then governing sects) and a free-school within the township. Thus, what is commonly called Presbyterianism became the *established religion* of that country. All went on well in this way while the same religious opinions were general, the support of minister and school being raised by a proportionate tax on the lands. But in process of time, some becoming Quakers, some Baptists, and, of late years some returning to the Church of England (through the laudable endeavours and a *proper application* of their funds by the society for propagating the gospel) objections were made to the payment of a tax appropriated to the support of a church they disapproved and had forsaken. The civil magistrates, however, continued for a time to collect and apply the tax according to the original laws which remained in force; and they did it the more freely, as thinking it just and equitable that the holders of lands should pay what was contracted to be paid when they were granted, as the only consideration for the grant, and what had been considered by all subsequent-purchasers as a perpetual incumbrance on the estate, bought therefore at a proportionably cheaper rate; a payment which it was thought no honest man ought to avoid under the pretence of his having changed his religious persuasion. And this I suppose is one of the best grounds of demanding tythes of dissenters now in England. But the practice being clamoured against by the episcopalians as persecution, the legislature of the Province of the Massachusets-Bay, near thirty years since, passed an act for their relief, requiring indeed the tax to be paid as usual, but directing that the several sums levied from members of the Church of England, should be paid over to the Minister of that Church, with whom such members usually attended divine worship, which Minister had power given him to receive and on occasion *to recover the same by law.*

It seems that legislature considered the *end* of the tax was, to secure and improve the morals of the people, and promote their happiness, by supporting among them the public worship of God and the preaching of the gospel; that where particular people fancied a particular mode, that mode might probably therefore be of most use to those people; and that if the good was done, it was not so material in what mode or by whom it was done. The consideration that their brethren the dissenters in England were still compelled to pay tythes to the clergy of the Church, had not weight enough with the legislature to prevent this moderate act, which still continues in full force, and I hope no uncharitable conduct of the church toward the dissenters will ever provoke them to repeal it.

With regard to a bishop, I know not upon what ground the dissenters, either here or in America, are charged with refusing the benefit of such an officer to the church in that country. *Here* they seem to have naturally no concern in the affair. *There* they have no power to prevent it, if government should think fit to send one. They would probably *dislike,* indeed, to see an order of men established among them, from whose persecutions their fathers fled into that wilderness, and whose future domination they may possibly fear, *not knowing that their natures are changed.* But the non-appointment of bishops for America seems to arise from another quarter. The same wisdom of government, probably, that prevents the sitting of convocations, and forbids, by *noli prosequi*'s, the persecutions of Dissenters for non-subscription, avoids establishing bishops where the minds of people are not are not yet prepared to receive them cordially, lest the public peace should be endangered.

And now let us see how this *persecution-account* stands between the parties.

In New-England, where the legislative bodies are almost to a man Dissenters from the Church of England,

1. There is no test to prevent Churchmen holding offices.

2. The sons of Churchmen have the full benefit of the Universities.

3. The taxes for support of public worship, when paid by Churchmen, are given to the Episcopal minister.

In Old England,

1. Dissenters are excluded from all offices of profit and honour.

2. The benefits of education in the Universities are appropriated to the sons of Churchmen.

3. The clergy of the Dissenters receive none of the tythes paid by their people, who must be at the additional charge of maintaining their own separate worship.

But it is said, the Dissenters of America *oppose* the introduction of a Bishop.

In fact, it is not alone the Dissenters there that give the opposition (if *not encouraging* must be termed *opposing*) but the laity in general dislike the project, and some even of the clergy. The inhabitants of Virginia are almost all Episcopalians. The Church is fully established there, and the Council and General Assembly are perhaps to a man its members, yet when lately at a meeting of the clergy, a resolution was taken to apply for a Bishop, against which several however protested; the assembly of the province at their next meeting, expressed their disapprobation of the thing in the strongest manner, by unanimously ordering the thanks of the house to the protesters: for many of the American laity of the church think it some advantage, whether their own young men come to England for ordination, and improve themselves at the same time by conversation with the learned here, or the congregations are supplied by Englishmen, who have had the benefit of education in English universities, and are ordained before they come abroad. They do not therefore see the necessity of a Bishop merely for ordination, and confirmation is among them deemed a ceremony of no very great importance, since few seek it in England where Bishops are in plenty. These sentiments prevail with many churchmen there, not to promote a design, which they think must sooner or later saddle them with great expences to support it. As to the Dissenters, their minds might probably be more conciliated to the measure, if the Bishops here should, in their wisdom and goodness, think fit to set their sacred character in a more friendly light, by dropping their opposition to the Dissenters application for relief in subscription, and declaring their willingness that Dissenters should be capable of offices, enjoy the benefit of education in the universities, and the privilege of appropriating their tythes to the support of their own clergy. In all these points of toleration, they appear far behind the present Dissenters of New-England, and it may seem to some a step below the dignity of Bishops, to follow the example of such inferiors. I do not, however, despair of their doing it some time or other, since nothing of the kind is too hard for *true christian humility.* I am, Sir, your's, &c. [175]

Preface to an Abridgement of the Book of Common Prayer – 1773

The Editor of the following Abridgement of the Liturgy of the Church of England thinks it but decent and respectful to all, (more particularly to the reverend body of Clergy who adorn the Protestant Religion by their good works, preaching, and example) that he should humbly offer some reasons for such an undertaking. He addresses himself to the serious and discerning. He professes himself to be a Protestant of the Church of England, and holds in the highest veneration the doctrines of Jesus Christ. He is a sincere lover of social worship, deeply sensible of its usefulness to society; and he aims at doing some service to religion, by proposing such abbreviations and omissions in the forms of our Liturgy (retaining every thing he thinks essential) as might, if adopted, procure a more general attendance.[176] For, besides the differing sentiments of many

---

[175] It appears from this essay that Franklin was not opposed to using tax money to pay for churches and ministers as long as those funds were given to the ministers chosen by the people.

[176] Franklin is not the editor being spoken of in this paragraph. Most of the abridgement being referred to was written by Sir Francis Dashwood. Franklin's

pious and well-disposed persons in some speculative points, who in general have a good opinion of our Church, it has often been observed and complained of, that the Morning and Evening Service, as practised in the Churches of England and elsewhere, are so long, and filled with so many repetitions, that the continued attention suitable to so serious a duty becomes impracticable, the mind wanders, and the fervency of devotion is slackened. Also the propriety of saying the same prayer more than once in the same service is doubted, as the service is thereby lengthened without apparent necessity; our Lord having given us a short prayer as an example,[177] and censured the Heathen for thinking to be heard because of much speaking.[178] Moreover, many pious and devout Persons, whose age or infirmities will not suffer them to remain for hours in a cold church, especially in the winter season, are obliged to forego the comfort and edification they would receive by their attendance on divine service. These, by shortening the time, would be relieved: and the younger sort, who have had some principles of religion instilled into them, and who have been educated in a belief of the necessity of adoring their Maker, would probably more frequently, as well as cheerfully, attend divine service, if they were not detained so long at any one time. Also many well-disposed tradesmen, shopkeepers, artificers, and others, whose habitations are not remote from churches, could, and would (more frequently at least) find time to attend divine service on other than Sundays, if the prayers were reduced into a much narrower compass. Formerly there were three services performed at different times of the day, which three services are now usually joined in one. This may suit the conveniency of the person who officiates, but is too often inconvenient and tiresome to the congregation. If this Abridgement, therefore, should ever meet with acceptance, the well-disposed Clergy, who are laudably desirous to encourage the *frequency* of divine service, may promote so great and good a purpose, by

---

contribution to the project was this preface, an abridgement of the catechism, and an abridgement of the Psalms.

[177] Matthew 6:9-15

[178] Matthew 6:7

repeating it three times on a Sunday, without so much fatigue to themselves as at present. Suppose, at Nine o'clock, at Eleven, and at One in the Evening; and by preaching no more sermons than usual, of a moderate length; and thereby accommodate a greater number of people with convenient hours.

These were general reasons for wishing and proposing an Abridgement. In attempting it we do not presume to dictate even to a single Christian: we are sensible there is a proper authority in the rulers of the Church for ordering such matters; and whenever the time shall come when it may be thought not unseasonable to revise our Liturgy, there is no doubt but every suitable improvement will be made, under the care and direction of so much learning, wisdom, and piety, in one body of men collected. Such a work as this must then be much better executed. In the mean time, this humble performance may serve to shew the practicability of shortening the service near one half, without the omission of what is essentially necessary: and we hope, moreover, that the book may be occasionally of some use to families, or private assemblies of Christians.

To give now some account of particulars. We have presumed upon this plan of Abridgement to omit the First Lesson, which is taken from the Old Testament, and retain only the Second from the New Testament; which, we apprehend, is more suitable to teach the so-much-to-be-revered doctrine of Christ, and of more immediate importance to Christians; altho' the Old Testament is allowed by all to be an accurate and concise history, and, as such, may more properly be read at home.[179]

We do not conceive it necessary for Christians to make use of more than one creed. Therefore in this Abridgement are omitted the Nicene Creed, and that of St. Athanasius. Of the Apostles' Creed we have retained the parts that are most intelligible, and most essential.

---

[179] Franklin's reverence for the doctrines of Christ and his veneration of the historical accuracy of the Old Testament stands in sharp contrast to his views as a teenager when he doubted the validity of any revelation.

And as the *Father, Son,* and *Holy Ghost,* are there confessedly and avowedly a part of the Belief,[180] it does not appear necessary, after so solemn a confession, to repeat again in the Litany, the *Son* and *Holy Ghost,* as that part of the Service is otherwise very prolix.

The Psalms, being a collection of Odes, written by different persons, it hath happened that many of them are on the same subject, and repeat the same sentiments; such as those that complain of enemies and persecutors, call upon God for protection, express a confidence therein, and thank him for it when afforded. A very great part of the book consists of repetitions of this kind, which may therefore well bear abridgement. Other parts are merely historical, repeating the mention of facts more fully narrated in the preceding books, and which, relating to the ancestors of the Jews, were more interesting to them than to us. Other parts are *local,* and allude to places of which we have no knowledge, and therefore do not affect us. Others are *personal,* relating to the particular circumstances of David or Solomon, as kings; and can therefore seldom be rehearsed with any propriety by private Christians. Others imprecate, in the most bitter terms, the vengeance of God on our Adversaries, contrary to the spirit of Christianity, which commands us to love our enemies, and to pray for those that hate us, and despitefully use us.[181] For these reasons it is to be wished, that the same liberty were, by the governors of our Church, allowed to the minister with regard to the *reading Psalms,* as is taken by the clerk, with regard to those that are to be sung, in directing the parts that he may judge most suitable to be read at the time, from the present circumstances of the congregation, or the tenor of his sermon, by saying, Let us *read* such and such parts of the Psalms named. Until this is done, our Abridgement, it is hoped, will be found to contain what may be most

---

[180] The abridged Apostle's Creed reads as:

"I Believe in God the Father Almighty, Maker of Heaven and Earth:
And in Jesus Christ, his Son, our Lord;
I believe in the Holy Ghost; The Forgiveness of Sins; and the life everlasting.
Amen." (Dashwood, 4)

[181] Matthew 5:44

generally proper to be joined in by an assembly of Christian people. The Psalms are still apportioned to the days of the month, as heretofore, though the several parts for each day are generally a full third shorter.

We humbly suppose the same service contained in this Abridgement might properly serve for all the Saints Days, Fasts, and Feasts, reading only the Epistle and Gospel appropriated to each day of the month.

The Communion is greatly abridged, on account of its great length; nevertheless, it is hoped and believed, that all those parts are retained which are material and necessary.

Infant Baptism in Churches being performed during divine service, would greatly add to the length of that service, if it were not abridged. We have ventured, therefore, to leave out the less material parts.

The Catechism, as a compendium of systematic theology, which learned divines have written folio volumes to explain, and which therefore, it may be presumed, they thought scarce intelligible without such expositions; is, perhaps, taken altogether, not so well adapted to the capacities of children as might be wished. Only those plain answers, therefore, which express our duty towards God, and our duty towards our neighbour, are retained here. The rest is recommended to their reading and serious consideration, when more years shall have ripened their understanding.

The Confirmation is here shortened.

The Commination, and all cursing of mankind, is (we think) best omitted in this Abridgement.

The form of solemnization of Matrimony is often abbreviated by the officiating Minister, at his discretion. We have selected what appear to us the material parts, and which, we humbly hope, will be deemed sufficient.

The long prayers in the service for the Visitation of the Sick, seem not so proper when the afflicted person is very weak, and in distress.

The Order for the Burial of the Dead is very solemn and moving; nevertheless, to preserve the health and lives of the living, it appeared to us that this service ought particularly to be shortened. For numbers, standing in the open air with their hats off, often in tempestuous weather, during the celebration, it's great length is not only inconvenient, but may be dangerous to the attendants. We hope, therefore, that our Abridgement of it will be approved by the Rational and Prudent.

The Thanksgiving of Women, after Child-birth being, when read, part of the Service of the day, we have also, in some measure, abridged that.

Having thus stated very briefly our motives and reasons, and our manner of proceeding in the prosecution of this work, we hope to be believed, when we declare the rectitude of our intentions. We mean not to lessen or prevent the Practice of Religion, but to honour and promote it. We acknowledge the excellency of our present Liturgy; and, though we have shortened it, we have not presumed to alter a word in the remaining Text; not even to substitute *who* for *which* in the Lord's Prayer, and elsewhere, altho' it would be more correct. We respect the characters of bishops, and other dignitaries of our Church; and with regard to the inferior clergy, we wish that they were more equally provided for, than by that odious and vexatious, as well as unjust method, of gathering tythes in kind, which creates animosities and litigations, to the interruption of the good harmony and respect which might otherwise subsist between the rectors and their parishioners.

And thus, conscious of upright meaning, we submit this Abridgement to the serious consideration of the prudent and dispassionate, and not to enthusiasts and bigots; being convinced in our own breasts, that this shortened method, or one of the same kind better executed, would further religion, increase unanimity, and occasion a more frequent attendance on the worship of God.

On a Proposed Acts to Prevent Emigration – Dec. 1773

God has given to the Beasts of the Forest and to the Birds of the Air a Right when their Subsistence fails in one Country, to migrate into another, where they can get a more comfortable Living; and shall Man be denied a Privilege enjoyed by Brutes, merely to gratify a few avaricious Landlords? Must Misery be made *permanent,* and suffered by *many* for the Emolument of One? While the Increase of Human Beings is prevented, and thousands of their Offspring stifled as it were in the Birth, that this petty Pharaoh may enjoy an *Excess* of Opulence? God commands to increase and replenish the Earth:[182] The proposed Law would forbid increasing, and confine Britons to their present Number, keeping half that Number too, in wretchedness. The Common People of Britain and of Ireland, contributed by the Taxes they paid, and by the Blood they lost, to the Success of that War, which brought into our Hands the vast unpeopled Territories of North America; a Country favoured by Heaven with all the Advantages of Soil and Climate; Germans are now pouring into it, to take Possession of it, and fill it with their Posterity; and shall Britons, and Irelanders, who have a much better Right to it, be forbidden a Share of it, and instead of enjoying there the Plenty and Happiness that might reward their Industry, be compelled to remain here in Poverty and Misery? Considerations such as these persuade me, that the proposed Law would be both unjust and inhuman.

Proposed Preamble to a Congressional Resolution on Privateering – March 23, 1776

Whereas the british Nation, through great Corruption of Manners, and extream Dissipation and Profusion both private and publick, have found all honest Resources insufficient to supply their excessive Luxury and Prodigality, and thereby have been driven to the practice of every Injustice which Avarice could dictate or rapacity execute, and wheras, not satisfied with the immence plunder of the East, obtained by sacrificing Millions of the human

---

[182] Genesis 1:28 and Genesis 9:1

Species, they have lately turned their Eyes to the West, and grudging us the peaceable enjoyment of the Fruits of our hard Labour and virtuous Industry, have for Years past been endeavouring to extort the same from us under Colour of Laws regulating trade; and have thereby actually succeeded in draining us of large sums to our great Loss and detriment, and wheras impatient to seize the whole they have at length proceeded to open Robbery, declaring by a solemn Act of Parliament that all our Estates are theirs and all our Property found upon the Sea divisible among such of their armed plunderers as shall take the same; and have even dared in the same Act to declare that all the Spoilings, Thefts, burnings of Houses and Towns, and murders of innocent People perpetrated by their wicked and inhuman Corsairs on our Coasts, previous to any War declared against us were just Actions, and shall be so deemed, contrary to several of the Commandments of God,[183] which by this Act they presume to repeal, and to all the Principles of Right and all the Ideas of Justice entertained heretofore by every other Nation Savage as well as Civilized thereby manifesting themselves to be *hostes humani generis*: And whereas it is not possible for the People of America to subsist under such continual Ravages without making some Reprisals: therefore Resolved

Proposal for the Great Seal of the United States

Moses standing on the Shore, and extending his Hand over the Sea, thereby causing the same to overwhelm Pharoah who is sitting in an open Chariot, a Crown on his Head and a Sword in his hand. Rays from a Pillar of Fire in the Clouds reaching to Moses, to express that he acts by Command of the Deity.

Motto, *Rebellion to Tyrants Is Obedience to God.*[184]

---

[183] Franklin did not hesitate to propose an act of Congress which expressed approval for the Commandments of God.

[184] Frazer argues very strongly against the validity of Franklin's proposed motto. According to Frazer, "the Bible *never* discusses political freedom," (Frazer, *Religious Beliefs*, 81 emphasis in original) and he devoted the next five pages of

his book to a refutation of the view expressed in Franklin's motto. Frazer's position echoes that of his pastor, John MacArthur who once famously wrote:

"Over the past several centuries, people have mistakenly linked democracy and political freedom to Christianity. That's why many contemporary evangelicals believe the American Revolution was completely justified, both politically and scripturally ... But such a position is contrary to the clear teachings and commands of Romans 13:1-7. So the United States was actually born out of a violation of New Testament principles, and any blessings that God has bestowed on America have come in spite of that disobedience by the Founding Fathers." MacArthur, *Why Government Can't Save You*, 6-7)

Frazer and MacArthur are mistaken on two points. First, according to British law, the colonies were made independent of British rule with the passage of the Prohibitory Act in December of 1775. This was recognized by John Adams, and he wrote of this act that:

"It is a complete dismemberment of the British empire. It throws thirteen colonies out of the royal protection, levels all distinctions, and makes us independent in spite of our supplications and entreaties." (Adams, 207)

After the passage of this act, the actions of the American colonists were the actions of an independent nation, and their war against Britain was a war of self-defense against foreign invaders.

The second error held by Frazer and MacArthur is their belief that rebellion against authority is never justified in Scripture. I have dealt with this error at length in my book *We the People: The Biblical Precedent for Popular Sovereignty* in which I pointed out that the actions of the Judges in Israel and the rebellion against Rehoboam recorded in I Kings 12 both demonstrate that God recognizes a right of the people to resist kings who become tyrannical. Additionally, Wayne Grudem addressed Franklin's motto and answered the arguments against it with three justifications. Grudem's third justification was:

"A third reason why it is sometimes right to attempt to change the existing government is that the Bible gives some examples where God raised up leaders to deliver his people from the rule of tyrants, such as Moses leading his people out of Egypt and out of the rule of Pharaoh (see Exod. 1-14). The book of Judges records many stories showing how foreign rulers oppressed the people of Israel but then God delivered them through judges whom he had appointed: 'The Lord raised up judges, who saved them out of the hand of those who plundered them' (2:16).

To Madame Brillon – March 10, 1778

People commonly speak of *Ten* Commandments. I have been taught that there are *twelve*. The *first* was, *Increase and multiply*[185] and replenish the Earth. The *twelfth* is, A new Commandment I give unto you, *that ye love one another*.[186] It seems to me that they are a little misplac'd, and that the last should have been the first. However, I never made any Difficulty about that, but was always willing to obey them both whenever I had an Opportunity. Pray tell me, my dear Casuist, whether my keeping religiously these two Commandments, tho' not in the Decalogue, may not be accepted in Compensation for my breaking so often one of the Ten, I mean that which forbids Coveting my Neighbour's Wife, and which *I confess* I break constantly, God forgive me, as often as I see or think of my lovely Confessor: And I am afraid I should never be able to repent of the Sin, even if I had the full Possession of her.

And now I am consulting you upon a Case of Conscience, I will mention the Opinion of a certain Father of the Church, which I find myself willing to adopt, tho' I am not sure it is orthodox. It is this, That the most effectual Way to get rid of a certain Temptation, is, as often as it returns, to comply with and Satisfy it. Pray instruct me how far, I may venture to practice upon this Principle?

But why should I be so scrupulous, when you have promised to absolve me of the *future!* Adieu, my charming Conductress, and

---

"In the New Testament, one author speaks of some Old Testament heroes 'who through faith conquered kingdoms' (Heb. 11:33), which meant that by military action they overthrew governments and established other ruling powers." (Grudem, 91)

[185] Genesis 1:28

[186] Mark 12:31

believe me ever, with the sincerest Esteem and Affection, Your most obedient humble Servant.[187]

To Montaudouin – March 17, 1779

I received your favour of the 4th inst. by M. David with much Pleasure; as it informed me of the well fare of Friends I love, and who are indeed beloved by every Body. I thank you for your kind Congratulations, & for the Prayer you use in my Behalf. Tho' the Form is heathen, there is a good Christian Spirit in it: and I feel myself very well disposed to be content with this World, which I have found hitherto a tolerable good one, & to wait for Heaven (which will not be the worse for keeping) as long as God pleases.[188]

To Josiah Quincy Sr. – Apr. 22, 1779

It is with great Sincerity I join you in acknowledging and admiring the Dispensations of Providence in our Favour. America has only to be thankful and to persevere. God will finish his Work, and establish their Freedom: And the Lovers of Liberty will flock, from all Parts of Europe with their Fortunes to participate with us of that Freedom, as soon as the Peace is restored.[189]

---

[187] Pangle refers to this letter in speaking of "Franklin's laxness in sexual morals," (Pangle, 70) but Walter Isaacson correctly notes that:

"Despite a reputation for lecherousness that he did little to dispel, there is no evidence of any serious sexual affair he had after his marriage to Deborah." (Isaacson, 165)

[188] It is interesting to note that, when Franklin was presented with a heathen prayer, he did not praise it as being equal to that of a Christian prayer but rather said that it was acceptable because it contained things which agreed with Christian theology. If Franklin really thought that all religions were equal as many historians claim, then he would have simply praised this prayer for its own merit rather than comparing it to Christian theology.

[189] Franklin often credited God with the success of the American Revolution.

To Thomas Viny – May, 1779

We have had a hard Struggle, but the Almighty has favour'd the just Cause, and I join most heartily with you in your Prayers that he may perfect his Work, and establish Freedom in the New World, as an Asylum for those of the Old who deserve it.— I find that many worthy and wealthy Families of this Continent are determined to remove thither and partake of it, as soon as Peace shall make the Passage safer; for which Peace I also join your Prayers most cordially. As I think the War a detestable One: and grieve much at the Mischief & Misery it occasions to many; my only Consolation being that I did all in my Power to prevent it.

To Benjamin Vaughan – Nov. 9, 1779

I did not write the Pamphlet you mention. I know nothing of it. I suppose it is the same concerning which Dr Priestly formerly ask'd me the same Question.— That for which he took it, was intitled, *A Dissertation on Liberty and Necessity, Pleasure & Pain,* with the Lines in the Title Page

Whatever is, is right. But purblind Man
Sees but a Part o' the Chain, the nearest Link;
His Eye not carrying to that equal Beam
That poises all above.——— Dryden. London: Printed mdccxxv.

It was address'd to Mr J.R. that is James Ralph, then a Youth of about my Age, and my intimate Friend, afterwards a political Writer and Historian. The purport of it was to prove the Doctrine of Fate, from the suppos'd Attributes of God; in some such Manner as this. That in creating & governing the World, as he was infinitely wise he knew what would be best; infinitely good, he must be dispos'd; and infinitely powerful, he must be able to execute it. Consequently *all is right.*— There were only a hundred Copies printed, of which I gave a few to Friends, and afterwards disliking the Piece, as conceiving it might have an ill Tendency, I burnt the rest, except one Copy the Margin of which was fill'd with manuscript Notes by *Lyons* Author of the *Infallibility of Human Judgement,* who was at that time another of my Acquaintance in London. I was not 19 Years of Age when it was written. In 1730 I wrote a Piece on the other side of the Question, which began with laying for its Foundation this Fact, *That almost all Men in all Ages and Countrys, do have at times made use of* Prayer. Thence I reasoned, that if all things are ordain'd, Prayer must among the rest be ordain'd. But as Prayer can procure no Change in Things that are ordain'd, Praying must then be useless and an Absurdity. God would therefore not ordain Praying if every thing else was ordain'd. But Praying exists; therefore all other Things are not ordain'd, &c. This Pamphlet was never printed, & the Manuscript has been long lost. The great Uncertainty I found in Metaphysical Reasonings, disgusted me, and I quitted that kind of Reading & Study, for others more satisfactory.[190]

To Richard Price – Oct. 9. 1780

I do not expect that your new Parliament will be either wiser or honester than the last. All Projects to procure an Honest one, by Place Bills, &c appear to me vain and Impracticable. The true Cure I imagine is to be found only in rendring all Places unprofitable, and the King too poor to give Bribes & Pensions. Till this is done, which can only be by a Revolution, and I think you have not Virtue enough left to procure one, your Nation will always be plundered; & obliged to pay by Taxes the Plunderers for Plundering & Ruining. Liberty & Virtue therefore join in the Call, COME OUT OF HER, MY PEOPLE![191]

I am fully of your Opinion respecting Religious Tests; but tho' the People of Massachusetts have not in their new Constitution kept quite clear of them; yet if we consider what that People were 100 Years ago, we must allow they have gone great Lengths in Liberality of Sentiment, on religious Subjects; and we may hope for

---

[190] As I mentioned previously, it is remarkable that so many historians present Franklin's *Dissertation* as if he had agreed with the contents of that pamphlet throughout his entire life. Here, Franklin directly refutes that idea and states that his *Dissertation* was a mere passing folly of his youth.

[191] Revelation 18:14

greater Degrees of Perfection when their Constitution some years hence shall be revised. If Christian Preachers had continued to teach as Christ & his Apostles did, without Salaries, and as the Quakers now do, I imagine Tests would never have existed: For I think they were invented not so much to secure Religion itself, as the Emoluments of it.— When a Religion is good, I conceive that it will support itself; and when it cannot support itself, and God does not take care to support, so that its Professors are oblig'd to call for the help of the Civil Power, 'tis a Sign, I apprehend, of its being a bad one.[192] But I shall be out of my Depth if I wade any deeper in Theology, & I will not trouble you with Politicks, nor with News which are almost as uncertain: But conclude with a heartfelt Wish, to embrace you once more, & enjoy your sweet Society in Peace, among our honest, worthy, ingenious Friends at the London.

To John Adams – Feb. 22, 1781

I received the Letter your Excellency did me the honour of writing to me the 15th Instant, respecting Bills presented to you for Acceptance, drawn by Congress in favour of N. Tracey for 10,000 £ Sterling, payable at 90 Days sight; and desiring to know if I can furnish Funds for the Payment. I have lately made a fresh & strong Application for more Money. I have not yet received a positive Answer. I have, however, two of the Christian Graces, Faith and Hope: But my Faith is only that of which the Apostle speaks, the Evidence of Things not seen. For in Truth I do not see at present how so many Bills drawn at random on our Ministers in France,

---

[192] Franklin here appears to endorse another tenet of the Baptists, for his statement regarding a religion that supports itself is identical to the position advocated by the Baptists of that day. William Fristoe, a Baptist historian of that time, wrote that:

"It has been believed by us that that Almighty Power that instituted religion will support his own cause; that in the course of divine Providence events will be overruled and the influence of grace on the hearts of the Lord's people will incline them to afford and contribute what is necessary for the support of religion, and therefore there is no need for compulsory measures." (James, 133)

Spain and Holland, are to be paid; nor that any thing but omnipotent Necessity can excuse the Imprudence of it.[193]

To Samuel Cooper – May 15, 1781

It gives me great Pleasure to learn that your new Constitution is at length settled with so great a Degree of Unanimity & general Satisfaction. It seems to me upon the whole an excellent one; and that if there are some particulars that one might have wish'd a little different, they are such as could not in the present State of things have been well obtain'd otherwise than they are, and if by Experience found inconvenient will probably be chang'd hereafter.— I would only mention at present one Article, that of Maintenance for the Clergy. It seems to me that by the Constitution the Quakers may be obliged to pay the Tax for that purpose. But as the great End in imposing it, is professedly the Promotion of Piety, Religion & Morality, and those People have found means of securing that End among themselves, without a regular Clergy, and their Teachers are not allow'd to receive Money; I should think it not right to tax them and give the Money to the Teacher of the Parish; But I imagine that in the Laws to be made for levying Parish Taxes, this Matter may be regulated to their Contentment...

Your excellent Sermon gave me abundance of Pleasure, and is much admired by several of my Friends who understand English. I purpose to get it translated & printed at Geneva at the End of a Translation of your new Constitution. Nothing could be happier than your Choice of a Text, & your Application of it. It was not necessary in New England where every body reads the Bible, and is acquainted with Scripture Phrases, that you should note the Texts from which you took them; but I have observed in England as well as in France, that Verses and Expressions taken from the sacred Writings, and not known to be such, appear very strange and

---

[193] Hebrews 11:1

awkward to some Readers; and I shall therefore in my Edition take the Liberty of marking the quoted Texts in the Margin.[194]

---

[194] The sermon that Franklin references here was a sermon preached by Samuel Cooper to which he gave the very lengthy and descriptive title of:

"A Sermon Preached Before His Excellency John Hancock, Esq; Governor, The Honourable Senate, and House of Representatives of the Commonwealth of Massachusetts, October 25th, 1780. Being the day of the Commencement of the Constitution and Inauguration of the New Government."

This was one of the most widely read sermons in America, and it presented a theme that was commonly acknowledged in our nation at that time. Cooper preached that:

"The form of government originally established in the Hebrew nation by a charter from heaven, was that of a free republic, over which God himself, in peculiar favour to that people, was pleased to preside. It consisted of three parts; a chief magistrate who was called judge or leader, such as Joshua and others, a council of seventy chosen men, and the general assemblies of the people. Of these the two last were the most essential and permanent, and the first more occasional, according to the particular circumstances of the nation. Their council or Sanhedrim, remained with but little suspension, through all the vicissitudes they experienced, till after the commencement of the christian æra. And as to the assemblies of the people, that they were frequently held by divine appointment, and considered as the fountain of civil power, which they exerted by their own decrees, or distributed into various channels as they judged most conducive to their own security, order, and happiness, is evident beyond contradiction from the sacred history. Even the law of Moses, though framed by God himself, was not imposed upon that people against their will; it was laid open before the whole congregation of Israel; they freely adopted it, and it became their law, not only by divine appointment, but by their own voluntary and express consent. Upon this account it is called in the sacred writings a covenant, compact, or mutual stipulation...

"To mention all the passages in sacred writ which prove that the Hebrew government, tho' a theocracy, was yet as to the outward part of it, a free republic, and that the sovereignty resided in the people, would be to recite a large part of its history...

"Such a constitution, twice established by the hand of heaven in that nation, so far as it respects civil and religious liberty in general, ought to be regarded as a solemn recognition from the Supreme Ruler himself of the rights of human

256

My Ink with a Little Loaf Sugar – July 11, 1781

So the pure limpid Stream &c
So when some Angel, by divine Command,
With rising Tempests shakes a guilty Land,
(Such as of late o'er pale Britannia past)
Calm and serene he drives the furious Blast,
And, pleas'd th' Almighty's Orders to perform,
Rides in the Whirlwind, and directs the Storm.

The Levee – March 1782

In the first chapter of Job we have an account of a transaction said to have arisen in the court, or at the *levée,* of the best of all possible princes, or of governments by a single person, viz. that of God himself.

At this *levée,* in which the sons of God were assembled, Satan also appeared.

It is probable the writer of that ancient book took his idea of this *levée* from those of the eastern monarchs of the age he lived in.

It is to this day usual at the *levées* of princes, to have persons assembled who are enemies to each other, who seek to obtain favor by whispering calumny and detraction, and thereby ruining those that distinguish themselves by their virtue and merit. And kings frequently ask a familiar question or two, of every one in the circle, merely to show their benignity. These circumstances are particularly exemplified in this relation.

---

nature. Abstracted from those appendages and formalities which were peculiar to the Jews, and designed to answer some particular purposes of divine Providence, it points out in general what kind of government infinite wisdom and goodness would establish among mankind." (Cooper, 634-637)

Franklin heartily agreed with Cooper and sought to have his sermon published throughout Europe as well as in America.

If a modern king, for instance, finds a person in the circle who has not lately been there, he naturally asks him how he has passed his time since he last had the pleasure of seeing him? the gentleman perhaps replies that he has been in the country to view his estates, and visit some friends. Thus Satan being asked whence he cometh? answers, "From going to and fro in the earth, and walking up and down in it." And being further asked, whether he had considered the uprightness and fidelity of the prince's servant Job, he immediately displays all the malignance of the designing courtier, by answering with another question: "Doth Job serve God for nought? Hast thou not given him immense wealth, and protected him in the possession of it? Deprive him of that, and he will curse thee to thy face." In modern phrase, Take away his places and his pensions, and your Majesty will soon find him in the opposition.

This whisper against Job had its effect. He was delivered into the power of his adversary, who deprived him of his fortune, destroyed his family, and completely ruined him.

The book of Job is called by divines a sacred poem, and with the rest of the Holy Scriptures, is understood to be written for our instruction.

What then is the instruction to be gathered from this supposed transaction?

Trust not a single person with the government of your state. For if the Deity himself, being the monarch, may for a time give way to calumny, and suffer it to operate the destruction of the best of subjects; what mischief may you not expect from such power in a mere man, though the best of men, from whom the truth is often industriously hidden, and to whom falsehood is often presented in its place, by artful, interested, and malicious courtiers?[195]

---

[195] Pangle makes the following remark on Franklin's conclusion:

"Consider the writing that is probably Franklin's most blasphemous, an allegory based on the Book of Job in which God's part is played by a king surrounded by

258

And be cautious in trusting him even with limited powers, lest sooner or later he sap and destroy those limits, and render himself absolute.

For by the disposal of places, he attaches to himself all the placeholders, with their numerous connexions, and also all the expecters and hopers of places, which will form a strong party in promoting his views. By various political engagements for the interest of neighboring states or princes, he procures their aid in establishing his own personal power. So that, through the hopes of emolument in one part of his subjects, and the fear of his resentment in the other, all opposition falls before him.

Proposed New Version of the Bible – 1782

It is now more than 170 years since the translation of our common English Bible. The language in that time is much changed, and the stile being obsolete, and thence less agreeable, is perhaps one reason why the reading of that excellent book is of late so much neglected. I have therefore thought it would be well to procure a new version, in which, preserving the sense, the turn of phrase and manner of expression should be modern. I do not pretend to have the necessary abilities for such a work myself; I throw out the hint for the consideration of the learned: and only venture to send you a few verses of the first chapter of Job, which may serve as a sample of the kind of version I would recommend.

---

flattering courtiers and the moral is that even 'the best of all possible princes' will be a tyrant if his power is unlimited." (Pangle, 260)

But there is nothing in Franklin's comment to indicate that he considered God's actions to be tyrannical or even wrong in any sense. He is merely pointing out that just as God has the authority to allow evil to come into our lives, even so an earthly monarch whom we cannot trust to have a good purpose in all his actions will also have power to bring evil upon the people over whom he rules. This is not an aspersion against God as Pangle asserts but rather an observation of fact. Every monarch has the power to allow his subjects to suffer; therefore, men, of whom none can be trusted to always have wise and good purposes for the suffering of their subjects, should not be permitted to reign as monarchs.

A.B.

Part of the First Chapter of Job Modernised.

Verse 6 And it being *levée* day in heaven, all God's nobility came to court, to present themselves before him; and Satan also appeared in the circle, as one of the ministry.

7 And God said to Satan, You have been some time absent; where was you? And Satan answered, I have been at my country-seat, and in different places visiting my friends.

8 And the Lord said unto Satan, Hast thou considered my servant Job, that there is none like him in the earth, a perfect and an upright man, one that feareth God, and escheweth evil?

8 And God said, Well, what think you of Lord Job? You see he is my best friend, a perfectly honest man, full of respect for me, and avoiding every thing that might offend me.

9 Then Satan answered the Lord, and said, Doth Job fear God for nought?

9 And Satan answered, Does your Majesty imagine that his good conduct is the effect of mere personal attachment and affection?

10 Have you not protected him, and heaped your benefits upon him, till he is grown enormously rich?

11 Try him; only withdraw your favor, turn him out of his places, and with-hold his pensions; and you will soon find him in the opposition.

To James Hutton – July 7, 1782

A Letter written by you to M. Bertin, Ministre d'Etat, containing an Account of the abominable Murders committed by some of the frontier People on the poor Moravian Indians, has given me infinite

Pain and Vexation. The Dispensations of Providence in this World puzzle my weak Reason. I cannot comprehend why cruel Men should have been permitted thus to destroy their Fellow Creatures. Some of the Indians may be suppos'd to have committed Sins, but one cannot think the little Children had committed any worthy of Death. Why has a single Man in England, who happens to love Blood, and to hate Americans; been permitted to gratify that bad Temper, by hiring German Murderers, and joining them with his own, to destroy in a continued Course of bloody Years, near 100,000 human Creatures, many of them possessed of useful Talents, Virtues and Abilities to which he has no Pretension! It is he who has furnished the Savages with Hatchets and Scalping Knives, and engages them to fall upon our defenceless Farmers, and murder them with their Wives and Children paying for their Scalps, of which the Account kept already amounts as I have heard, to near *two Thousand.* Perhaps the People of the Frontier exasperated by the Cruelties of the Indians have in their [*torn*] been induced to kill all Indians that fall into their Hands, without Distinction, so that even these horrid Murders of our poor Moravians may be laid to his Charge; And yet this Man lives, enjoys all the good Things this World can afford, and is surrounded by Flatterers, who keep even his Conscience quiet, by telling him he is the best of Princes! I wonder at this, but I cannot therefore part with the comfortable Belief of a divine Providence; and the more I see the Impossibility, from the number & Extent of his Crimes of giving equivalent Punishment to a wicked Man in this Life, the more I am convinc'd of a future State, in which all that here appears to be wrong shall be set right, all that is crooked made straight. In this Faith let you & I, my dear Friend, comfort ourselves. It is the only Comfort in the present dark Scene of Things, that is allow'd us.

To David Hartley – Oct 16, 1783

How many excellent things might have been done to promote the internal welfare of each Country; What Bridges roads canals and other usefull public works, and institutions tending to the common felicity might have been made and established with the money and men foolishly spent during the last seven centuries by our mad wars in doing one another mischief. You are near neighbours and each have very respectable qualities. Learn to be quiet and to respect each others rights. You are all Christians. One is the most Christian King, and the other defender of the faith. Manifest the propriety of these titles by your future conduct. By this says Christ shall all men know that ye are my Disciples if ye Love one another.[196] Seek peace and ensue it.[197] Adieu yours most affectionately

Remarks Concerning the Savages - 1784

The Politeness of the Savages in Conversation is indeed carried to Excess, since it does not permit them to contradict or deny the Truth of what is asserted in their Presence; By this means they indeed avoid Disputes, but then it becomes difficult to know their Minds, or what Impression you make upon them. The Missionaries who have attempted to convert them to Christianity, all complain of this as one of the great difficulties of their Mission: The Indians hear with Patience the Truths of the Gospel explain'd to them, and give their usual Tokens of Assent & Approbation: You would think they were convinc'd. No such Matter. It is mere Civility. A Suedish Minister, having assembled the Chiefs of the Saquehanah Indians, made a Sermon to them, acquainting them with the principal historical Facts on which our Religion is founded, such as the Fall of our first Parents by eating an Apple; the Coming of Christ, to repair the Mischief; his Miracles & Suffering, &c. When he had finished, an Indian Orator stood up to thank him. What you have told us, says he, is all very good. It is indeed a bad Thing to eat Apples. It is better to make them all into Cyder. We are much oblig'd by your Kindness in coming so far to tell us these Things which you have heard from your Mothers; in return I will tell you some of those we have heard from ours.[198]

---

[196] John 13:35

[197] I Peter 3:11

[198] By using the pronoun "our," Franklin again claims to be a Christian, and he correctly presents the doctrines of the fall of man and the sacrifice of Christ as the foundation of Christianity.

To Sarah Bache – Jan. 26, 1784

I wish therefore that the Cincinnati, if they must go on with their Project, would direct the Badges of their Order to be worn by their Parents instead of handing them down to their Children. It would be a good Precedent, and might have good Effects. It would also be a kind of Obedience to the fourth Commandment, in which God enjoins us to *honour* our Father and Mother, but has no where directed us to *honour* our Children.[199] And certainly no Mode of honouring those immediate Authors of our Being can be more effectual, than that of doing praiseworthy Actions, which reflect honour on those who gave us our Education; or more becoming than that of manifesting by some public Expression or Token that it is to their Instruction and Example we ascribe the Merit of those Actions.

Information for those who would Remove to America – March 9, 1784

To this may be truly added, that serious Religion under its various Denominations, is not only tolerated but respected and practised. Atheism is unknown there, Infidelity rare & secret, so that Persons may live to a great Age in that Country without having their Piety shock'd by meeting with either an Atheist or an Infidel. And the Divine Being seems to have manifested his Approbation of the mutual Forbearance and Kindness with which the different Sects treat each other, by the remarkable Prosperity with which he has been pleased to favour the whole Country.

To William Strahan – Aug. 4, 1784

But after all my dear Friend, do not imagine that I am vain enough to ascribe our Success to any superiority in any of those Points. I am too well acquainted with all the Springs and Levers of our Machine, not to see that our human means were unequal to our undertaking, and that if it had not been for the Justice of our Cause, and the consequent Interposition of Providence in which we had Faith we

---

[199] Exodus 20:12

must have been ruined. If I had ever before been an Atheist I should now have been convinced of the Being and Government of a Deity. It is he who abases the Proud and favors the Humble![200] May we never forget his Goodness to us, and may our future Conduct manifest our Gratitude.[201]

To John Calder – Aug. 21, 1784

I agreed with you in Sentiments concerning the Old Testament, and thought the Clause in our Constitution, which required the Members of Assembly to declare their belief that the whole of it was given by divine Inspiration, had better have been omitted. That I had opposed the Clause but being overpower'd by Numbers, and fearing might in future times be grafted on it, I Prevailed to have the additional Clause that no further or more extended Profession of Faith should ever be exacted. I observ'd to you, too, that the Evil of it was the less, as no Inhabitant, nor any Officer of Government except the Members of Assembly, were oblig'd to make that Declaration.

So much for that Letter. To which I may now add, that there are several Things in the old Testament impossible to be given by divine Inspiration, such as the Approbation ascrib'd to the Angel of the Lord, of that abominably wicked and detestable Action of Jael the Wife of Heber the Kenite. If the rest of the Book were like that, I should rather suppose it given by Inspiration from another Quarter, and renounce the whole.[202]

---

[200] Luke 18:14

[201] It is apparent from Franklin's request for prayer at the Constitutional Convention that he followed his own advice and never forgot that America owed her very existence to the grace of God.

[202] Frazer's response to this letter is typical of modern scholars. He wrote:

"At times, Franklin was overtly critical of Scripture ... In a letter to Priestley, Franklin agreed with the minister that 'there are several things in the Old Testament, impossible to be given by *divine* inspiration.' After giving a specific example from Judges 4, Franklin added, 'If the rest of the Book were like that, I should rather suppose it given by Inspiration from another Quarter, and

264

To William Temple Franklin – Aug. 25, 1784

The Report is publish'd and makes a great deal of Talk. Every body agrees that it is well written; but many wonder at the Force of Imagination describ'd in it, as occasioning Convulsions, &c. and some fear that Consequences may be drawn from it by Infidels to weaken our Faith in some of the Miracles of the New Testament. I send you two more Copies. You would do well to give one to the French Ambassador, if he has not had it. Some think it will put an End to Mesmerism. But there is a wonderful deal of Credulity in the

---

renounce the whole.' In other words, his inclination was to consider portions of the Bible that did not conform to his reason to be satanic in origin." (Frazer, *Religious Beliefs*, 141 emphasis his)

And on page 18 of the same book, Frazer identified this flaw in Franklin as evidence that he was not a true Christian. There, Frazer wrote:

"Christians believed that the whole Bible was divinely inspired, was God's special revelation of Himself, and was the only infallible authority in all matters that it treated."

What Frazer did not mention in his book is that he is just as guilty of this as Franklin was, for he uses a translation of the Bible which teaches that Mark 16:9-20 and John 7:53-8:11 were not inspired by God. If Frazer were to present his Bible to the theologians of the eighteenth century, he would have been proclaimed just as much of a heretic as he claims that Franklin was, and if he were to present that same Bible to the theologians of the thirteenth century he could very well be in danger of losing his life.

Instead of drawing aspersions against Franklin for denying the inspiration of a few obscure verses of the Old Testament, Frazer should have noted that Franklin also proclaimed his belief that all of the rest of the Old Testament was directly inspired by God. It is only if the rest of the book were like the story of Jael, that Franklin would think it inspired by Satan instead of God, and it is evident from other comments that Franklin made in veneration of various Old Testament teachings that he did not see the rest of it as similar to the account in Judges 4.

265

World, and Deceptions as absurd, have supported themselves for Ages. [203]

To Benjamin Vaughan – March 1785

Among the Pamphlets you lately sent me, was one intitled *Thoughts on Executive Justice*. In return for that I send you a French one on the same Subject, *Observations concernant l'Execution de l'Article II de la Declaration sur le Vol*. They are both address'd to the Judges, but written as you will see in a very different Spirit. The English Author is for hanging all Thieves. The Frenchman is for proportioning punishments to Offences.

If we really believe, as we profess to believe, that the Law of Moses was the Law of God, the Dictate of divine Wisdom infinitely superior to human, on what Principles do we ordain Death at the Punishment of an Offense, which according to that Law was to be punish'd by a Restitution of Fourfold? To put a Man to Death for an Offence which does not deserve Death, is it not Murder? [204]

---

[203] The report referenced here is the *Secret Report on Mesmerism* which was prepared for the King of France by Franklin and several others who had investigated the claims of animal magnetism made by Franz Mesmer. The important thing to note from this letter, however, is that Franklin here claims to have faith in the miracles of the New Testament and to be concerned that his report might lessen that faith in others.

[204] Lemay wrote of Franklin's beliefs regarding the Bible that he was "no believer in the Bible," (Lemay, 3:8) and Morgan similarly wrote that "he never came to accept the Bible as a divine revelation." (Morgan, 19) But in this letter, we not only find Franklin praising the Law of Moses as a divinely inspired revelation but also claiming that it is "infinitely superior" to human reasoning.

This letter also reveals that Franklin thought that human laws should be subordinate to the laws of God. This demonstrates that he agreed with the sermon by Samuel Cooper which we looked at previously.

To Richard Price – May 18, 1785

My Nephew, Mr. Williams, will have the honour of delivering you this Line. It is to request from you a List of a few good Books to the Value of about Twenty-five Pounds, such as are most proper to inculcate Principles of sound Religion and just Government. A new Town in the State of Massachusetts, having done me the honour of naming itself after me, and proposing to build a Steeple to their Meeting House if I would give them a Bell, I have advis'd the sparing themselves the Expence of a Steeple at present, and that they would accept of Books instead of a Bell, Sense being preferable to Sound. These are therefore intended as the Commencement of a little Parochial Library, for the Use of a Society of intelligent respectable Farmers, such as our Country People generally consist of. Besides your own Works I would only mention, on the Recommendation of my Sister, Stennet's Discourses on personal Religion, which may be one Book of the Number, if you know it and approve of it.[205]

To George Whatley – May 23, 1785

You see I have some reason to wish that in a future State I may not only be *as well as I was,* but a little better. And I hope it: For I too, with your Poet, *trust in God.* And when I observe that there is great Frugality as well as Wisdom in his Works, since he has been evidently sparing both of Labour and Materials; for by the various

---

[205] Remsburg cited this letter as evidence that Franklin denied Christianity. He wrote:

"The fact that Franklin selected a man who denied the infallibility of the Bible and the divinity of Christ, to make a collection of books 'to inculcate principles of sound religion,' to say nothing of his expressed preference of sense to sound, is of itself sufficient to prove his disbelief in popular Christianity." (Remsburg, 169)

What Remsburg failed to point out, however, is that while Price did recommend several books by unitarians, his list also included the works of trinitarians such as Isaac Barrow, Thomas Ridgeley, Samuel Stennett, Isaac Backus, Isaac Watts, David Brainerd, Joseph Bellamy, Jonathan Edwards, and Jonathan Dickinson. (Thorpe, 109)

wonderful Inventions of Propagation he has provided for the continual peopling his World with Plants and Animals without being at the Trouble of repeated new Creations; and by the natural Reduction of compound Substances to their original Elements, capable of being employ'd in new Compositions, he has presented the Necessity of creating new Matter; for that the Earth, Water, Air and perhaps fire which, being compounded, from Wood, do when the Wood is dissolved return and again become Air, Earth, Fire and Water: I say that when I see nothing annihilated, and not even a Drop of Water wasted, I cannot suspect the Annihilation of Souls, or believe that he will suffer the daily Waste of Millions of Minds ready made that now exist, and put himself to the continual Trouble of making new ones. Thus finding myself to exist in the World, I believe I shall in some Shape or other always exist: And with all the Inconveniences human Life is liable to, I shall not object to a new edition of mine; hoping however that the Errata of the last may be corrected.

To Granville Sharp – July 5, 1785

The Liturgy you mention, was an Abridgement of the Prayers made by a noble Lord of my Acquaintance, who requested me to assist him by taking the rest of the Book, viz. the Catechism and the reading and singing Psalms. These I abridg'd, by retaining of the Catechism only the two Questions, *What is your Duty to God? What is your Duty to your Neighbour?* with their Answers. The Psalms were much contracted by leaving out the Repetitions (of which I found more than I could have imagined) and the Imprecations, which appear'd not to suit well the Christian Doctrine of Forgiveness of Injuries, and doing good to Enemies. The Book was printed for Wilkie in Paul's Churchyard, but never much notic'd. Some were given away, very few sold, and I suppose the Bulk became Waste Paper. In the Prayers so much was retrench'd that Approbation would hardly be expected; but I think with you, a moderate Abridgement might not only be useful but generally acceptable.[206]

---

[206] Franklin has often been criticized for his abridgement of the liturgy, but it should be remembered that there were many Christians who agreed with him

268

that the liturgy needed to be shortened. Granville Sharp is an excellent example of this. He was an ardent defender of Christianity, and his response to Franklin's abridged liturgy demonstrates that Franklin's efforts were not contrary to Christianity. Here is Sharp's response to Franklin's letter:

"My best thanks are due to you for the candid information you have given me concerning the abbreviated Liturgy. Your directions enabled me to procure the … The Character you gave me of it seems perfectly just: it is certainly too much retrenched; and I am very happy to have the concurrence of your judgment in favour of a more "moderate abridgement." I must also remark further that the Repetition of the book of Psalms are of a very different nature from the objectionable tautology too [often] found in Liturgies of mere human composition. The Psalms are Odes, and as such are certainly intended to be chanted, or set to Musick for the public Service of the Temple, so that the Repetitions therein are most commonly of the same nature as that kind of poetical recapitulation which in other Odes is called "the burthen of the Song," and which is intended to have its proper effect by being repeated in Chorus by the M of Worshippers. But these Odes are also highly Prophetic: revealing to us many of the most important purposese of Divine Providence to the end of the World, with assurances of a glorious interference at length in behalf of popular Rights, Justice, and Peace. And therefore as a Lover of Liberty, jealous for the natural Rights of Man I chant my Hebrew Psalter to my Harp in the exultation of Hope that the happy times perhaps are not far distant, but always with confidence that they will surely come! for the predictions already fulfilled insure to us by their clear accomplishment the literal completion also of the other glorious changes which the World has not yet seen, such as the universal establishement of Truth, Justice, and Peace even on a general vindication of the Poor; the entire destruction of all wicked and arbitrary Governments with their standing Armies; nay and exemplary vengeance also … wicked individuals in this world. But indeed, these predictions of Retribution are liable to be mistaken for "imprecations," which even to many worthy persons have "appeared not to suit well the Christian doctrine of forgiveness of injuries, and doing good to enemies," but a more attentive examination must convince them that these supposed imprecations are really predictions of the Holy Spirit against Judas and other persecutors of Christ as in the 35, 69, 70, and 109th Psalms, and against the Enemies of Religion in general in the 68, 72, 75, 76, 94, 144 and 149. Psalms &ca &ca so that the Psalms cannot be curtailed without risque of losing not only the sublime element of the poetry but also the Prophetic information with which they abound." (Hale, 367-369)

Convention Speech Proposing Prayers – Jun 28, 1787

The small Progress we have made after 4 or 5 Weeks close Attendance and continual Reasonings with each other, our different Sentiments on almost every Question, several of the last producing as many *Noes* as *Ayes,* is methinks a melancholy Proof of the Imperfection of the Human Understanding. We indeed seem to feel our own Want of political Wisdom, since we have been running all about in search of it. We have gone back to ancient History for Models of Government, and examin'd the different Forms of those Republicks, which, having been originally form'd with the Seeds of their own Dissolution, now no longer exist. And we have view'd modern States all round Europe, but find none of their Constitutions suitable to our Circumstances.

In this Situation of this Assembly, groping, as it were, in the dark, to find Political Truth, and scarce able to distinguish it when presented to us, how has it happened, Sir, that we have not, hitherto once thought of humbly applying to the Father of Lights to illuminate our Understandings? In the Beginning of the Contest with Britain, when we were sensible of Danger, we had daily Prayers in this Room for the Divine Protection! Our Prayers, Sir, were heard; and they were graciously answered. All of us, who were engag'd in the Struggle, must have observ'd frequent Instances of a Superintending Providence in our Favour. To that kind Providence we owe this happy Opportunity of Consulting in Peace on the Means of establishing our future national Felicity. And have we now forgotten that powerful Friend? or do we imagine we no longer need its Assistance? I have lived, Sir, a long time; and the longer I live, the more convincing Proofs I see of this Truth, *That GOD governs in the Affairs of Men!* And if a Sparrow cannot fall to the Ground without his Notice,[207] is it probable that an Empire can rise without his Aid? We have been assured, Sir, in the Sacred Writings, that "except the Lord build the House, they labor in vain that build it."[208]

---

[207] Matthew 10:29

[208] Psalm 127:1

I firmly believe this; and I also believe that without his concurring Aid, we shall succeed in this political Building no better than the Builders of Babel:[209] We shall be divided by our little partial local Interests, our Projects will be confounded and we ourselves shall become a Reproach and a Byeword down to future Ages. And what is worse, Mankind may hereafter, from this unfortunate Instance, despair of establishing Government by human Wisdom, and leave it to Chance, War and Conquest. I therefore beg leave to move,

That henceforth Prayers, imploring the Assistance of Heaven, and its Blessing on our Deliberations, be held in this Assembly every Morning before we proceed to Business; and that one or more of the Clergy of this City be requested to officiate in that Service.[210]

Speech before the Constitutional Convention – August 10, 1787

We should remember the character which the Scripture requires in rulers, that they should be men hating covetousness.[211]

---

[209] Genesis 11:1-9

[210] Most historians focus on the fact that Franklin's proposal was not accepted by the convention, but it is important for our study to note that it was Franklin who made the proposal in the first place.

[211] There are many who argue that there was no significant reference to the Bible during the Constitutional Convention. Frazer, for example, wrote that:

"There was precious little reference to God or the Bible in the Constitutional debates. There were a few casual references to Scripture, but they were offered only to illustrate points already made, not as a basis for principle – despite the Bible's supposed role as the foundation for the whole document and all its parts." (Frazer, *Religious Beliefs*, 219)

Claims such as this one are more than a little deceptive for the simple reason that we do not have a complete record of the debates of the Constitutional Convention. All that we have are a few collections of abbreviated notes and a random sampling of pre-written speeches. The most comprehensive record available comes from the notes of James Madison, but even this account is filled with short summarizations of lengthy speeches and debates. In fact, there is one place in which Madison wrote a single paragraph about a speech given by Mr.

271

To Alexander Small – Sept. 28, 1787

I have made no Attempt to introduce the Form of Prayer here, which you and good Mrs. Baldwin do me the Honour to approve. The Things of *this* World take up too much of my Time, of which indeed I have too little left to undertake any thing like a Reformation in Matters of Religion. When we can sow good Seed we should however do it, and wait, when we can do no better, with Patience Nature's Time for their Sprouting. Some lie many Years in the Ground, and at length certain favourable Seasons or Circumstances bring them forth with vigorous Shoots and plentiful Productions.

Martin and then said, "This was the substance of a speech which was continued more than three hours." (Madison, 249)

The deception of this claim is further emphasized by the fact that there is also no mention of Locke, Montesquieu, Sydney or Harrington and only two passing references to Blackstone in Madison's notes, and yet it is common to hear the same historians claim that the Constitution was founded on the works of these men. In reality, Madison made few references to any of the sources which may have been cited in the various debates. His purpose appears to have been to keep a record of the bare essence of each day's proceedings for his own personal benefit. He made no attempt to preserve an accurate account for posterity.

In light of these facts it is very significant to note that Madison recorded Franklin's quotation of Exodus 18:21. In direct contradiction to Frazer's claim, this reference to Scripture played a major role in the debates regarding the Constitution. Franklin quoted this passage in response to a proposal by Mr. Pinckney that the ownership of a significant amount of property be one of the requirements for those seeking to represent their state in the House of Representatives. This proposal had been debated unsuccessfully for several days when Franklin finally stood up and presented his biblical argument against it. Madison records that after Franklin finished speaking:

"The motion of Mr. Pinckney was rejected by so general a no, that the states were not called." (Madison, 403)

Franklin's reference to the teachings of Scripture was the deciding factor in the decision to reject a property requirement for Representatives.

To the Editor of the Federal Gazette – April 8, 1788

A zealous Advocate for the propos'd federal Constitution, in a certain public Assembly, said, that the Repugnance of a great part of Mankind to good Government, was such, that he believ'd if an Angel from Heaven were to bring down a Constitution, form'd there for our Use, it would nevertheless meet with violent Opposition. He was reprov'd for the suppos'd Extravagance of the Sentiments; and he did not justify it. Probably it might have not immediately occur'd to him, that the Experiment had actually been try'd, and that the Event was rewarded in the most faithful of all Histories, the Holy Bible; otherwise he might, as it seems to me, have supported his Opinion by that unexceptionable Authority.[212]

The Supreme Being had been pleased to nourish up a single Family, by continu'd Acts of his attentive Providence, 'till it became a great People; and having rescued them from Bondage by many Miracles perform'd by his Servant Moses, he personally deliver'd to that chosen Servant, in the Presence of the whole Nation, a Constitution, and Code of Laws for their Observance, accompained and sanction'd with Promises of great Rewards, and Threats of severe Punishments, as the Consequence of their Obedience or Disobedience.

This Constitution, tho' the Deity himself was to be at its Head, and it is therefore call'd by Political Writers a Theocracy, could not be carried into Execution but by the Means of his Ministers, Aaron and his Sons were therefore commission'd to be, with Moses, the first establish'd Ministry of the new Government.

One would have thought that this Appointment of Men, who had distinguish'd themselves in procuring the Liberty of their Nation, and had hazarded their Lives in openly opposing the Will of a powerful Monarch, who would have retain'd that Nation in Slavery, might have been an Appointment acceptable to a grateful People; and that a Constitution fram'd for them by the Deity himself, might

---

[212] Once again, Franklin states his praise for the Bible. In this instance, he refers to it as the most accurate history book ever written.

on that Account have been secure of an universal welcome Reception: yet there were, in every one of the thirteen Tribes, some discontented restless Spirits, who were continually exciting them to reject the propos'd new Government; and this from various Motives. Many still retain'd an Affection for Egypt, the Land of their Nativity; and these whenever they felt any Inconvenience or Hardship, tho' the natural and unavoidable Effect of their Change of Situation, exclaim'd against their Leaders as the Authors of their Trouble, and were not only for returning into Egypt, but for Stoning their Deliverers.

Numbers, ch. XI [torn]

Those inclin'd to Idolatry, were displeas'd that their Golden Calf was destroy'd. Many of the Chiefs thought the new Constitution might be injurious to their particular Interests, that the profitable Places would be engross'd by the Families and Friends of Moses and Aaron, and others equally well-born excluded.

Numbers, ch. XVI, 1.3.

And they gathered themselves together against Moses and against Aaron, and said unto them, Ye take too much upon you, seeing all the Congregation are holy, every one of them, wherefore then lift ye up yourselves above the Congregation? In Josephus, and the Talmud, we learn some Particulars, not so fully narrated in the Scripture. We are there told that Corah was ambitious of the Priesthood, and offended that it was conferred on Aaron, and this as he said, by the Authority of Moses only, without the Consent of the People. He accus'd Moses of having by various Artifices fraudulently obtain'd the Government, and depriv'd the People of their Liberties; and of Conspiring with Aaron to perpetuate the Tyranny in their Family. Thus tho' Corah's real Motive was the supplanting of Aaron, he persuaded the People that he meant only the Public Good; and they mov'd by his Insinuations, began to cry out, "Let us maintain the common Liberty of our respective Tribes; we have freed ourselves from the Slavery impos'd on us by the Egyptians, and shall we now suffer ourselves to be made Slaves by

Moses? If we must have a Master, it were better to return to Pharaoh, who at least fed us with Bread and Onions, than to serve this new Tyrant, who by his Operations has often brought us into Danger of Famine." Then they call'd in question the Reality of his Conferences with God, and objected the Privacy of the Meetings, and the preventing any of the People from being present at the Colloquies, or even approaching the Place, as Grounds of great Suspicion. They accused Moses also of Peculation, as embezzeling Part of the Golden Spoons and the Silves Chargers that the Princes had offer'd at the Dedication of the Altar,

Numb. ch. VII.

and the Offerings of Gold by the common People,

Exod. ch. XXXV. 22.

as well as most of the Poll-Tax;

Numb. ch. III. and Exod. ch. XXX.

and Aaron they accus'd of pocketing much of the Gold of which he pretended to have made a molten Calf. Besides Peculation, they charg'd Moses with Ambition; to gratify which Passion, he had, they said, deceiv'd the People, by promising to bring them to a Land flowing with Milk and Honey, instead of doing which, he had brought them from such a Land; and that he though light of all this Mischief provided he could make himself an absolute Prince.

Numb. ch. XVI. v. 13. Is it a [torn] that thou had brought us up out of a Land flowing with Milk and Honey [torn] Wilderness thyself altogether a Prince over us?

That to support the new Dignity with Splendor in his Family, the partial Poll-Tax already levied and given to Aaron,

Numb. ch. III.

was to be follow'd by a general one,

Exod. ch. XXX.

which would probably be augmented from time to time, if he were suffered to go on promulgating new Laws on pretence of new occasional Revelations of the divine Will, 'till their whole Fortunes were devour'd by that Aristocracy.

Moses deny'd the Charge of Peculation; and his Accusers were destitute of Proofs to support it; tho' Facts, if real, are in their Nature capable of Proof. "I have not, said he (with holy Confidence in the Presence of his God) I have not taken from this People the Value of an Ass, nor done them any other Injury. But his Enemies had made the Charge, and with some Success among the Populace, for no kind of Accusation is so readily made, or easily believ'd, by Knaves, as the Accusation of Knavery.

In fine, no less than two hundred and fifty of the principal Men, "famous in the Congregation, Men of Renown,

Numb. ch. XVI

heading and exciting the Mob, work'd them up to such a Pitch of Frenzy, that they called out Stone 'em, Stone 'em, and thereby secure our Liberties; and let us chuse other Captains that may lead us back into Egypt in case we do not succeed in reducing the Canaanites.

On the whole it appear, that the Israelites were a People jealous of their newly-acquired Liberty, which Jealousy was in itself no Fault; but, that when they suffer'd it to be work'd upon by artful Men, pretending Public Good, with nothing really in view but private Interest, they were led to oppose the Establishment of the New Constitution, whereby they brought upon themselves much Inconvenience and Misfortune. It appears farther from the same inestimable History, that when, after many Ages, that Constitution was become old and much abus'd, and an Amendment of it was propos'd, the Populace, as they had accus'd Moses of the Ambition of making himself a Prince, and cry'd out Stone him, stone him, so, excited by their High Priests and Scribes, they exclaim'd against the Messiah,[213] that he aim'd at becoming King of the Jews, and cry'd out Crucify him, Crucify him, From all which we may gather, that popular Opposition to a public Measure is no Proof of its Impropriety, even tho' the Opposition be excited and headed by Men of Distinction.

To conclude, I beg I may not be understood to infer, that our general Convention was divinely inspired when it form'd the new federal Constitution, merely because that Constitution has been unreasonably and vehemently opposed; yet I must own I have so much Faith in the general Government of the World by Providence, that I can hardly conceive a Transaction of such momentous Importance to the Welfare of Millions now existing, and to exist in the Posterity of a great Nation, should be suffered to pass without being in some degree influenc'd, guided and governed by that omnipotent, omnipresent and beneficent Ruler, in whom all inferior Spirits live and move and have their Being.[214]

To Benjamin Vaughan – Oct. 24, 1788

Remember me affectionately to good Dr. Price and to the honest heretic Dr. Priestly. I do not call him honest by way of distinction; for I think all the heretics I have known have been virtuous men. They have the virtue of fortitude or they would not venture to own their heresy; and they cannot afford to be deficient in any of the other virtues, as that would give advantage to their many enemies; and they have not like orthodox sinners, such a number of friends to excuse or justify them. Do not, however mistake me. It is not to my

---

[213] Here Franklin refers to Jesus as the Messiah.

[214] This essay stands as further evidence of Franklin's agreement with the sermon that Samuel Cooper preached in 1780.

good friend's heresy that I impute his honesty. On the contrary, 'tis his honesty that has brought upon him the character of heretic.[215]

To Ezra Stiles – March 9, 1790

You desire to know something of my Religion. *It is the first time I have been questioned upon it*: But I do not take your Curiosity amiss, and shall endeavour in a few Words to gratify it. Here is my Creed: I believe in one God, Creator of the Universe. That He governs it by his Providence. That he ought to be worshipped. That the most acceptable Service we can render to him, is doing Good to his other Children. That the Soul of Man is immortal, and will be treated with Justice in another Life respecting its Conduct in this. These I take to be the fundamental Principles of all sound Religion, and I regard them as you do, in whatever Sect I meet with them.[216]

---

[215] The last two sentences of this paragraph reveal that Franklin may not have approved of the heresies of Price and Priestly as much as he approved of their boldness in defending those heresies.

[216] Most of the criticisms of the creed which Franklin presents here are merely arguments from silence. Franklin's creed is condemned because it does not say everything that various authors think it should say in order to qualify as a Christian creed. But if we limit our judgment to what Franklin actually said instead of speculating about why he did not say other things, we can see that his creed consisted of several true statements. It is true that:

- There is one God (Deuteronomy 6:4)
- He created the universe (Genesis 1:1)
- He governs by His providence (Psalm 22:28)
- He ought to be worshiped (Psalm 29:2)
- We serve Him by serving others (Matthew 25:40)
- The soul of man is immortal (Matthew 25:46)
- We are judged according to our conduct (I Corinthians 3:11-15)

Everything that Franklin chose to place in his creed is true and scriptural. The fact that he did not include other statements which are also true and scriptural does not mean that he denied the truth of those additional statements.

The criticisms of Franklin's creed can be compared to the fact that the Nicene Creed does not mention that Christ was born of a virgin nor that He shed His

As to Jesus of Nazareth,[217] my Opinion of whom you particularly desire, I think the System of Morals and his Religion as he left them to us, the best the World ever saw, or is likely to see; but I apprehend it has received various corrupting Changes, and I have with most of the present Dissenters in England, some Doubts as to

---

blood for our sins nor that the Scriptures are inerrant. Do these glaring absences mean that the Council of Nicea denied these truths? Of course not. We do not know exactly why these things were left out of their creed, but the simple fact that they were left out does not in any way imply that they were rejected as false. The same can be said for the creed of Benjamin Franklin. We do not know why he chose to list the items that he did nor why he chose not to list other items, but it is very wrong to conclude that he was not a Christian simply because he did not mention some things in this particular place which another man might have mentioned.

[217] Frazer has latched onto Franklin's use of the term "Jesus of Nazareth" in this letter as evidence of Franklin's rejection of Christianity. In his book, he writes that:

"Franklin referred to 'Jesus of *Nazareth*,' which was a common method used to emphasize His mere humanity." (Frazer, *Religious Beliefs*, 149. Emphasis his)

And in his lectures on the founders, Frazer often follows his quotation of this letter with this statement:

"Now, first of all, I want to point out 'Jesus of Nazareth.' That was a way of emphasizing the humanity of Jesus. They didn't talk about Jesus Christ. They didn't talk about Christ. It was just Jesus or Jesus of Nazareth to emphasize His humanity." (Frazer, "One Nation," 34:00)

What Frazer has neglected to point out, however, is that Franklin was answering Stiles in the same language that was used in order to ask the question. Stiles wrote to Franklin, "I wish to know the Opinion of my venerable Friend concerning JESUS of Nazareth." (Dexter, 387) And Franklin responded with, "As to Jesus of Nazareth, my Opinion of whom you particularly desire..." There is no attempt here to avoid using the name of Christ, and indeed, such an attempt would be out of character for Franklin who, as we have seen, often referred to Jesus with such titles as Christ, Lord, Messiah, and Savior.

his Divinity:[218] tho' it is a Question I do not dogmatise upon, having never studied it, and think it needless to busy myself with it now, when I expect soon an Opportunity of knowing the Truth with less Trouble. I see no harm however in its being believed, if that Belief has the good Consequence as probably it has, of making his Doctrines more respected and better observed, especially as I do not perceive that the Supreme takes it amiss, by distinguishing the Believers, in his Government of the World, with any particular Marks of his Displeasure. I shall only add respecting myself, that having experienced the Goodness of that Being, in conducting me prosperously thro' a long Life, I have no doubt of its Continuance in the next, tho' without the smallest Conceit of meriting such Goodness. My Sentiments in this Head you will see in the Copy of an old Letter enclosed, which I wrote in answer to one from a zealous Religionist whom I had relieved in a paralitic Case by Electricity, and who being afraid I should grow proud upon it, sent me his serious, tho' rather impertinent, Cautions. I send you also the Copy of another Letter, which will shew something of my Disposition relating to Religion. With great and sincere Esteem and Affection, I am, Dear Sir, Your obliged old Friend and most obedient humble Servant

---

[218] Frazer also wrote that:

"Expressing 'some doubts' to someone who believed was the polite eighteenth-century way of saying that one did not share the belief." (Frazer, *Religious Beliefs*, 149)

But if that is the case, then I find myself wondering how someone in the eighteenth-century would express himself if he really did have some doubts about a particular belief. Frazer did not provide any consideration for that question in his book. After reading all that Franklin wrote about Jesus including the numerous examples of him referring to Jesus in terms which could only apply to God, I am of the opinion that Franklin did believe in the deity of Christ, and that he merely began having doubts about that belief after many years of association with unitarians. But even if he did come to deny the Trinity by the end of his life, that would still leave us with the question of whether such a denial would condemn him to an eternity in hell. I have provided an answer to that question in the appendix, and I trust that you will take the time to give it your full consideration.

280

Appendix

What is it that makes an individual a Christian? This simple question has been asked and answered alternatively for nearly two millennia, and, in recent years, it has been brought once again to the forefront of academic thought by a book on the founders of America by historian Gregg Frazer who postulated a list of ten beliefs which an individual must accept in order to be of the Christian faith. (Frazer, *Religious Beliefs,* 18-19) How one answers this question will have profound implications in his life, his ministry and his future estate. It is imperative that every individual come to a realization of the minimal beliefs with which he must agree in order to obtain salvation.

To truly understand the faith by which an individual becomes a Christian, it is necessary to consider Christianity not as a movement within Western culture but rather as a specific religion in history. In an article for the Harvard Theological Journal, B. B. Warfield once wrote that: "Clearly, Christianity being a historical religion, its content can be determined only on historical grounds." Warfield then cited H. H. Went as coming to the same conclusion when he wrote that the Christian religion "is a historically given religion" and that we must determine its essence "by such an objective historical examination as we should give it were we dealing with the determination of the essence of some other historical religion." (Warfield, 482)

To obtain an accurate definition of Christianity, therefore, it is necessary to consider the original usage of that term as recorded in the Book of Acts. In that portion of Scripture, we read that "the disciples were called Christians first in Antioch," (Acts 11:26) and from this we can see that the name of Christian was given to those who were in another place called "the disciples of the Lord." (Acts 9:1) This, however, is not to be understood as a reference to the original twelve disciples only, for none of the original twelve were in Antioch at this time, and further, it is stated earlier in the Scriptures that the number of disciples on the morning of Pentecost was "about an hundred and twenty." (Acts 1:15) The proper understanding of which individuals were called Christians in Antioch can be seen in the phrase which precedes that statement. Just before we are told that the disciples were called Christians, we are informed that Paul and Barnabas traveled to that city and "assembled themselves with the church." It was thus the members of the church that are here said to have been previously known as disciples and which were, from then on, known among the heathen as Christians.

Consideration must now be given to the means by which these disciples became members of the church. This is also explained in the Book of Acts where we read that "the Lord added to the church daily such as should be saved." (Acts 2:47) The means of this salvation by which individuals are made Christians and added to the church is stated in another place to be "the gospel of Christ" (Romans 1:16) which is clearly defined in Paul's first letter to the Corinthians.

> Moreover, brethren, I declare unto you the gospel which I preached unto you, which also ye have received, and wherein ye stand; By which also ye are saved, if ye keep in memory what I preached unto you, unless ye have believed in vain. For I delivered unto you first of all that which I also received, how that Christ died for our sins according to the scriptures; And that he was buried, and that he rose again the third day according to the scriptures.
> (I Corinthians 15:1-4)

This gospel, or good news, is the means by which an individual is able to become a Christian, but he must first believe it to be true as is stated in the Epistle to the Hebrews.

> For unto us was the gospel preached, as well as unto them: but the word preached did not profit them, not being mixed with faith in them that heard it.
> (Hebrews 4:2)

It is for this reason that we read in the Epistle to the Romans that this gospel is "the power of God unto salvation to every one that believeth" (Romans 1:16) and not simply to everyone regardless of his belief. Of those who refuse to believe this gospel, the Scriptures tell us that the Lord will come "in flaming fire taking vengeance on them that know not God, and that obey not the gospel of our Lord Jesus Christ." (II Thessalonians 1:8) But all of those who believe are promised salvation by which they are made members of the church, disciples of Christ and Christians in the purest meaning of the word.

This brief survey of the New Testament teaching on salvation settles the historical foundation of Christianity upon the belief in the death, burial and resurrection of Jesus Christ, but that is not how the religion of Christ has always been viewed. In the early part of the fourth century, Emperor Constantine assembled at Nicea the first ecumenical council of the Catholic Church in order to address the heresy of Arianism. Athanasius wrote of this council that:

> Heretics have assembled together with the Emperor
> Constantius, so that he, by alleging the authority of
> the bishops, may exercise his power against
> whomsoever he will, and while he persecutes may yet
> avoid the name of persecutor. (Jurgens, 326)

Of course, the council decided against the Arians, but Athanasius' fear of sanctioning persecution was fully realized, for in the decision of the Council of Nicea is found the first departure from the historical definition of Christianity and, consequently, the first official denial of the title of "Christian" on grounds other than the gospel.

The decisions of the Council of Nicea were set forth to the public in the form of a creed, which has come to be known as the Nicene Creed, a list of twenty canons and a synodal letter which was published throughout the churches. Both the Nicene Creed and the synodal letter pronounce a condemnation of anathema against individuals who reject a particular belief in regards to the Trinity.

Here is the text of the creed in which this anathema was first pronounced:

> We believe in one God, the Father Almighty, maker of all things visible and invisible; and in one Lord Jesus Christ, the Son of God, the only-begotten of his Father, of the substance of the Father, God of God, Light of Light, very God of very God, begotten (γεννηθέντα), not made, being of one substance (ὁμοούσιον, consubstantialem) with the Father. By whom all things were made, both which be in heaven and in earth. Who for us men and for our salvation came down [from heaven] and was incarnate and was made man. He suffered and the third day he rose again, and ascended into heaven. And he shall come again to judge both the quick and the dead. And [we believe] in the Holy Ghost. And whosoever shall say that there was a time when the Son of God was not (ἦν ποτε ὅτε οὐκ ἦν), or that before he was begotten he was not, or that he was made of things that were not, or that he is of a different substance or essence [from the Father] or that he is a creature, or subject to change or conversion — all that so say, the Catholic and Apostolic Church anathematizes them.
> (Percival, 3)

According to this creed, anyone who suggests that Colossians 1:15 and Revelation 3:14 could be viewed as saying that Christ was created by God; and then, as God and with God, He created everything else – anyone who makes this suggestion is anathematized. Or if anyone were to claim that Christ could have chosen to sin when He "was in all points tempted like as we are," (Hebrews 4:15) that person would likewise be anathematized.

The *Catholic Encyclopedia* explains that to anathematize someone is to "separate him from the society of all Christians" and to "judge him condemned to eternal fire with Satan and his angels and all the reprobate." (Cignac, 456) In other words, to anathematize someone is to declare that individual to not be a Christian. This judgment is not to be taken lightly, and the Bible provides only two justifications for its pronouncement. In his letter to the Galatians, the Apostle Paul said that anyone who preaches a gospel other than the gospel which he and the other apostles preached, then that preacher is to be anathematized; (Galatians 1:8-9) and in his first letter to the church at Corinth, he proclaimed the same judgment against anyone who does not love the Lord Jesus Christ. (I Corinthians 16:22) There is no other justification given in Scripture for declaring that someone is not a Christian. This judgment is to be reserved for those who do not love the Lord and those who preach a means of salvation other than faith in the death, burial and resurrection of Christ.

The Council of Nicea abandoned the example of Scripture. They chose to reject certain individuals from being Christians simply because those individuals did not hold to the exact same view of the Trinity as the majority of the bishops of the Catholic church. This act of straying from the authority of the Scriptures placed the Catholic church on a slippery slope producing anathema upon anathema until anyone who dared to disagree with the Catholics on practically any point of doctrine was condemned by them to an eternity in hell.

In fact, less than sixty years after the Council of Nicea, the Catholic church formed another council at Constantinople where it was declared that "Every heresy is to be anathematized." The title of heretic was defined by this council as:

> Those who were aforetime cast out and those whom
> we ourselves have since anathematized, and also
> those professing to hold the true faith who have
> separated from our canonical bishops, and have set
> up conventicles in opposition [to them].
> (Percival, 183)

One of the sects anathematized by the Council of Constantinople as heretics was identified in the eighth canon of the Council of Nicea as the Cathari. John T. Christian identified the Cathari as being the followers of Novatian. He wrote of them that:

> On account of the purity of their lives they were
> called the Cathari, that is, the pure. "What is still
> more," says Mosheim, "they rebaptized such as came
> over to them from the Catholics" (Mosheim,
> Institutes of Ecclesiastical History I. p. 203. New
> York, 1871). Since they baptized those who came to
> them from other communions they were called
> Anabaptists. The fourth Lateran Council decreed that
> these rebaptizers should be punished by death.
> Accordingly, Albanus, a zealous minister, and others,
> were punished with death. They were, says Robinson,
> "trinitarian Baptists." They held to the independence
> of the churches; and recognized the equality of all
> pastors in respect to dignity and authority. (Christian,
> *History of the Baptists*)

These "trinitarian Baptists" were condemned to hell by the Council of Constantinople for no other crime than that of seceding from the Catholic church. This is a far departure from the biblical example of anathematizing only those who do not love the Lord and those who preach another gospel, and one would think that it would be difficult to stray any further from the clear teaching of the Scriptures. The Council of Ephesus, however, caused the Catholic church to slip even further away from the truth.

A mere fifty years after the Council of Constantinople, the Catholic church assembled another council at Ephesus to discuss the hypostatic union of Christ. In the sixth session of this council, it was declared that the Nicene Creed was to be the only creed of the church. It was also said that:

> Those who shall dare to compose a different faith, or
> to introduce or offer it to persons desiring to turn to
> the acknowledgment of the truth, whether from
> Heathenism or from Judaism, or from any heresy

whatsoever, shall be deposed, if they be bishops or clergymen ... and if they be laymen, they shall be anathematized. (Percival, 231)

The interesting aspect of this particular anathema is that it is a direct reversal of the proclamation found in Scripture. When Paul wrote to the Galatians, he was very direct in saying that those who were preaching a false gospel were to be anathematized, but the believers who had accepted this false gospel were still referred to by Paul as brethren. The Council of Ephesus reversed this process. They proclaimed the laymen who believed heresies to be anathema, but the bishops who taught those heresies to the people were merely removed from office, and the Catholic church moved even farther from historical and biblical definition of Christianity.

The Council of Ephesus was very quickly followed by the Council of Chalcedon which adopted the same formula of anathematizing laymen while only disrobing clergy for an identical offense. In the canons of the Council of Chalcedon, the punishment of anathema was applied to four different offenses. The first of these was mentioned in the second canon:

> IF any Bishop should ordain for money, and put to sale a grace which cannot be sold, and for money ordain a bishop, or chorepiscopus, or presbyters, or deacons, or any other of those who are counted among the clergy; or if through lust of gain he should nominate for money a steward, or advocate, or prosmonarius, or any one whatever who is on the roll of the Church, let him who is convicted of this forfeit his own rank; and let him who is ordained be nothing profited by the purchased ordination or promotion; but let him be removed from the dignity or charge he has obtained for money. And if any one should be found negotiating such shameful and unlawful transactions, let him also, if he is a clergyman, be deposed from his rank, and if he is a layman or monk, let him be anathematized. (Percival, 268)

In this canon, a layman or a monk was to be anathematized if he even appeared to assist a bishop in procuring money in exchange for appointments within the church. There was to be no trial, no provision for determining whether the accused was actually guilty or not. The mere presence of suspicion was enough for him to be condemned to eternity in hell.

The seventh canon applied to members of the clergy who chose to leave the service of the church and take up service in the military or in some other capacity under a secular ruler.

> WE have decreed that those who have once been
> enrolled among the clergy, or have been made
> monks, shall accept neither a military charge nor any
> secular dignity; and if they shall presume to do so
> and not repent in such wise as to turn again to that
> which they had first chosen for the love of God, they
> shall be anathematized. (Percival, 272)

The fifteenth canon concerned women who were given in marriage after being ordained as deacons.

> A WOMAN shall not receive the laying on of hands
> as a deaconess under forty years of age, and then only
> after searching examination. And if, after she has had
> hands laid on her and has continued for a time to
> minister, she shall despise the grace of God and give
> herself in marriage, she shall be anathematized and
> the man united to her. (Percival, 279)

And the twenty-seventh canon pronounced anathema against any layman who chose to elope instead of receiving a proper marriage:

> THE holy Synod has decreed that those who forcibly
> carry off women under pretence of marriage, and the
> alders or abettors of such ravishers, shall be degraded

if clergymen, and if laymen be anathematized. (Percival, 287)

The Second Council of Constantinople extended the list of anathemas by twenty-nine anathemas from the council and nine anathemas from the Emperor. These included anathemas against anyone who did not anathematize heretics, who did not anathematize those who defended Theodore, who did not anathematize those who wrote against the writings of Cyril, or who claimed that any part of the letter from Ibas to Maris was correct.

These pronunciations were made in the last four capitulas of this council. The eleventh capitula states:

> If anyone does not anathematize Arius, Eunomius, Macedonius, Apollinaris, Nestorius, Eutyches and Origen, as well as their impious writings, as also all other heretics already condemned and anathematized by the Holy Catholic and Apostolic Church, and by the aforesaid four Holy Synods and [if anyone does not equally anathematize] all those who have held and hold or who in their impiety persist in holding to the end the same opinion as those heretics just mentioned: let him be anathema. (Percival, 314)

This is followed by the twelfth capitula:

> If anyone defends the impious Theodore of Mopsuestia ... if anyone does not anathematize him or his impious writings, as well as all those who protect or defend him, or who assert that his exegesis is orthodox, or who write in favour of him and of his impious works, or those who share the same opinions, or those who have shared them and still continue unto the end in this heresy: let him be anathema. (Percival, 315)

Then the thirteenth capitula concludes:

> If anyone does not anathematize these impious
> writings and those who have held or who hold these
> sentiments, and all those who have written contrary
> to the true faith or against St. Cyril and his XII.
> Chapters, and who die in their impiety: let him be
> anathema. (Percival, 315)

And the final capitula states:

> If anyone shall defend that letter which Ibas is said to
> have written to Maris the Persian ... If anyone
> therefore shall defend the aforementioned epistle and
> shall not anathematize it and those who defend it and
> say that it is right or that a part of it is right, or if
> anyone shall defend those who have written or shall
> write in its favour, or in defence of the impieties
> which are contained in it, as well as those who shall
> presume to defend it or the impieties which it
> contains in the name of the Holy Fathers or of the
> Holy Synod of Chalcedon, and shall remain in these
> offenses unto the end: let him be anathema.
> (Percival, 315-316)

In these four capitulas, the Catholic church progressed so far from the teaching of Scripture that they condemned to hell not only those who dared to disagree with Catholic doctrine but also anyone who did not agree with the decision to condemn "heretics" to hell or even those who did not agree with condemning to hell those who did not condemn "heretics" to hell. According to the standard put forth by this council, the Apostle Paul himself should be anathematized for his failure to anathematize the Galatian believers who had been deceived by a false gospel.

The Third Council of Constantinople was mostly just a direct application of the decisions of the previous council to a particular list of men culminating in the exclamation, "To all heretics, anathema! To all who side with heretics, anathema!" (Percival, 343)

Then, the seventh of the great ecumenical councils of the Catholic church, the Second Council of Nicea, embraced the ultimate departure from the biblical view of anathemas by anathematizing all those who did not accept the false gospel of Mariology. This council pronounced that:

> If anyone shall not confess the holy ever-virgin Mary, truly and properly the Mother of God, to be higher than every creature whether visible or invisible, and does not with sincere faith seek her intercessions as of one having confidence in her access to our God, since she bare him ... let him be anathema from the Father and the Son and the Holy Ghost, and from the seven holy Ecumenical Synods! (Percival, 546)

Thus, over a period of less than four hundred years, the simple gospel of the death, burial and resurrection of Christ was perverted by the Catholic church to a gospel of strict adherence to Catholic dogma and to the veneration of Mary, but the true message of the gospel was not lost. It was preserved throughout this time in the patient teachings of the churches of those called the Anabaptists. These churches included the Cathari, the Donatists, the Albigenses, the Waldensians and many others. According to John T. Christian:

> The footsteps of the Baptists of the ages can more easily be traced by blood than by baptism. It is a lineage of suffering rather than a succession of bishops; a martyrdom of principle, rather than a dogmatic decree of councils; a golden chord of love, rather than an iron chain of succession, which, while attempting to rattle its links back to the apostles, has been of more service in chaining some protesting Baptist to the stake than in proclaiming the truth of the New Testament. It is, nevertheless, a right royal succession, that in every age the Baptists have been advocates of liberty for all, and have held that the gospel of the Son of God makes every man a free

man in Christ Jesus. (Christian, *History of the Baptists*)

The true doctrine of salvation by faith in the finished work of Christ was preserved by these Baptists in the face of great persecution until it was made the rallying cry of the Protestant Reformation. B. B. Warfield noted that "In the mind of Jesus as truly in the mind of His followers, the religion which He founded was by way of eminence the religion of redemption," (Warfield, 524) and it was a return to the true gospel of redemption which marked the success of the Reformation.

In the formation of the ideology which produced the freedoms of America, there is a marked progression from the declaration of Robert Persons that a man can be a Christian only if "he believe unfainedly the total sum of documents and mysteries, left by Jesus and his disciples in the Catholic Church" (Persons, 299) to the recognition of the true gospel by the great puritan preachers such as Thomas Watson who taught that:

> If you would enter into the bond of the covenant, get
> faith in the blood of the covenant. Christ's blood is
> the blood of atonement; believe in this blood, and
> you are safely arked in God's mercy. (Watson, 149)

This theme was picked up by the patriot preachers of the revolution who echoed the words of John Witherspoon that:

> Through this man is preached unto you the
> forgiveness of sins. There is a fulness of merit in his
> obedience and death to procure your pardon. There
> is no sin of so deep a dye, or so infectious a stain, but
> his blood is sufficient to wash it out. This is no new
> doctrine, or modern discovery, to gratify a curious
> mind. Perhaps you have heard such things so often,
> that you nauseate and disdain the repetition. But they
> are the words of eternal life, on which your souls
> salvation depends; and therefore, though this call

should come but once more to be rejected, it is yet
again within your offer. (Witherspoon, 45)

The pure gospel message was carried throughout the nineteenth
century by theologians such as Albert Barnes who proclaimed, "To
all, I say, if you believe the gospel, heaven is yours." (Barnes, 37)
And in the twentieth century, this message was defended in the
writings of men like Lewis Sperry Chafer, J. Dwight Pentecost, Josh
McDowell and numerous others. Chafer wrote of the gospel that
"The believer, in contrast to the unsaved, has consented to the
atonement as the basis of his salvation, and has thus appropriated by
faith the propitiation made for him." (Chafer, 34) Pentecost claimed
that "The Word of God tells us that a man who does no more than
believe that Jesus Christ is his personal Saviour passes from death
into life." (Pentecost, 35) And McDowell emphatically stated that
"Christian conversion is based upon something objective, the
resurrection of Christ." (McDowell, 120)

The history of America, more than that of any other nation, has
exemplified the conclusion of Paul Feine that:

> The Christian Church is an inevitable product of the
> declaration of the expiatory effect of His death for
> many. For those who have experienced redemption
> and reconciliation through the death of Jesus must by
> virtue of this gift of grace draw together and
> distinguish themselves over against other
> communities. (Warfield, 530)

What is it that makes an individual a Christian? What belief must
one hold to in order to be delivered from the curse of sin? The
answer is not to be found in the adherence to a set of accepted
doctrines, nor is it discovered in the creeds of the ancient church.
The key which admits the believer into the community of Christ is
his acceptance of the true gospel of the death, burial and resurrection
of Jesus Christ for the remission of sins.

Works Cited

Adams, John. *The Works of John Adams, Second President of the United States*. vol 1. Boston: Little, Brown and Company. 1856. Print.

Augustine of Hippo. *The City of God*. vol. 2. Trans. Marcus Dods. Edinborough: T & T Clark. 1871. Print.

Barnes, Alfred. *The Way of Salvation*. New York: Leavitt, Lord & Co. 1836. Print.

Baxter, Richard. *A Treatise of Justifying Righteousness*. London: Nevil Simons. 1676. Print.

Baxter, Richard. *The Reasons of the Christian Religion*. London: R. White. 1667. Print.

Bartlet, Andrew. *An Inquiry into the Nature of the Human Soul.* vol. 1. London: A. Millar. 1737. Print.

Bryce, John. *The Confession of Faith*. Glasgow: John Bryce. 1764. Print.

Campbell, Sir Hugh. *A Collection of Letters Relative to an Essay upon the Lord's Prayer*. Edinburgh: Andrew Symson. 1709. Print.

Chafer, Lewis Sperry. *True Evangelism*. Wheaton: Von Kampen Press. 1919. Print.

Chalmers, Alexander, F.S.A. *The General Biographical Dictionary*. London: Nichols, Son, and Bentley. 1815. Print.

Chillingworth, William. *The Works W. Chillingworth, M.A.* London: B Blake. 1836. Print.

Christensen, Merton A. "Franklin on the Hemphill Trial: Deism Versus Presbyterian Orthodoxy." *The William and Marry Quarterly.* 10.3 (1953): 422-440. Print.

Christian, John T. *A History of the Baptists,* vol. 1. Providence Baptist Ministries. n.d. Web. 18 August 2013.

Cignac, Joseph N. "Anathema." *The Catholic Encyclopedia.* vol. 1. 1913. Print.

Cooper, Samuel. "A Sermon on the Day of the Commencement of the Constitution." *Political Sermons of the American Founding Era: 1730-1805.* Ed. Ellis Sandoz. Indianapolis: Liberty Fund. 1998. 627-656. Print.

Dashwood, Sir Francis. *Abridgement of the Book of Common Prayer.* London. 1773. Print.

Dexter, Franklin Bowditch. *The Literary Diary of Ezra Stiles.* vol. 3. New York: Charles Scribner's Sons. 1901. Print.

Dunn, Elizabeth E. "From a Bold Youth to a Reflective Sage: A Reevaluation of Benjamin Franklin's Religion." *The Pennsylvania Magazine of History and Biography.* 111.4 (1987): 501-524. Print.

Edwards, Jonathan. *Some Thoughts Concerning the Present Revival of Religion in New England.* Boston: S. Kneeland and T. Green. 1742. Print.

Fea, John. *Was America Founded as a Christian Nation?* Louisville, KY: Westminster John Knox Press. 2011. Print.

Ford, Paul Leicester. *The Many Sided Franklin.* New York. The Century Co. 1899. Print.

Fortenberry, Bill. "Frazer, Fortenberry and Franklin." *Increasing Learning.* n.p. 17 June 2014. Web. 19 December 2014.

Foster, James. *The Usefulness, Truth, and Excellency of the Christian Revelation*. London: J. Noon. 1731. Print.

Frazer, Gregg. "One Nation Under God." Shepherd's Conference. Grace Community Church. Sun Valley, CA. 6 March 2014.

Frazer, Gregg. *The Religious Beliefs of America's Founders*. Lawrence, KS: University Press of Kansas. 2012. Print.

Frazer, Gregg. "Seminar 3: The Religious Beliefs of America's Founders." The Master's College. Santa Clarita, CA. 18 January, 2013.

Grudem, Wayne. *Politics According to the Bible*. Grand Rapids, MI: Zondervan. 2010. Print.

Hale, Edward Everett. *Franklin in France*. vol. 2. Boston: Roberts Brothers. 1888. Print.

Hankins, Eric. "A Statement of the Traditional Southern Baptist Understanding of God's Plan of Salvation." *Journal for Baptist Theology and Ministry*. 9.2 (2012): 14-18. Print.

Harwood, Adam. "Commentary on Article 2: The Sinfulness of Man." *Journal for Baptist Theology and Ministry*. 9.2 (2012): 28-40. Print.

Ibbot, Benjamin, D.D. *Thirty Discourses on Practical Subjects*. Dublin: Geo. and Alex. Ewing, Booksellers. 1751. Print.

Isaacson, Walter. *Benjamin Franklin: An American Life*. New York: Simon and Schuster Paperbacks. 2003. Print.

James, Charles F. *Documentary History of the Struggle for Religious Liberty in Virginia*. Fort Worth, TX: RDMc Publishing. 2006. Print.

Jurgens, William A. *The Faith of the Early Fathers: Pre-Nicene and Nicene Eras*. Collegeville, MN: The Order of St. Benedict, Inc. 1970. Print.

Labaree, Leonard W., ed. *The Papers of Benjamin Franklin*. vol. 3. New Haven: Yale University Press. 1961. Print.

Lemay, J. A. Leo. *The Life of Benjamin Franklin*. vol. 1. Philadelphia: University of Pennsylvania Press. 2006. Print.

Lemay, J. A. Leo. *The Life of Benjamin Franklin*. vol. 2. Philadelphia: University of Pennsylvania Press. 2006. Print.

Lemay, J. A. Leo. *The Life of Benjamin Franklin*. vol. 3. Philadelphia: University of Pennsylvania Press. 2009. Print.

Locke, John. *The Works of John Locke*. vol. 6. London: C. Baldwin. 1824. Print

Lubert, Howard L. "Benjamin Franklin and the Role of Religion in Governing Democracy." *The Founders on God and Government*. Ed. Daniel L. Dreisbach, Mark D. Hall. Jeffry H, Morrison. Lanham, MD: The Rowman & Littlefield Publishing Group. 2004. 147-180. Print.

MacArthur, John. *The Gospel According to Jesus*. Grand Rapids, MI: Zondervan. 2008. Print.

MacArthur, John. *Why Government Can't Save You*. Nashville, TN: Thomas Nelson Publishing. 2000. Print.

Madison, James. *Debates on the Adoption of the Federal Constitution*. New York: Burt Franklin. 1888. Print.

Marsden, George M. *Jonathan Edwards: A Life*. Harrisonburg, VA: R. R. Donnelley and Sons. 2003. Print.

McDowell, Josh and Don Stewart. *Answers to Tough Questions Skeptics Ask about the Christian Faith.* San Bernadino: Here's Life Publishers, Inc. 1980. Print.

Mead, Sidney E. *The Lively Experiment.* Eugene, OR: Wipf and Stock Publishers. 1963. Print.

Melton, J. Gordon. *Unbelief.* San Diego: San Diego University, Department of Religious Studies. 2011. Print.

Moody, Charles. *Biographical Sketches of the Moody Family.* Boston: Samuel G. Drake. 1847. Print.

Morgan, Edmund S. *Benjamin Franklin.* New Haven, CT: Yale University Press. 2002. Print.

Pangle, Loraine Smith. *The Political Philosophy of Benjamin Franklin.* Baltimore: Johns Hopkins University Press. 2007. Print.

Parton, James. *The Life and Times of Benjamin Franklin.* vol. 1. Boston: Ticknor and Fields. 1867. Print.

Pentecost, J. Dwight. *Things Which Become Sound Doctrine.* Grand Rapids, MI: Zondervan Publishing House. 1969. Print.

Percival, Henry R. *The Seven Ecumenical Councils of the Undivided Church.* Oxford: James Parker & Co. 1900. Print.

Persons, Robert. *A Christian Directorie Guiding Men to Their Salvation.* 1585. Print.

Pink, Arthur W. *The Sovereignty of God.* Lafayett, IN: Sovereign Grace Publishers. 2008. Print.

Remsberg, John E. *Six Historic Americans.* New York: The Truth Seeker Company. 1943. Print.

Schaff, Philip. *A Select Library of Nicene and Post-Nicene Fathers*. vol. 1. New York: The Christian Literature Company. 1892. Print.

Sharp, John. *Eight Discourses on Several Subjects*. London: W. Parker. 1734. Print.

Sherlock, William. *A Discourse Concerning a Judge of Controversies in Matters of Religion*. London: Robert Clavell. 1686. Print.

Stewart, Matthew. *Nature's God*. New York: W. W. Norton & Company. 2014. Kindle.

Stout, Harry S. *The Divine Dramatist: George Whitefield and the Rise of Modern Evangelicalism*. Grand Rapids, MI: Wm. B. Eerdman's Publishing Co. 1991. Print.

Thorpe, Francis Newton. *Benjamin Frnaklin and the University of Pennsylvania*. Washington: Government Printing Office. 1893. Print.

Tillotson, John. *The Works of the Most Reverend John Tillotson*. London: T. Goodwin. 1720. Print.

Trumble, George. *Observations Upon Liberal Education, in all its Branches*. London: A. Millar. 1742. Print.

Walters, Kerry. *Benjamin Franklin and His Gods*. Chicago: University of Illinois Press. 1999. Print.

Warfield, Benjamin B. *The Person and Work of Christ*. ed. Samuel G. Craig. Phillipsburg, NJ: The Presbyterian and Reformed Publishing Company. 1950. Print.

Watson, Thomas. *A Body of Practical Divinity*. Aberdeen: George King. 1838. Print.

Watts, Isaac. *The Redeemer and the Sanctifier*. London: J. Oswald. 1737. Print.

Watts, Isaac. *A Caveat against Infidelity*. London: The Bible and Crown. 1729. Print.

Wells, Edward. *An Help for the Right Understanding of the Several Laws and Covenants*. Oxford: Will. Wells Bookseller. 1729. Print.

Whitefield, George. *The Puritan Revived.* Lewes: Sussex Press. 1829. Print.

Williams, John R. "The Strange Case of Dr. Franklin and Mr. Whitefield." *Pennsylvania Magazine of History and Biography* 1978. 399-421. Print.

Wilson, James. *The Works of James Wilson*. vol. 1. Chicago: Callaghan and Co. 1896. Print.

Witherspoon, John. *The Absolute Necessity of Salvation Through Christ*. Edinburgh: W. Miller 1758. Print.

39496801R00188

Made in the USA
Lexington, KY
26 February 2015